EDUCATION AND THE POLITICAL ORDER

Education and the Political Order

Changing Patterns of Class Control

Ted Tapper and Brian Salter

M

First published 1978 by
THE MACMILLAN PRESS LTD
London and Basingstoke
Associated companies in Delhi Dublin
Hong Kong Johannesburg Lagos Melbourne
New York Singapore and Tokyo

Typeset by Santype International Limited
Salisbury, Wiltshire

Printed and bound in Great Britain by
REDWOOD BURN LIMITED
Trowbridge & Esher

British Library Cataloguing in Publication Data

Tapper, Ted
    Education and the political order.
    1. Education – Great Britain 2.   Politics and
    education
    I. Title II. Salter, Brian
    379.41   LA632

    ISBN 0–333–22691–7
    ISBN 0–333–22692–5   Pbk.

Contents

Preface

In Britain it has been customary to assume that education and politics do not mix, that educational issues are more readily and satisfactorily resolved if they do not enter the political arena. The past decade has seen the shattering of this convention and several important educational issues have become a focus for intense partisan political conflict. The intensity of the debate has been matched by the range of interested parties it has attracted and serious contributions are no longer contained within a narrow liberal consensus. The general purpose of this book is to provide a context which will help to make these developments more intelligible. We examine the changing relationship between class, education and politics in Britain; more specifically, how the educational system has been used to shape the way social class influences the acquisition of political behaviour. As such we would like this book to be seen as a serious statement about the nature of contemporary educational ideology. To this end we have reinterpreted a wide range of secondary source literature as well as presenting primary evidence gleaned from social survey data, demographic trends and government reports.

We have received assistance from many persons, in several different ways, in the writing of this book. For intellectual support we would like to thank R. Benewick, N. Bowles, I. Goodson, and B. D. Graham of the University of Sussex; D. Hutchison of the University of Kent; R. Dowse of the University of Exeter; and P. Goldstene of California State University, Sacramento. R. Flynn and L. McDowell helped with the collection of the data on which part of one chapter is based. Secretarial assistance has come from: J. Arnott, A. Hooper, B. Nicolson, J. Suggett, F. Touch and above all Kate Tapper, who also tried — but alas has not entirely succeeded — to rectify our worst abuses of the English language. We are grateful for the help provided by the Documents Section of the University of Sussex Library in easing the burden of tracking down relevant material. For general moral support in times of crises our thanks go to the clientele of Beverley Farm of the University of Kent, The Monument of Canterbury and The Hervey of Kemp Town.

TED TAPPER AND BRIAN SALTER

Brighton, Sussex
February, 1977

To those members of the working class
who will never read this book

Introduction

Education today is in the melting pot. Or is it? As a political issue it has undoubtedly arrived — the 1976 Education Act, Tameside, William Tyndale, and, last but not least, the unforgettable Great Debate have seen to that. Its visibility has rarely been higher and never before have its functions been so programmatically examined in the public arena as in 1977. But what does it all mean? Are we at a crossroads in educational history, about to embark on new educational directions through democratic debate and re-assessment or is all the talk so much hot air, a political manoeuvre by the government and the Department of Education and Science (D.E.S.) to legitimate pre-determined policies? In any case, what precisely constitutes 'significant' educational change and what criteria can be used to measure it?

In this book we argue that to answer these and related questions about the role of education in society it is necessary to place education in a basically political perspective: a perspective which demonstrates its ultimate purpose as the reinforcement of established patterns of power. In setting ourselves the task of developing such a perspective we recognise that, as political scientists, we can scarcely be said to be following a well-beaten political science path. Political scientists have till now been remarkably coy about committing resources to the study of the links between formal education and the political order and where they have, as with political socialisation research, the results have been less than inspiring. Instead, the field has been dominated by educationalists and sociologists who, while frequently alluding to the political implications of education, have done so intermittently rather than systematically, in line with the natural preoccupations of their disciplines. In contrast to this, our approach assumes the reality of élite power in society and then enquires into the relationship of education to that power. What it does not assume, however, is that the buttressing of power by education is inevitably successful. The attempt will always be made but whether or not it succeeds is dependent both on the internal efficiency of the power reinforcement process and on its capacity to adapt to changing economic and social factors. What we are witnessing today in the contemporary educational crisis, we argue, is a struggle caused by the need for such an adaptive shift counterposed against an educational system reluctant to change.

The individual's progress through the educational system to a position of societal power or powerlessness can be charted along three main dimensions all of which are designed to produce and maintain a differential class effect. The educational system, then, provides structures for: (i) the differential conceptual education of children and hence the preservation of class based conceptual horizons and skills; (ii) the differential political role socialisation of children and hence the creation of different capacities for the use of power; (iii) the differential allocation of individuals to positions of societal power (for example, via public schools).

None of this is news to educational sociologists since they have been playing variations on these themes for some time. It is a neat and apparently accurate set of constructs. It isolates certain educational mechanisms which act as instruments of class control and demonstrates their operation. It shows how class cultures are preserved and marked off by educational parameters and how social mobility between them is carefully monitored to avoid confrontation between class cultures. It is altogether too neat, too exclusive and too predictable.

But from the point of view of those who wield power this interpretation must be highly reassuring since whatever educational change occurs can be shown to be to their advantage. The mechanisms of class control simply adjust to preserve the pre-ordained pattern of élite dominance: even progressive teaching methods have been cast in the role of ensuring a more subtle and extensive form of social control. As an interpretation which begins with a notion of underlying class conflict it ironically ends with affinities to the traditionally more conservative equilibrium model of society with its perpetually self-balancing social forces.

While accepting that education is an instrument of class control, we do not accept that it will always be a successful instrument. It is necessary to be alive to the possibility of substantial inefficiencies and discontinuities in the process of power reinforcement through education, of education's capacity to supply socially disruptive knowledge to groups capable of using it, and of wider economic and political forces which can place education's social control function under substantial stress. There is no convenient symbiosis between élite needs and education's response to these needs as a loyal supporter of élite power. The relationship is undeniably there but its strength and consistency varies from the unquestioning to the precarious.

Even if education is, at a given point in time, creating or perpetuating the kinds of social inequalities which mesh most effectively with the existing distribution of political power, it is another matter altogether whether this inequality is simultaneously legitimated. Merely because people are born or made unequal is no guarantee that they will be happy with their inequality. They need to be persuaded that their situation is in some sense either just or inevitable, that there is a 'rational' explanation for inequality which they can either wholeheartedly accept or fatalistically tolerate. In other words, because of its close connections with the political order, education has to have an ideology which links individual capacities, teaching methods, educational structures and desired educational product (that is differentially educated individuals) in a convincing chain of reasoning. Without such an umbrella of legitimating ideas education has little chance of performing its task of maintaining inequality without finding itself constantly under attack from those who are losing out.

Does this mean, then, that the current educational crisis can be seen as a failure of the dominant educational ideology? The answer is ambiguous. The ideology is undoubtedly weakening, if not collapsing, but not because those who lose out as a consequence of its hegemony are rejecting it. It is the élite, or rather one of several élites, who are themselves seeking to redefine it. This is the immediate reason for its sudden political visibility, though the more interesting question is why its redefinition has become necessary.

A primary factor is undoubtedly Britain's economic problems and the feeling of 'all hands to the pumps' which has lately gripped certain sections of the élite (though other sections, as we shall show, remain relatively unmoved). This has prompted a hasty reassessment of education's functions and the rapid promotion of the new ideology based on a manpower planning approach which incorporates a directly economic definition of inequality.

However, developing a new ideology is one thing but implementing it, as the D.E.S. and government are well aware, is quite another. They are faced with a decentralised education system over which they have only weak lines of control, an ensconced ideology with pockets of radical opinion neither of which are going to give up without a fight, and last but not least, the prospect of disrupting existing mechanisms of class control should they interfere too vigorously: scarcely an example of an efficient ruling class in action. In this country there is something less than a dynamic relationship between education and the political order. Education is not the automatic servicing agency of the ruling class that some Marxists believe it to be; it *is* an instrument of class control but not one which operates in a blanket fashion to the permanent and inevitable advantage of that alleged ruling class. It can promote anti-system attitudes and behaviour (for example, student radicalism), develop an institutional lethargy at times oblivious to the needs of the dominant political order and fall back on its traditional claim to be non-political when the going gets rough and the élite attempts to bring it into line.

Our exploration of the consequent tensions between education and the political order is both interdisciplinary in its consideration of educational, sociological and political science theory, and eclectic in its use of data drawn from a range of secondary and primary sources. We begin in Chapter 1 with a critical overview of the predominantly sociological literature concerned with the relationship between class, education and politics, identify the main points of articulation between the various positions, and establish their common limitations in terms of the primary components of our own fundamentally political perspective. From an emphasis in this first chapter on the social stratification and sociology of knowledge approaches to the role of education in the maintenance and legitimation of inequality, we move in Chapters 2 and 3 to an evaluation of the treatment given to this question by political socialisation and ruling class theories respectively. Our contention is that both these theories have an over-integrated view of society and an over-socialised conception of man which combine to produce a far too simplistic picture of British political society. Power and inequality are linked by a much more subtle and tenuous educational chain than either side realises.

While these first three chapters deal with the more implicit and informal processes of political education, Chapter 4 analyses the history, rationale and political import of recent attempts to introduce political education in explicit form as a curriculum innovation. Not all attempts at political education are necessarily adult sponsored, however. Self-taught political activism by school students has also increased in recent years and Chapter 5 traces its emergence in the face of overwhelming ideological odds, the range of wild, humorous and sad reactions it evoked, and its chances for survival and progress in the future. The explanations advanced for the parallel phenomenon of university student unrest are then tested in Chapter 6 on data gathered in a survey of sixth formers and technical college students, all between the ages of sixteen and nineteen, to try and discern the origins of school discontent. Particular attention is paid to the idea that youth cultures can provide cultural support for such discontent.

From the secondary and further education sectors, we turn in Chapters 7 and 8 to higher education and consider two important issues associated with its massive expansion over the past fifteen years. First, in Chapter 7 we examine the bitter conflict which has developed between two élite ideologies of education, the traditional university ideal and the manpower planning approach to education, establish the incompatibility of their principal components and demonstrate how both relate directly to different conceptions of the political order. Following this, in Chapter 8 we explore the effect of the expansion on higher education's function as a class control mechanism, employing both government and other pertinent survey data.

Our claim is that this book is the first to place formal education firmly within a political perspective on such a broad range of issues. In the final chapter we test the importance of this claim by placing the current educational crisis squarely within this perspective and predicting the direction of future attempts at élite manipulation and legitimation of inequality. Whether or not we are successful is for both the reader and the future to judge.

Chapter 1

Class, Education and Politics in Britain

Education and Politics: Some Established Themes

In an introduction to a section entitled 'Education and Politics' of an Open University set text B. R. Cosin has written, 'What I am attempting, therefore, in this part of the Reader, is less to set out even a basic introduction to one conceptual scheme than to outline elements of *three* such schemes, which may be displayed as more or less common to both sociology and the study of politics. This is a fortunate overlap, since the socio-political study of education is overwhelmingly sociological rather than political.'[1] Although the disciplinary overlap of these conceptual schemes may have helped Cosin to overcome a dilemma in the organisation of his book, it is to be regretted that he was forced to pursue such a tactic in order to incorporate material on education and politics. In spite of our regrets Cosin is undoubtedly correct in his assessment of the paucity of political material in the socio-political study of education. The purpose of this book is to increase the percentage of that political material in three complementary ways: by collating and analysing the information that already exists (the field is not quite as barren as Cosin implies), by drawing out clearly and systematically the political elements that are to be found within the literature of educational sociology, and by presenting collections of our own data. Although each chapter has its particular emphasis, we continuously interrelate these objectives. In this chapter the stress is upon the first and second goals. A considerable body of literature demonstrates the allegedly beneficial influence of formal education upon individual political behaviour.[2] Those who have received more formal education tend to have stronger participatory predispositions, higher levels of actual participation, and are engaged in the more committed and time-consuming forms of participation than those who have received less formal education. Perhaps even more significant is the fact that exposure to formal education directs the working-class voter towards the conservative parties.[3] The most common explanation as to why formal education should have these effects upon individual political behaviour is to point to its influence upon social mobility. If political participation and conservative political orientations are closely associated with middle-class membership then formal education, in as much as it stimulates social mobility, will steer the working class in these directions. Changes in political behaviour, therefore, accompany a pattern of life-style changes that are apparently dependent upon levels of formal education.

Of greater interest to us is the fact that this approach to relating class, education and politics reflects a particular style in describing their mutual links. The stress is upon the political attitudes and behaviour of *individuals* who have different kinds and levels of formal education so that political behaviour is the inevitable product of an educational experience. It is in the political socialisation literature that this notion of an unseen guiding hand is most thoroughly developed. Political man is portrayed as the product of a socialisation process that gradually unfolds as the individual matures. The socialising agents, of which the school is one of the most central, harmoniously interrelate to produce the well-rounded citizen.[4] In fairness to the political socialisation literature, an early stress upon universal and internally reinforcing learning experiences gave way to a more realistic picture which illustrated the fragmentation and tensions that occurred within many individual political learning cycles. None the less the stress was still upon how *individuals* acquired their political behaviour, even if it was increasingly recognised that this learning took place within different boundaries for different individuals.

Obviously the future citizen is socialised into particular societal norms, and presumably he will act as they dictate as long as his socialisation has been successful (that is, the norms have been internalised) and he has the means to enable him to structure his behaviour accordingly.[5] In other words political socialisation is not a neutral process but one which contains cultural and ideological biases. Milbrath has argued that levels of political participation in the United States are dependent upon individual proximity to the political mainstream; that is, the closer one is to the centre of political life the more one is likely to participate.[6] The fact that participation correlated positively with formal education was a consequence of its shifting the individual's social location closer to the political mainstream. The cultural pressures that are associated with high political participation in the United States appear to be replicated in most of the industrialised liberal democratic polities, which reflects that in this kind of society political life is structured in ways conducive to those with middle-class economic and cultural resources.

If it is socio-cultural forces that stimulate participation, then it is ideological pressures (that may be contained within socio-cultural forces) that determine the direction of that participation. In the United States writing about civics education is almost as big an industry as civics education itself. Whether civics education imparts a blind patriotism, an apolitical constitutionalism, or a reformist spirit, and whether it has much impact upon individual behaviour regardless of what it may impart, are all matters of controversy. What is quite clear, however, is that civics education does not offer a serious discussion of possible alternatives to the *status quo*, political or otherwise.[7] Within the past decade a lobby in favour of the teaching of politics in British schools has emerged.[8] Although its various members would be upset to see themselves labelled as a pro-civics education pressure group, the affinities with the American experience are quite close. The main aim is to increase the political literacy of adolescents with a view to securing their more informed participation in the polity.[9] The approach to linking class, education and politics is still conceived in individualistic terms, for it is hoped that the emerging citizen acquires beneficial behavioural characteristics within a favourable context.

The most significant linking of class, education and politics is found in that body of literature which describes the context within which behaviour is acquired as ideologically biased. The suggestion is that learning is directed not so much to develop the individual's political talents but rather to ensure the perpetuation of the character of the established order. The assumption is that all polities will attempt to create patterns of political behaviour that are conducive to their continuing stability, which means ensuring the acceptance of, or less positively compliance to, existing structures of political power. Undoubtedly the system-stabilising functions of political socialisation provide the sub-discipline with its theoretical origins, but most of the subsequent empirical research has stressed the lack of direction within the political learning process and the implicit acquisition of political behaviour within the family. Even if one believes that the political learning process has ideological biases and an ideological goal, it does not follow that one also believes that the state directly controls every aspect of this process. What it does mean, however, is that one sees ideological biases within the societal institutions that may control the learning process.[10]

In this debate on the relationship of state to society, and more specifically the state direction of the societal socialising agents, the educational system occupies a sensitive position. In Britain the state is paramount in the provision of funds for formal education and centrally designated guidelines determine what is an 'efficient' school.[11] But the room for manoeuvre is considerable: there is little state control of the curriculum (religious instruction is the one compulsory subject), local education authorities exercise their discretion within nationally determined policies, the head-master is rarely constrained in how he runs his school, private institutions, most notably the churches, still have a powerful voice in deciding educational policy, and a small but important private sector continues to thrive. In Britain, therefore, the educational system occupies an ambivalent position between state and society which makes it difficult for the state to intervene directly in educational matters, and a strong norm exists that educational policy should be above party politics.[12] The opponents of comprehensive secondary education have sought legitimacy for their stand partly on the grounds that the case for a universal system of comprehensive schools is politically motivated.[13] If the educational system provides an ideologically biased guide to political learning then these biases are to be sought within the character of society and cannot be seen solely as a strait-jacket superimposed upon the schools by the state, or more personally, the class that controls the state.

Expressed in its boldest form there are those who maintain that the educational system is part of the ideological state apparatus and as such it is one of the instruments by which the ruling class perpetuates its hegemony, economic or cultural — and perhaps even both.[14] The structure of the British educational system gives this thesis a certain amount of superficial credibility. In the first place the public schools continue to dominate recruitment into many branches of the establishment which ensures their hold over the social, economic and political life of the country.[15] As important as the stratification implications of the private sector of education are its cultural consequences. All the work on the sociology of the public schools stresses the peculiarity of their internal rituals and educational experiences which reinforce the structural isolation of their members from the rest of the community. The implication is straightforward: the public schools help to create and perpetuate a coherent ruling-class identity. The educational system complements what it does *for* future members of the ruling class by what it does *to* future members of the working class. The traditional stratification of the state schools has resulted in the subjection of the British working class to an educational experience which ensures that most of its members will remain within the confines of their class of origin. This social segregation is buttressed by the content of the knowledge they receive, which is designed to ensure their compliance in their unequal control of resources.

In future chapters we will be examining in some detail the ways in which the past literature has related class, education and politics in Britain. We hope that this brief review has shown that there are two basic approaches to the problem. On the one hand it is possible to conceive of the relationship as a series of correlations arrived at almost fortuitously which stem from the individual's exposure to particular kinds and lengths of formal education. This perspective stresses the pattern of individual learning experiences and the passivity of the educational system, with the individual acquiring certain behavioural characteristics as he or she matures. In complete contrast to this, others have attempted to demonstrate that class influences intrude dramatically into the political learning cycle and the class pattern that is established relies heavily upon the structure and processes of formal education. This assumes one of two forms: either the educational institutions are an integral part of the ideological state apparatus or they occupy a nebulous position on the boundaries of the state and society. In practice, however, this distinction is undermined, for in both cases the individual is exposed to similar ideological biases which are aimed at preserving the *status quo* and the power of the ruling class. What differs is the means by which this hegemony is ensured and although means are not without their significance, it is valid to ask whether a 'tyrannical' society is preferable to a 'tyrannical' state.

The Political Implications of British Educational Sociology

Until comparatively recently British educational sociology has concentrated most of its resources upon demonstrating how formal education acts as an agent of social selection and social stratification.[16] In a sympathetic review of the emergence of this particular perspective Basil Bernstein has noted, 'The approach bore the hallmarks of British applied sociology: atheoretical, pragmatic, descriptive, and policy-focused. Yet if we look back to the mid-1950s, it is not easy to see how there could have been an alternative.'[17] Bernstein then proceeds to relate that period of British educational sociology to wider forces in sociology, in particular the theoretical influence of structural–functionalism and the professional dominance of industrial sociology in British universities, especially at the London School of Economics.

In certain respects Bernstein's work bridges the earlier emphasis upon social selection and the more recent concern with the social control of knowledge. His work in the field of socio-linguistics could be used to explain *how* the educational system acted as such an effective agent of social selection. If the educational experience transmitted knowledge in ways that made its acquisition more possible for those with certain linguistic skills then this was an explanation of the selection process, that is, how some 'succeeded' and others 'failed'. But at the same time Bernstein's work provided a direct lead into the more recent concern with the social control of knowledge — how the educational system selects, organises, transmits and thus controls patterns of knowledge. By moving beyond a description of the social stratification function of formal education to posing questions, and indeed an answer, to how this function is accomplished, Bernstein opened up a whole series of questions on the content of education and how this is related to the wider social structure.

The newer interest in the social control of knowledge complements the earlier concern with the social stratification implications of formal education. In the first place the social divisiveness of British education has been so visible that educational sociologists could scarcely ignore it. This visibility made the social stratification approach an important area of study in its own right. What a theory of knowledge should do is provide the stratification debate with a theoretical rationale, for the aim is to provide explanations of how the social structure relates to the educational system rather than simply to describe the patterns that emerge from that interrelationship. As Ioan Davies has written, 'Without a theory of knowledge it is difficult to see what the stratification debate is about.'[18]

Most significantly from the point of view of drawing out the political implications of this literature, is their common overwhelming concern with the impact of social class upon their respective orientations. As we shall see in more detail shortly, the main emphasis in the social stratification literature is how the British educational system has been structured in ways that ensure the working class fails to receive an equitable distribution of educational resources. Initially Bernstein was interpreted as providing an explanation of working-class educational failure that was dependent upon linguistic skills. However, once he had rid himself of this 'taint' he was able to point to a *social* explanation of that failure, that is, the way knowledge was transmitted by the schools. As Michael Young writes: 'Thus the direction of research for a sociology of educational knowledge becomes to explore how and why certain dominant categories persist and the nature of their possible links to sets of interests or activities such as occupational groupings.'[19] Within contemporary Britain it is possible to relate the organisation of knowledge within the schools to various aspects of the social structure — for example, ethnic differences, national groupings or even sexual identities — but given the past stress upon the educational significance of the British class structure there is little doubt where most of the bridges will be built. This is to be expected if one fully believes that the organisation of knowledge in the schools is dependent upon the character of the British class structure, but it means that the central concern of educational sociology has not basically changed. The emphasis has switched merely from describing to explaining the pattern of working-class exploitation.

Nevertheless educational sociology has undoubtedly benefited from this change in direction. There was clearly a limit to the kinds of questions that the social stratification approach could stimulate and it acted as an intellectual strait-jacket upon new educational problems. The comprehensive schools, for example, were initially investigated in terms of their ability to escape the stratification pressures that had existed in the selective secondary system.[20] There was little consideration as to what would enable the comprehensive schools to forge a new relationship between education and class, simply because the basis of this relationship had never been seriously considered in the selective framework. It is a major advance in disciplinary maturity to move from describing the patterns that emerge from the interaction of variables to explaining how these patterns emerge. In spite of the gains a sense of perspective must be maintained and this is why we have stressed the complementary, rather than the mutually exclusive nature of the two approaches. At the same time the new approach has its own inherent limitations. Ioan Davies has written, 'Unfortunately what is often taken to be the sociology of education is not primarily about education at all — but about selection and stratification, socialisation and organisations.'[21] Davies does not elaborate why this is unfortunate, and one may query whether it is much more beneficial to the long-term development of educational sociology to relate it to the sociology of knowledge as opposed to the other interests he enumerates.

It is ironic that Davies' quote should raise the spectre of subdisciplinary inbreeding, for one of the main aims of those (including Davies) who have been concerned with the content of educational knowledge is to widen the horizons of those working in the field of educational sociology. The sociology of knowledge would provide an intellectual framework for educational sociology while the search for a definition of what education is would flow from an analysis of its socio-cultural context. However, this grand vision fails to penetrate much of the work in the field of curriculum studies where the interests have remained narrowly pedagogical in scope, form and style.[22] In order to ensure that the 'narrowness' of the social stratification approach to educational sociology is not replaced by an equally 'narrow' organisation of knowledge approach we would argue that a stronger political dimension needs to be included within the subdiscipline. In fact this political dimension already exists in different guises and the rest of this chapter will attempt to identify it and expand it.

Pierre Bordieu has commented

> Indeed, among all the solutions put forward throughout history to the problem of the transmission of power and privileges, there surely does not exist one that is better concealed, and therefore better adapted to societies which tend to refuse the most patent forms of hereditary transmission of power and privileges, than that solution which the educational system provides by contributing to the reproduction of the structure of class relations and by concealing, by an apparently neutral attitude, the fact that it fills this function.[23]

Put in simpler language what Bordieu is saying is that formal education is central to the process by which most industrialised societies attempt to legitimate inequality. This is a vital political function because unless the control of scarce resources is legitimated, those who have access to and control of a disproportionate share of status, income and power cannot feel safe in their position of relative privilege. Without this feeling of safety a society is likely to suffer from that most pressing of political problems, social instability.

Before tackling the central question of how the educational

system fulfils, or perhaps in the light of recent events it would be more accurate to say 'fails to fulfil', its legitimating functions, we need to consider the actual creation and maintenance of inequality as opposed to its legitimation. It has been a powerful myth in most industrialised societies that inequality is distributed on the basis of individual merit.[24] Formal schooling is the institution which has the primary responsibility in industrialised societies for discovering this merit, developing it, certifying it, and ensuring that it is duly rewarded by the society at large. The reason why Jencks' work was received with such incredulity in the United States was because it attacked this central myth: individuals react strongly when their total myth structure is threatened.[25] If formal education is not responsible for either creating or maintaining differentials in income and status can it none the less still legitimate the unequal distribution of those variables? The truly powerful myths are undoubtedly those that are firmly believed to have a basis in reality, but whether they in fact have that basis in reality is another matter. In relation to formal education, therefore, it is not so much what its actual bearing upon inequality may be but rather what its influence is thought to be. The difficulty is ascertaining how long this belief is likely to hold up in the face of onslaughts upon its basis in reality launched by scholars such as Jencks. It is reasonable to postulate that one of the explanations for the tense political debates that have surrounded several educational issues in recent years is this increasing uncertainty regarding both what schooling should achieve and what it actually accomplishes. Central to this is the battle over the old structures and processes that legitimated inequality — whether they should be retained, replaced or destroyed along with the society that they flow out of and in return help to sustain.

Just as the social stratification approach to studying education is severely undermined by the findings that the actual impact of schooling upon stratification is limited, so the 'cultural' equivalent of Jencks' research may well demonstrate that the schools have little impact upon the cultural boundaries of their pupils; in effect that the schools neither create inequality nor the cultural divisions that sustain individuals in inegalitarian roles. Bordieu, one of the strongest advocates of the thesis that formal education maintains social control through an organisation of knowledge that leads to differing class cultural horizons, has hinted as much. He notes,

The existence of such a powerful and exclusive relationship between the level of education and cultural practice should not conceal the fact that, in view of the implicit pre-suppositions that govern it, the action of the educational system can attain full effectiveness only to the extent that it bears upon individuals who have been previously granted a certain familiarity with the world of art by their family upbringing. Indeed, it would seem that the action of the school ... tends to reinforce and to consecrate by its sanctions the initial inequalities.[26]

Bordieu's position is contradicted by Bernstein (or at least by the Bernstein of 1972). Bernstein writes: 'What the school does, its rituals, its ceremonies, its authority relations, its stratification, its procedure for learning, its incentives, rewards and punishments, its very image of conduct, character and manner, can modify or change the pupils' role as this has been initially shaped by the family. Thus the number of pupils initially involved in a particular role can be modified or changed by the school itself.'[27] Regardless of where the truth may lie, and neither Bordieu nor Bernstein have undertaken the necessary empirical work to establish this with confidence, this uncertainty concerning the cultural impact of the school must reflect upon its ability to legitimate, let alone create and maintain, inequality.

So far we have been discussing this central political function of schooling solely in terms of the educational legitimations of inequality. The way knowledge is controlled in the schools may provide pertinent ideas as to *how* formal education performs its class control functions but another question needs to be asked and that is *why* it performs these functions. The 'why' question can only be answered by seeking out the various social, economic and political explanations of the educational legitimations, in other words by placing the structure and processes of formal education within their power context. It is our contention that for the most part these wider explanations of the educational legitimations of inequality remain hidden, and that they are only likely to reveal their true nature during periods of societal stress. In this respect we agree with Bordieu that education is a sophisticated legitimator of inequality because its purpose is disguised by an educational as opposed to a political analysis of its structure and processes. But the educational legitimations have a pedagogical as well as a socio-political form and purpose, that is they are meant to be carried out in certain ways and to attain certain academic goals. If it can be shown that this is not happening then efforts will be made to change it and the ensuing conflict could have immense educational as well as political repercussions. In fact in recent years we have witnessed the impossibility of restricting the debate to the educational level and we have seen many fascinating interplays of educational and political themes.[28]

The simple answer as to why the schools perform class control functions is that they have been dominated by those interests which benefit from this. As we have already pointed out many Marxists believe that formal education is one of the instruments by which a capitalist ruling class imposes a cultural hegemony upon society.[29] The structure and processes of formal education reflect an attempt on the part of the ruling class to maintain patterns of power, prestige and income/wealth that are conducive to its continuing domination of state and society; yet the schools allegedly perform this function in ways which conceal their true purpose. We fully agree that formal education has this social control function as one of its tasks, but it is the fact that this function has to be disguised by educational legitimations that undermines the very effectiveness with which it can be performed. These educational legitimations enable the school to become a power centre in its own right which helps its personnel to resist wider societal pressures for change. Contemporarily we have seen attempts to increase the interdependence of the school and the economy, but certain power centres within the educational system have been very successful at resisting these pressures.[30] Although we are reluctant to go as far as Davies who proclaims, 'After all, education is as much about *the creation* of ideologies as it is about anything else',[31] we would accept that education can be a powerful proponent of old 'ideologies' when dominant interests may deem that new ones are necessary. So even if formal education is an instrument at the disposal of the ruling class it is by no means a malleable instrument.

The possibility that education may not successfully legitimate inequality is, therefore, greatly heightened by the likelihood of conflict between the socio-political implications of the prevailing educational legitimations of inequality, and the debate in the political arena as to how the society and state should be structured and run. In other words it is the schools that may need to be changed if they are to perform the tasks that some think essential for the proper functioning of society. So far we have posited the potential conflict as one between powerful educational interests and powerful political interests, but the debate is much wider than this. Although we would agree that some interests are in a better position than others to influence the structure of society and how this should be reflected in education, the debate is by no means a closed one. In the past decade many people on the political right have argued that educational institutions, and universities in particular, have provided a comfortable refuge for those who are bent on overthrowing the established order. Even more heinous in the eyes of those who find this reprehensible is the fact that these subversive individuals are prepared to use the educational institutions as a base for attacking the *status quo*. The educational process is being politicised in ways that run counter to its traditional function of promoting social control by legitimating established patterns of inequality. One may cast aspersions upon the extent of this trend, and the likelihood of its having much impact, but that it is taking place is beyond dispute.

Examples of the ideological implications of progressive educational reforms do exist. Davies has briefly considered the differing interpretations associated with the new mathematics movement in schools.[32] The development could be seen in straightforward pedagogical terms — as an attempt to increase the understanding of mathematics — or in ideological terms — as an attempt to change teaching methods and classroom structures. If it were the latter the ultimate goal must have been to change the pattern of social and power relations within the school, which obviously would have wider societal implications. Of course the two goals are not necessarily exclusive and if one believes that learning potential is determined by the way knowledge is controlled then it is impossible to increase that potential without also changing power relationships.

So far we have posed two obstacles preventing the schools from successfully fulfilling their central political objective of legitimating inequality: the conflict between what they actually do and what they are supposed to do, and potential tensions between the political goals that have been set for the schools and the educational legitimations of inequality. A substantial problem is ascertaining whether the schools are actually successful in legitimating inequality which naturally depends upon the definition of success. If one believes that formal education is central to the means by which the ruling class perpetuates its cultural hegemony then the definition of success is demanding. Hegemony implies that little opposition exists and that the working classes accept the consequences of inequality so internalising as legitimate their failure to control an equitable share of scarce resources. If one believes there is active and substantial opposition to the ruling class then it has failed to establish its hegemony. In other words where there is active opposition there is no hegemony.

The acceptance of inequality can be understood in two different ways. To legitimate inequality fully, those who are losing out in the struggle for scarce resources have to accept that it is just that others are entitled to a bigger share than themselves; they have internalised the norm that their comparative failure is legitimate. Where this occurs a hegemonic value structure is effectively enforced, but where such a situation cannot be created powerful opposing values are likely to emerge and the at best fragile acceptance of inequality is more accurately described as compliance. As we will maintain in our chapter on the ruling class, compliance is a much more realistic interpretation of the responses of the British working class to inequality than the more positive term acceptance.[33]

In ascertaining whether the schools are an effective agent of social control part of the problem is deciding what constitutes opposition to the patterns of control they are attempting to legitimate. If the school's attempts to legitimate inequality are a response to external political pressures then the only effective challenge to this must be one that has political dimensions, that attacks the political power structure which favours some and handicaps others. Seen in these terms it is only in recent years that significant political opposition to the social control function of schooling has emerged within the educational system itself. But what is one to make of the considerable working-class antipathy to schooling that has existed for decades?[34] Are not truancy, classroom violence, vandalism, and more significantly, early leaving all forms of opposition to formal education? Although the working classes may not be opposed to education, considerable working-class antagonism to schooling exists. In fact one question begs another for these are clear forms of opposition, but whether they can be described as *political* opposition depends upon what is meant by political. If we confine our definition to attacks upon the political power structure then this is not political opposition, although it may be opposition to the power structure of the school itself. The situation is complicated by the possible links between political and educational power structures, but even if such links exist these are none the less undeveloped forms of political opposition for they are individualistic, have a crude theoretical and tactical rationale, and are invariably self-defeating. They are classic symptoms of a working class that is complying with inequality, but is far from satisfied with the consequences of that compliance. Some of the chapters in this book will trace and analyse the growth of effective political opposition within the educational system itself. It differs from much of the previous opposition because it creates organisations, is evolving a coherent strategy and theoretical rationale, and poses a challenge to established authority — political and educational — that is hard to ignore and dangerous to devalue.

Legitimating Inequality: Social Stratification

The social stratification research tradition in British educational sociology has demonstrated quite conclusively that formal education in this country is organised along class lines. This is reflected in both the access to educational resources and the way in which those resources are distributed within the schools after the point of access. The main features of these findings are straightforward: different classes attend different kinds of schools, social class correlates strongly with selection patterns even when — as in the case of the grammar schools — admission is supposedly according to meritocratic criteria, and within the schools it is the working-class child who is most clearly discriminated against by internal methods of selection (various forms of streaming), and who is most prone to leave school as soon as the law permits. Often it is too readily assumed that to analyse the stratification patterns that emerge from relating social class and education is to provide a mere description of reality. It is understandable that the relationship should be viewed in this light because those who have been responsible for constructing it have rarely moved beyond the descriptive level of analysis. But as long ago as 1922 Tawney could write, 'The organization of education on the lines of class, though qualified in the last twenty years, has characterized the English system of public education since its very inception, and has been a symptom, an effect and a cause of the control of the lives of the mass of men and women by a privileged minority.'[35] What Tawney is saying is that the organisation of formal education along class lines is within itself an explanation of patterns of socio-political control in British society.

Tawney suggests that the class basis of formal education not only reflected and was a product of a class distribution of power, but also helped to cause that distribution of power. We would like to suggest a different but related line of argument: that a class-based educational system helped to legitimate a class biased distribution of power because it was considered just to distribute educational resources along class lines. So the fact that resources are distributed on the basis of social class is not simply descriptive sociology if it is recognised that the basis of resource allocation (in this case social class) also provides the legitimating criteria.

What is startling about the British educational system is the longevity of the notion that social class provides a reasonable criteria for the allocation of resources. This begs the question of who considered this to be either 'just' or even 'reasonable' and quite obviously the answer is those who stood to gain most by it. Evidence presented to several nineteenth-century education commissions contains strong streaks of naturally assumed class superiority which was manifested in statements to the effect that working-class education should be severely limited in both its length and scope.[36]

In spite of the fact that social class is still seen by many as an acceptable basis for the inegalitarian distribution of resources, the legitimating criteria have changed. They have become more personalised rather than class based. This change in emphasis came to fruition with the 1944 Education Act in which the state guaranteed everyone an education commensurate with his or her age, aptitude and ability. One of the central debates in the social stratification literature is whether these new legitimations of inequality are merely a disguise for the old social basis of resource allocation. The intelligence tests which formed the core of the 11+ examination have given rise to the greatest controversy, with their opponents arguing that cultural biases explain the lower test scores of working-class adolescents while their proponents suggest that this is due to a lower distribution of intelligence within the working class.[37] We will leave others more competent than ourselves to pass judgement on this issue, but we want to note that even if there is an entity known as intelligence, which can be accurately measured by intelligence tests, this is not automatically a sufficient justification for an inegalitarian distribution of educational resources. What the intelligence tests do is provide a rationalisation, perhaps even an ideology if they are related to wider aspects of man and society, for those who want to secure certain patterns of social control.

A fascinating question is why the basis for legitimating inequality should have changed from social class to more personalised criteria like intelligence. The answer can be found only in an examination of the changing character of the social structure. In this case we would have to point to the growing power of the trade unions, whereby it became politically untenable to discriminate blatantly against the working class. At the same time the political voice of the trade unions, the Labour Party, was arguing for greater 'equality of educational opportunity', which necessitated a shift in the basis of resource allocation from class to personal criteria. As the industrial base grew more complex so the demand for greater and more varied forms of skills increased. If the educational system was to control the competition for the acquisition of these skills it had to expand educational opportunities for the working class, thus stimulating limited amounts of social mobility. Life opportunities could still be segregated along class lines but the emphasis on individual 'merit' would decide who in the working class was to be socially mobile and who was not. This enabled formal education to continue its traditional function of class control in a much more subtle fashion for its old class prejudices were disguised and the potential solidarity of the working class was eroded by the creation of individual channels of social mobility.

In an article that questions both the descriptive validity and ideological implications of Basil Bernstein's work, Harold Rosen writes:

> It was just when this theory [that 'intelligence' was a real and measurable entity] was looking sadly tattered and when the high priest of the psychometric ideology himself, Professor Vernon, felt obliged to publish a self-critical restatement of his position (Vernon, 1960) that the theories of Bernstein began to be available. These early papers . . . which were the only ones available for several years, were readily seized upon, not only because of the great upsurge of interest in linguistics, but also because they seemed to offer theoretical respectability to the widespread notion among teachers and others that an intrinsic feature of working class language, rooted in their way of life, disqualified working class children educationally and, by the same token, justified the notion of the superior educational potential of the middle class. Whereas in the fifties children had their I.Q.s branded on their forehead, in the sixties more and more of them had the brand changed to 'restricted' or 'elaborated' The ideology vacuum had been filled.[38]

With the shift from class to I.Q., and then to language, the legitimations of inequality are becoming more narrowly educational in their focus. But by assuming this narrowness their effectiveness (that is, the extent to which it is believed that they have a basis in reality) is restricted to fewer individuals. Rosen claims that teachers and others (Just who are these unspecified others?) saw in Bernstein's theories an explanation of the superior educational potential of the middle class. Even if this is true, (and Rosen fails to substantiate it) there is no evidence that anyone else — particularly working-class children and their parents — believed this. The fact that I.Q. tests were used on such a wide scale for decades *suggests* that they were widely accepted as a legitimate means of segregating children into different kinds of schools. But even in the case of the I.Q. tests the record is by no means one-sided. Many psychologists (long before Vernon's 1960 statement to which Rosen refers) were disenchanted with intelligence testing and plenty of evidence shows that many parents, both middle class and working class, were far from happy at the anxiety the 11+ caused them and their children.

Of course class itself could only be a legitimate basis for distributing inequality in a class-based society. If it was more widely acceptable as a basis for inequality than the notions of either intelligence or linguistic differences then this reflects the strength of social class differences in our society. The appeal of intelligence tests was twofold: they conventionally complemented the shift from a class-based to an allegedly meritocratic system and they placed the differences in access to educational resources on a scientific (some would say, pseudo-scientific) basis. Over time a number of different threads coalesced to form an effective challenge to this particular legitimation of inequality: the scientific pretensions of the tests were undermined; it was increasingly disputed that segregating pupils at the tender age of eleven was beneficial — in either educational or social terms — for the pupils themselves, regardless of whether they 'failed' or 'passed' the 11+; and the societal consequences of this were claimed to be harmful. The attack upon the educational use of intelligence testing has all but succeeded and, Rosen notwithstanding, it has not been replaced by an all-embracing socio-linguistic legitimation of inequality. Bernstein's research provides an explanation as to why working-class adolescents, particularly those from the lower working class, did not perform as well as their middle-class peers in the intelligence tests. As such it can be seen as one of the many assaults upon the validity of intelligence tests (which were meant to be free of cultural biases) rather than as a replacement for them. At the same time Bernstein has maintained, rather unconvincingly, that it is not linguistic skills *per se* that account for the poorer educational achievement of working-class pupils but rather how the schools are organised in relation to these contrasting linguistic patterns. The implication is that with different organisational structures, including new ways of controlling knowledge, the linguistic skills need not have the impact that they have at present.

The clearest manifestations of the continuing use of class as a means of distributing educational resources is to be found in the private sector. Here class inequality is not disguised by reference to the intelligence or the linguistic patterns of the pupils for it is accepted that, with few exceptions, they owe their privileged positions to the income, status and power of their parents. Whereas in the nineteenth century it was openly accepted by many that social classes required different kinds of educational experiences, not even the private sector can be justified in these terms today. Private education may result in particular patterns of class control, but it most certainly cannot be legitimated on these grounds. As in previous cases there is a subtle combination of political and educational legitimations. At the political level freedom of parental control over the education of their children is sacrosanct. This has much wider connotations: the individual has a right to dispose of his resources in a manner that suits him, and if this means buying a privileged education for his children then so be it. The implication is that to abolish private education, no matter how beneficial this may be in either educational or social terms (and naturally the defenders of private education would deny these possible gains), would undermine the principle of a free cultural market. A parallel argument has been raised in the debate over comprehensive education; those who wish to retain the grammar schools have argued that their abolition would reduce parental educational choice. The defenders of private education and selective secondary education are correct that the retention of these forms of schooling increases parental educational choices, but they are usually reluctant to make the further point that it is a minority of parents who gain considerably more choice than the majority. Retaining private schools and grammar schools increases the options of those parents who can either afford private education or who have children who have 'passed', or 'will pass', the 11+ examination. This dilemma is not necessarily resolved in a fully comprehensive educational system for conflict may well result from allocating pupils amongst the comprehensive schools if it is felt within the community that 'standards' vary from school to school.[39] A more important political point is whether the state is justified in restricting the educational choice of all parents because some can exercise that choice more effectively than others. There can only be a political answer to this question and it is dependent upon what particular values one wishes to maximise and what kind of society one wants to create.

In educational terms the private sector is usually defended because it allegedly helps to maintain educational standards and because, free from many of the pressures that state schools have to contend with, it is better placed to conduct educational experiments.[40] Again taken at face value both these points are valid, but it should be noted that 'standards' invariably refer to the traditional academic values of the better private and grammar schools, and that although some of these schools have been innovative, the majority are bastions of an educational conservatism which combines ancient rituals with the more recent fanaticism for academic excellence. These rationalisations of educational privilege cannot conceal the fact that many parents want their children to receive a private education because of the *quality* of the educational experience, in the widest sense of the word, to which they are exposed. The most prestigious sector of private education, the public school, has been noted for the esoteric quality of its schooling. It indelibly marks many of those in our society who control a disproportionate share of income, status and power. It is this which the political and educational rationalisations in favour of private education are concealing, although they do no better than provide a thin veneer of respectability to cover the perpetuation of blatant class privilege.

Legitimating Inequality: Schools and the Control of Knowledge

The whole purpose of selection in education is to provide individuals with differing educational experiences. In Britain the control of knowledge has depended upon the selection techniques, but in spite of this the analysis of how these techniques affect the control of knowledge has been limited, except to note that the *content* of educational experiences will differ from one kind of school to the next. The wider cultural environments that appear to be created by or at least are clearly defined by the various selection boundaries, have been more thoroughly researched. Jackson and Marsden's famous study of working-class children who were academically successful in the grammar schools traced their acculturation into the middle-class mores of their schools.[41] Many of them were apparently attuned to the process before entering the schools and it was only a question of time before their total integration into the bourgeoisie was complete.[42] Hargreaves' work on the creation of 'delinquescent' subcultures in the secondary modern schools provides another example of this process within a contrasting educational setting. Hargreaves' case study is interesting because the subculture arose out of opposition to the school, and in certain respects was a direct response to the exclusion of its members from the school's social and academic mainstream.[43] Research on the public schools provides the best evidence that education is a total cultural experience, but given the fact that they are mainly boarding schools they are in a better position to embrace the hearts, minds and bodies of their pupils. What is important about the educational experience transmitted by the public schools is the blending of knowledge and cultural ingredients to turn out pupils who are equipped to occupy élite roles in British society. In other words the educational experience is only a part— admittedly an important part—of a wider cultural experience, and not within itself a sufficient explanation of the political power of a public school education. Within the public schools knowledge has been defined in particular ways (note the traditional stress upon ancient languages and history) and transmitted within a structured framework to create a certain kind of mind (at its best or worst, depending on your taste, effortless scholasticism). However, this takes place within a hierarchically organised environment which stresses mutually reinforcing obligations, an idealisation of the well-rounded man, and a social code that excludes the uninitiated. Obviously the extent to which the organisation of knowledge plays a part in defining the cultural context of the individual's role varies from case to case. We have already implied that it is not very crucial in relation to anti-school cliques within secondary modern schools (and this is probably true of all schools with at least a significant minority of working-class pupils), that it blends with other cultural variables within the public schools, and probably exerts the greatest influence upon pupils, both working class and middle class, in the top streams of grammar schools, and probably comprehensive schools.

Although we have suggested that the way knowledge is understood has to be related to other factors in order to appreciate fully the content and social meaning of cultural roles, it does provide a powerful legitimation for the perpetuation of inequality. Bernstein has argued that knowledge is organised socially by deciding upon a content to the curriculum, transmitting that content in certain ways, and then constructing examination methods to ensure that those who are being taught have successfully internalised the designated content.[44] In Britain formal education has organised knowledge by emphasising the boundaries between academic subjects, stressing the need for early subject specialisation, isolating educational institutions from the wider society (especially from immediate community pressures), transmitting knowledge in well-regulated stages moving from the empirical to the theoretical, granting control over what knowledge 'is' to hierarchically structured professional groups who are organised within knowledge stratified institutions, and examining the acquisition of knowledge on an individual basis by ritualistic means.[45] These various features may be defended on the grounds that they help to preserve knowledge (which in common parlance usually ends up as 'standards'), but equally they help to preserve particular patterns of social control.

Organising knowledge along the above lines grants considerable power to those who are in control of the organisational structures and processes. This helps to account for the independence of the power base of the British teaching profession to which we have already alluded. More significant is the fact that knowledge is organised in ways that makes its acquisition easier for some social groups rather than others. It requires certain kinds of cultural supports to succeed within an educational environment that is both socially and to a greater extent individually selective. These are the cultural supports that have been strongly associated with middle-class families who stress individual achievement as the road to personal salvation. The emphasis upon a collective identity is much stronger within the public schools (and indeed within Hargreaves' 'delinquescent' subculture) than within this particular model of the social organisation of knowledge. By being organised along certain lines knowledge is socially controlled, but whether its acquisition results in power depends upon the wider cultural context. Furthermore, as we shall examine later, the understanding of what knowledge it is deemed desirable to possess is not static.

The relationship between how formal education controls social selection and how knowledge is defined is reinforced by the pattern of experimentation with educational codes (to use Bernstein's phrase). Michael Young has argued that most curriculum innovations have been made in the least prestigious parts of the educational system.[46] As William Taylor has shown in his fine book on the secondary modern schools, they were able to experiment with the curriculum because they were free from the examination constraints that bound the grammar schools.[47] At the same time the different curriculum content was a convenient way of fulfilling the promise of giving every child a secondary education; it was different from, but allegedly equal to, the established secondary school curriculum. The possibility of establishing a parity of esteem between the traditional and innovative secondary curricula was doomed from the start because the secondary modern schools accepted pupils who had 'failed' the 11+ and who on leaving school entered, for the most part, manual occupations. No matter how good their curricula may have been in pedagogical terms they could not overcome the 'stigma' of their social and academic selection functions.

It is the school's selection function that provides the key to the way in which it will control knowledge. Where the pressure of this function is low, one can expect more experimentation with educational codes. This pressure can be lowered by a variety of factors besides the school's location in the educational prestige hierarchy. Primary schools in Britain are removed from the selection pressures by the tender age of their pupils; they can be innovative because they do not have to prepare these pupils for selective examinations. The pressure is also lessened if a clear measure of *certainty* surrounds the institution's and its pupils' location in the prestige hierarchy. The fact that the secondary modern schools were of low prestige and their pupils' educational status was not initially further refined by competitive examinations encouraged them to introduce new curricula. The introduction of external examinations in the secondary modern schools, which enabled some of their pupils to show they had been wrongly selected, acted as a brake upon innovation. Prestigious educational institutions, such as Summerhill in the private sector and the University of Sussex in higher education, have also been active in forming new educational codes.[48] Admittedly their students are not free from further selective pressures but their mere presence within these institutions provides them with some certainty as to their position within the overall status hierarchy. The University of Sussex has experimented with its examination methods — extended essays, dissertations and take-away papers have replaced most of the traditional three-hour unseen examinations. Obviously status clarity does not automatically result in curriculum innovation — witness the difficulty of initiating changes at Oxford and Cambridge — but we are claiming that given other favourable factors it can provide the innovator with an assured base from which to proceed.[49] It has to be admitted that many prestige institutions change their educational codes with only the greatest reluctance because these codes represent to them an ideal from which many feel their status flows. In other words it is the way they control knowledge that results in their social exclusiveness and not vice versa. To claim that patterns of inequality in our society are a consequence of the transmission of knowledge is a powerful means of legitimating that inequality, for there are few people who are against the transmission of knowledge. The issue then is whether the imparting of knowledge can be accomplished in ways that do not result in established patterns of inequality and social control. This is one of the key debates in British education at the time of writing. The traditionalists are arguing that the move towards new educational structures (most noticeably the replacement of selective secondary schools by comprehensive education), new teaching methods, different examination techniques (note the controversy over the proposed 16+ examination which will be internally rather than externally controlled), and a lessening of emphasis upon the traditional subjects within the curriculum, is causing a decline in standards.[50] This can be interpreted either as idealistic protest or as selfish pragmatism — either a concern that knowledge is not being transmitted by formal education or a fear that ones own children are not obtaining the examination passes that are considered to be the key to success in later life. Although we are aware these are political issues, both in their own right and because of the way they affect the relationship between class, education and politics, we feel it is too early to pronounce, one way or the other, on how they will be resolved and what their political impact will be. It is of greater interest to us, and we believe of greater political significance, to clarify the main parameters within which this conflict is occurring.

Regardless of what the content of formal education may be, and how that content is transmitted, it is hard to imagine these educational factors as entirely detached from their societal context. Marxists are inclined to stress the importance of property relations as the central determinant of the character of the educational system, and more specifically, a reference to the social structure as determining the organisation of knowledge can invariably be taken to mean that this organisation reflects patterns of property ownership.[51] Non-Marxists look beyond property relationships to the technological basis of the society. Their argument is that technological societies, both capitalist and socialist, will have very similar educational codes. Obviously there will be some differences both within and between capitalist and socialist educational systems, but the similarities outweigh these, and over time the technological pressures lead to an increasing standardisation.[52] These influences are not mutually exclusive and both will be reflected in the educational system. The contemporary debates in British education may reflect an attempt to shift the system from its concern with class control and one set of property relations to technological efficiency and another set of property relations. Regardless of where one may stand in this controversy the important point is to recognise the extent to which the educational issues are constrained by wider societal forces, so that the conflict about educational codes becomes a conflict about the nature of society.[53]

To argue that the management of knowledge reflects the character of the societal structure, either its property relations or technological foundations, implies that the acquisition of knowledge can do little else but buttress the established social structure. But to maintain such an extreme case is patently absurd. No consensus prevails as to what the social structure is, let alone what it should be, and the pedagogical independence of the teaching profession has ensured that no harmony between educational codes and societal needs can be taken for granted. There is some confusion amongst those who believe that the curriculum should form the core of educational sociology as to whether educational institutions simply organise knowledge or whether they also define what knowledge is.[54] Obviously the two concepts are interrelated for if a body of knowledge is to gain credibility it has to receive the seal of approval from the professional intellectuals in the prestige educational institutions. Some evidence suggests that this is even true of areas like art which up to now have remained comparatively free from institutional controls and definitions.[55] But recognition of knowledge is not the same as defining knowledge, although without some recognition, which increasingly means institutional backing, it is hard to imagine that knowledge can be seen to exist, let alone have an impact. We are, therefore, more and more dependent upon reaching some understanding of what knowledge receives recognition and what does not. We would argue that although clear professional and political biases exist, knowledge is not narrowly defined within British educational institutions, especially at the higher levels, and that the definitions have widened in recent years.[56] The organisation of these differing definitions may follow similar lines, thus ensuring identical patterns of social control in the sense that the same kinds of persons are successful, but this does not rule out the possibility of political opposition emerging from within the educational institutions, for certain definitions of knowledge regardless of their structure may very well stimulate such a challenge.

Of course both the definition and control of knowledge have helped to legitimate patterns of socio-political control but what we are questioning is the degree of certainty with which this can be assumed. Up to now knowledge has been acquired on an individual basis, for example its acquisition has been the means by which many members of the working class have become socially mobile, thus ensuring their *personal* control of a larger share of scarce resources. At the same time the existence of competing definitions of knowledge has enabled some at least to question, and perhaps even effectively to challenge, the patterns of control that prevail in our society. So far this has been confined mainly to those who have received higher education, and below this level formal education has been a firmer instrument of social control.[57] Unless history can be rewritten, and all comparative standards erased (and not even Stalin succeeded in doing this), there will always be competing definitions of knowledge. In this sense exposing individuals to knowledge carries a threat to the social structure. The management of knowledge can limit that challenge by devaluing the status of threatening definitions and by establishing educational codes that result in personal rather than collectivist means of acquiring knowledge. But even if such strategies succeed in eliminating or rendering innocuous challenges to the *status quo* there is still no guarantee that formal education will help the society to achieve the goals that have been set for it, and in fact it may do precisely the opposite.[58] Furthermore, the consequence of temporary quiescence may well be more intense political conflict in the long run.

In this opening chapter we have analysed some of the main discussions within the literature of educational sociology on the relationship between class, education and politics in Britain. In subsequent chapters we draw upon different perspectives from the more politically based literature. Through this dissection of the published material and original data we will build our own understanding of the political functions of education in British society. It is our central contention that in the contemporary period the educational system is a hazardous agent of political control. We show why this is so, discuss certain of the implications of this for educational institutions as well as society at large, and make tentative predictions as to the outcome of the present turmoil in the educational world. In accomplishing these tasks our aim is to blend theoretical innovation with an analysis of the secondary sources and our own data. Basil Bernstein argues that 'the battle over curricula is also a conflict between different conceptions of social order and is therefore fundamentally moral'.[59] It is our guiding theme that the curricula battle is part of a more encompassing educational war and the purpose of this book is to illustrate that its central themes, patterns of development, and consequences are essentially political.

Chapter 2

From Political Socialisation to Political Education[1]

The Over-Socialised Conception of Man

In the 1960s the study of political socialisation blossomed into an important subdiscipline within the political science profession. Thanks to his synopsis of the pertinent literature, which was published in 1959 under the title *Political Socialization*, Herbert Hyman is invariably credited with triggering off this research boom.[2] After ten years of flourishing field work Fred Greenstein, probably the most prolific and sophisticated political scientist engaged in this subdiscipline, could still describe the research in political socialisation as a growth stock.[3] His quantitative measure was the number of American Political Science Association members who in 1968 listed political socialisation as one of their professional interests.[4] Furthermore as the 1960s progressed so the number of political socialisation publications increased.[5] On the basis of these kinds of quantitative measures this interest has not abated, and in 1973 Dennis felt that the foundations of political socialisation research were so secure that the future could be devoted to filling in 'the gaps in present empirical knowledge' and to crystallising 'current new developments'.[6]

The political socialisation literature is of considerable interest to us because it contains the most extensive body of information on the relationship between formal education and political behaviour. The purpose of this and the following chapter is to evaluate respectively the relationship between class and politics in the political socialisation literature and the ruling class model of British society. It is our contention that *both* the political socialisation and ruling class theorists have an over-integrated view of society and an over-socialised conception of man.[7] In the course of this chapter we will also present our own view of the political socialisation process with particular emphasis upon the part that the British educational system plays within it.

The Birth and Expansion of a Subdiscipline

Although Hyman did a first rate job of collating a wide range of research under the political socialisation umbrella, the empirical studies that flourished in the 1960s rely more upon various input–output models of the polity for their theoretical legitimation than Hyman's synthesis of the secondary source material.[8] Almond's functional model and Easton's systems models both posit a highly integrated society and each ascribes political socialisation the function of building support for the polity.[9] One would have expected the subsequent empirical research to demonstrate *how* political socialisation induces support for the political system, but in fact precisely the reverse has taken place, for individual attitudes have been surveyed and the polity characteristics (invariably political stability) assumed simply on the basis of these.

It is in its empirical work that political socialisation owes most to the legacy of Hyman. Hyman defined political socialisation in the following terms:

Regularities in the political behavior of adult individuals and stable differences between groups of adults have become commonplace in social research. Such patterns of behavior may be interpreted in terms of contemporaneous features present in the adult lives of particular individuals or groups. But, certainly it is true that the continuity of such patterns over time and place suggests that the individual has been modified in the course of his development in such a way that he is likely to exhibit certain persistent behavior apart from transient stimulation in his contemporary environment. One is naturally directed to the area of learning; more specifically to the socialization of the individual, his learning of social patterns corresponding to his societal positions as mediated through various agencies of society.[10]

The political socialisation literature has analysed, in increasing detail, these patterns of behaviour, or to be more accurate — as children have been its major subjects — it has presented ever more intricate attitudinal patterns. Once the information has been presented (for example, correlations between social class, sex and education and images of the president), the explanations of the trends have invariably depended upon tortuous and highly speculative inductive analysis. The finding that most American schoolchildren had benevolent images of the president was explained by their transference of positive attitudes of parental authority, and in particular of the father, to political authority. Occasionally this was supplemented by the intriguing titbit that parents tried to shield their children from the realities of political life so that they saw the world through rose-tinted spectacles![11]

This presentation of attitudinal patterns enabled the political socialisation research to fit into an empirical mould based upon social survey data. During the period in which the political socialisation studies have flourished the professional norms of American social science have decreed that research should be based upon quantifiable data, and more especially that the evidence should be subjected to statistical testing. With a captive audience — that is schoolchildren — it has been comparatively easy to conduct large-scale surveys once the controlling authorities have been persuaded of the utility of the research which has resulted in impressive empirical bases for some of the political socialisation studies.[12]

An equally important Hyman legacy is his view of a mainstream political socialisation process which embraces most of us, while small minorities are subjected to 'deviant' learning experiences. In the revised 1969 edition of his text he writes: 'The meaning [of political socialisation] I intended was narrower, more traditional. I hoped to preserve the terms for those processes that most members of a society or sub-group experience, in contrast with learning that is idiosyncratic in character.'[13] His reasons for the narrower focus are revealing: 'The former process produces the regularities, uniformities, that are directly relevant to the stability of political systems and that lend themselves to social and educational policy. The latter process produces endless variability, creates unpredictability, and defies institutional forms of control.'[14] Such claims represent an extreme variant of the over-socialised conception of man for not only do they say that man is a product of his socialisation experiences but also that those endproducts which aid political stability are somehow or other more 'normal' (and by implication more desirable) than those which do not. As we shall see this has important ramifications when it comes to ascertaining what political goals the educational system either fulfils or should fulfil.

The final guiding assumption of much of the early work was that the most important aspects of political behaviour (the basic orientations) were acquired in childhood.[15] It was believed that what the individual learned earliest stayed with him longest and that his later behaviour was based upon these initial foundations. With such a guiding principle the family had to be seen as the central agent of political socialisation for it is within families that nearly all of us experience our early learning. An implicit image of the American family was created: nuclear, father-dominated and stable. The alleged socialising power of the family was bolstered by various common-sense assumptions: the time spent in its confines, the immense power imbalance between parents (socialisers) and children (socialised), and the strength of the norm that parents are responsible for the behaviour of their offspring.

These initial parameters — that socialisation is an input into the political system helping to create diffuse support, that system characteristics and the influence of socialising agents can be deduced from attitudinal patterns, that there is a normal socialisation process that embraces the overwhelming majority of citizens, and that the most important political characteristics are acquired in the early years — have shaped the political view of the educational system. In most of the research, educational institutions are accorded second place to the family in the creation of diffuse support, although some of the more ambitious have placed them first.[16] Certainly the schools are more amenable than the family to state controls and over time their influence has become more pervasive. Schools now perform some of the functions previously undertaken by the family and academic qualifications are increasingly important in determining entry into prestige occupations. The consequence is that more time is being spent, by ever larger numbers of people, in educational institutions.[17] This is counterbalanced by the fact that in most societies there is no reason to suspect that the family is anything other than a loyal transmitter of socialisation messages that support the *status quo*. At the same time the family's influence is felt when it is widely believed that we are most amenable to pressure, that is during the early years of childhood. Historically the schools have been very important as *political* socialisation agents when governing élites have not trusted the family to impart the messages that they felt should be taught. Revolutionary regimes are often wary of the potentially conservative influence of the family for it is hard to penetrate its structure and ensure that the 'correct' messages are being taught.

In the United States the public school has been one of the primary means of building common citizenship patterns for it was in the schools that the immigrants learned both a new language and the part they were expected to play within the political system. It is not that the family is inevitably a conservative bulwark, and in fact it may be very active in bringing about revolutionary change, but ruling élites are likely to sleep sounder if they know that institutions more directly amenable to their control are advocating the official line.

Given the part he has played in constructing systems models, it comes as no surprise to discover that David Easton bears much of the responsibility for placing formal education firmly within this framework. In 1957 he wrote of formal education that 'it helps develop and transmit certain basic political orientations that must be shared, within a certain range of variation, by most members of any ongoing system'.[18] Subsequently the political socialisation agents, including the school, have been seen as building diffuse support which Easton views as a reservoir of citizen commitment to the regime which governing élites can draw upon in times of crisis.[19] In spite of the occasional word of warning many other political scientists and educationalists have placed their political socialisation studies within a systems model, believing that it provides a meaningful theoretical framework for what might otherwise be merely an interesting piece of descriptive research.[20]

Although it is in widespread use, it is exceedingly doubtful if Easton's systems model is an appropriate mould in which to cast the relationship between education and politics. He argues that it is an empirical question as to how much support a political system needs before it can be said to be stable which implies that as long as a polity persists it has the support of its citizens.[21] Only when political systems collapse does it seem that one can say that support has been withdrawn. Furthermore, couching the argument in these terms disguises the fact that political stability may be a consequence of numerous other forces besides diffuse support.[22] Much more significant, from the point of view of this chapter, is the fact that the empirical evidence does not substantiate the claim that the American educational system is building *rational* support for the polity amongst future citizens. Rather, in the words of Hess and Torney, 'The process of socialization in later years can best be understood in the context of this early establishment of unquestioning patriotism'.[23] Besides their success at inducing chauvinism the schools' other great achievement is in helping to create passive and compliant citizens. If compliance, passivity and chauvinism are termed support then the schools are accomplishing the function ascribed to them in the systems model. But this is scarcely a tenable interpretation for Easton claimed that stability was partially dependent upon citizen attachment to regime norms, and however one is going to interpret American political norms, they formally demand more of the citizen than the schools are imparting.

The impetus behind the early political socialisation research was generated by pressures both intellectual (in its relationship with the systems models) and professional (as an ever-expanding field for empirical work), but once the school became a serious focus of attention policy considerations added further momentum. This was especially so when one recollects how much political protest in the 1960s came from young people on both the campuses and in the urban ghettos. Feelings were widespread that educational institutions could make a better job of imparting civic virtues. Most attacks have been directed at the limited scope of established patterns of political education — their failure to supplement the successful building of national loyalty with the inculcation of participatory norms.[24] The civics curriculum has been attacked for its avoidance of controversy: its content has been blandly optimistic rather than dealing with such delicate issues as race relations, the values and structure of capitalism, or American intervention overseas.[25] The importance of political participation has been stressed but the emphasis has been upon individual forms of action and in particular the potential impact of voting has been grossly exaggerated.[26]

These criticisms naturally led to proposals for change and several political scientists were invited to present their own political education models. Some were more reluctant than others, either because of a greater sense of humility or a greater fear at transgressing their allegedly neutral postures.[27] Certainly the reform proposals have been far from startling; the call is for more realism, the introduction of conflict issues, and the greater use of social science approaches to the material. The aim is to break passivity and compliance and to stimulate responsible participation. Richard Merelman is an excellent example of this concerned liberalism: 'We are concerned only that there be enough democrats in the American system to permit it to learn from but not succumb to dissidence. We would differ from our hypothetical critics only in striking the balance between socialized commitment and creative discontinuity.'[28] As we shall see the movement for a reformed American civics curriculum closely parallels the major thrust behind the introduction of political education programmes in the United Kingdom.[29]

It is often assumed that because the civics curriculum does not have a significant impact upon political behaviour that formal education is not an influential agent of political socialisation.[30] The suggestion is that something is effective only when it is exerting a positive influence in the direction the researcher deems desirable. Nothing could be more misleading. By exuding a bland optimism the civics curriculum is in fact exerting political influence, and if the basic patriotism of American schoolchildren is anything to go by, it appears to be effective. Langton and Kent Jennings discovered that for the white schoolchildren in their study the civics curriculum presented redundant information, and as a consequence had little impact upon them, whereas for the lower status black schoolchildren this was new information which helped to stimulate both their political interest and patriotism.[31] The civics curriculum was extending a value consensus amongst groups which previously were excluded from that consensus. In terms of increasing the political effectiveness of such groups this may be precisely the opposite of what they need but this is quite different from claiming that the civics curriculum is ineffective as a political socialisation agent. Judgements on the effectiveness of socialisation processes are dependent on what goals are defined for them.

Edgar Litt has argued that the political messages the schools transmit to their students differ according to the community location of the school.[32] In the American working-class community the schools teach the basic democratic procedures without stressing the need for participation or illustrating societal conflict. In the lower-middle-class community an emphasis on the responsibilities of citizenship accompanies training in the elements of democratic government. It is only in the affluent and politically aware community that civics training is more sophisticated, teaching the students some of the realities of political life. Litt's research runs counter to most of the related studies which see a universal blandness in the civics curricula regardless of the community in which the school is located. The best that Merelman can say for good schools is that they 'help create a rudimentary democratic consensus'.[33] Even if the school is not actively in the business of discriminating against working-class students, it is certain that its neutrality operates against the long-term political interests of such students. Given their social location they are unlikely to receive many participatory stimulants and this passivity is reinforced if the schools do not perform this task for them. The problem that the schools face is that if they attempt to encourage participatory norms they run a high risk of becoming politically divisive institutions. For example, this will happen if they start to dissect the political problems that face contemporary America. Various groups will be concerned to see that teachers adopt the correct line, and if they seek their defence in an impossible neutrality then we are back to square one again. Even to encourage participation has its pitfalls for there are always the questions of what forms it is to take (especially if voting is seen as ineffectual), and what ends it is designed to achieve. In the light of these problems the current blandness of the schools' civics instruction in the U.S. is perhaps something of a defence mechanism on the part of teachers.

The problem of becoming a politically divisive institution is compounded for the American schools by the fact that for a long time they have been viewed as above political partisanship, serving the cause of spreading common citizenship values. This is the opposite to the United Kingdom where citizenship is very much class-based and the schools have helped to differentiate their pupils along a variety of dimensions. Of course the ideological foundations of central social institutions like schools can be changed but unless this has wider political support it will not occur, and even local experimentation can give rise to considerable political controversy.

In reference to participatory values, Jaros and Canon claim, 'Of course, in the United States, advocacy of this value as a keystone of democratic order has been nearly universal.'[34] If this is so then it suggests that the schools are failing to inculcate a basic societal value. The alternative approach is to question Jaros and Canon's claim by arguing that the commitment to participatory values is little more than ritualistic. The schools make the correct noises by stressing the importance of the franchise but rarely go beyond this by explaining to their students that there are participatory forms that enable some to exercise considerably more influence than those who are prepared merely to vote. Unless the societal commitment to participation is deeper than we have suggested then Jaros and Canon are faced with the problem of explaining the apparent gulf between the educational institutions and the rest of the society. In similar vein to Jaros and Canon, Wirt and Kirst have argued that the United States is a society with pluralist values and a pluralist power structure but that the schools portray a world of harmony and consensus.[35] Again Wirt and Kirst offer no satisfactory explanation of this apparent contradiction. The systems model seems to blind them to the fact that in spite of its pluralism there are also power distributions in American society: what the schools teach is very much in the interest of those who dominate the power hierarchy. Wirt and Kirst are prepared to admit that civics training is satisfactory to many elements in society but they fail to identify those elements in power terms. Political values can be taken seriously only if they are supported by structures and processes that ensure their implementation. However, the evidence on the effects of civics education in the United States indicates that it has failed to create citizen support for the regime by cultivating informed participation. Quite the contrary, for civics education is a mechanism of social control that aims to ensure the mass compliance of the citizenry to the *status quo* and to incorporate them within a broad value consensus. Heinz Eulau has raised the question of whether the polity determines the character of the educational system or vice versa.[36] A further question that needs to be asked affects the relationship between political change and educational reform. If, as we have maintained, the political functions of the schools reflect a societal power structure, then we need to know whether educational innovation is likely to have much effect without first directly undermining this power structure. Up to now the curriculum innovation in this field looks very much like it is tilting at windmills.

The school was of interest to political scientists not only because of its policy implications but also because it helped to further their professional interests. An enormous amount of time and energy was devoted to ascertaining the relative influence of socialising agents. This usually took the form of defining the agents in specific ways (for example, the school was inevitably measured by exposure or non-exposure to a formal civics curriculum!) and using statistical tests, of varying complexity, to ascertain which had the strongest relationship to the dependent variables (levels of political interest, cognition, efficacy, etc.).[37] This raised quantitative analysis to a higher level than the more usual presentation of simple correlations, thus placing political socialisation studies firmly in the behavioural school of social sciences. Apart from its statistical virtuosity (and perhaps even allowing for it), this approach has very little to recommend it. First, complex variables like the family and the school are usually over-simplified. Second, no reasons are presented as to why it is important to know whether the school is more influential than the family in shaping political behaviour, or vice versa. If one is interested in stimulating political change through educational reform then this has some possible relevance, but this has not been a major concern of the political scientists working in the field, and in any case we have already cast doubts upon the utility of this approach to change. Third, it ignores the fact that all of us are entangled in a complex socialisation web and to disentangle the various threads in this manner not merely simplifies reality but makes a mockery of it. Fourth, it concentrates attention upon the formal goals of education as well as the explicit content of educational programmes and these need to be reinterpreted in the light of what best serves the interests of the major power centres in the society. Finally, and this is a supplement to the fourth point, if the aim of the civics curriculum (to take one variable that is central to this kind of analysis) is to extend an uncontroversial value consensus then one would not expect radical attitudinal differences between those who have been exposed to it and those who have not.

So far we have argued that although the expansion of the subdiscipline of political socialisation led to an increasing interest in the school, this was primarily for professional and policy considerations. What has remained substantially intact is the initial systems framework of analysis and for the most part the expansion has enhanced this as the new studies have been placed within its context. This is surprising in view of the fact that the political violence that broke out in the 1960s made it increasingly untenable to hold on to the notion that a universal socialisation process was responsible for the vast majority of Americans internalising a convenient balance of subject and citizen roles to end up as well-rounded supportive adults.[38] Therefore the central issue raised by the new historical context was the viability of the intellectual rationalisation for political socialisation, that is, its ability to account for political stability. The eminent members of the discipline have proved themselves masters at fudging this relationship between political socialisation and system stability. In 1957 Easton referred to the importance of formal education in securing systems maintenance but at the same time he noted that a system could change, or, as he quaintly put it, 'fail to maintain itself'.[39] Subsequently Easton has been more likely to refer to systems persistence than systems maintenance. In a 1965 article he linked persistence and change by stating that we need to know how political systems persisted even as they changed.[40] By 1969 he was asserting neutrality for his definition, in claiming that political socialisation could perpetuate either stability or instability, depending upon the character of the polity.[41]

The increasing looseness of the theoretical discussion was matched by an equally haphazard extension of the empirical work. A process that encompassed white schoolchildren, took place within the family, and was completed in all its essentials in the childhood years, was broadened to cover different cultural groups, a myriad of socialisation agents, and the total life cycle. It is not that such developments were unwelcome, but that they took place in such a way that in the haste to discover untapped research areas the purpose of the search was forgotten. Two things remain: a tottering systems framework of analysis and a tendency to argue inductively about both the causes of data patterns as well as their wider impact. For example, Greenstein has on more than one occasion claimed, however tentatively, that because British working-class children were more likely than middle-class children to believe that the Queen ruled as well as reigned this partially explained the deference of certain sectors of the adult working class.[42] On another occasion Dennis and his collaborators were predicting a breakdown in the legitimacy of the British political system because of unexpectedly high levels of adolescent antipathy towards certain of its features.[43] Besides the naïvety of these interpretations they are a manifestation of American academic imperialism which has dominated the comparative dimension in political socialisation research.

Political Education in Britain

In his influential synopsis of the political socialisation literature Hyman failed to refer to the work of Charles Merriam and his associates.[44] This is an astounding omission for Merriam represents a whole tradition in the subdiscipline, one that examines the political control of the learning process and the way in which that learning process tries to structure political behaviour. It is within this tradition, which we prefer to term political education, that we intend to place our observations on the British educational system. There are three reasons why this approach to linking politics and education has remained dormant in the United States since Merriam's time. In the first place it does not readily lend itself to quantification but rather it requires making numerous qualitative judgements about the political impact of educational policies. Secondly, in spite of the strong emphasis in the civics curriculum upon training good citizens, American education has remained aloof from partisan politics throughout this century.[45] To impute a political motivation to educational policy could drag education into the political mire once again. Thirdly, as we have already discussed, the official function of American schools has been to extend a value consensus and because this is not politically divisive it has helped to disguise the political consequences of formal education.

Ironically it is much easier to attach political motivations to British educational institutions, although formal instruction in civics or similar subjects is a curriculum novelty. The societal motivations behind the state's intervention in formal education, and the subsequent expansion of its role are easy to document.[46] Education has always been conceived in terms which, although allegedly non-partisan, nevertheless have strong political implications, such as the need to expand certain categories of skilled manpower, or impart the rudiments of an education to newly enfranchised voters. More significant is the fact that the schools have been used to legitimise differential forms of citizenship while, at least at the level of myth, American schools have helped to create a common citizenship. In theory the differentiation that has appeared between students in American schools is not a consequence of the character of the educational experience but rather of the students making their own individual uses of the available opportunities. In other words success or failure is personalised, the result of individual effort or lack of effort. Parsons believes that the universal acceptance of an achievement norm legitimates, in the eyes of those who 'fail', the process of differentiation.[47]

In both Britain and the United States, therefore, formal education is part of the process by which inequality is legitimated. In the United States equality has been defined as equality of opportunity; theoretically the schools are institutions which attempt to maximise that principle. A large body of socialisation information illustrates a marked decline in the positive attitudes of American adolescents towards their political system.[48] This is particularly true of Afro–American adolescents who show remarkably positive attitudes in early childhood. The impression is that the values acquired in school are gradually put to the test and increasingly found wanting. In Britain there will be less of this 'reality-testing' of values because the educational system is more firmly locked into wider societal structures and values. More specifically formal education establishes boundaries to the concept of equality of opportunity by interlocking schools with the class structure and the job market.

T. H. Marshall has linked the expansion of formal education with the drive for the extension of citizenship rights.[49] This has a measure of historical validity in relation to Britain, but of equal significance is the way education has reinforced different forms of citizenship. Central to this task is the preservation of power patterns. This may not necessitate very much direct or explicit political indoctrination but it relates closely to all the prerequisites that are essential to obtaining power in British society. Children are allocated to schools that provide contrasting educational experiences. These experiences relate the individual to the structure of political power in both direct and indirect ways. The best example of a direct link is provided by the public schools and Oxbridge, for the pattern of recruitment from these institutions into various factions of the British political élite is sufficiently pronounced to talk of a structural relationship. Secondly, and as important, are the indirect links: the differential political role socialisation of the students (especially in terms of the stimulation of political activity), and the acquisition of conceptual skills, without which it is difficult to be politically literate.[50]

Educational institutions may not be the *cause* of this differentiation — their structures, processes and content may simply be a response to a stratified society.[51] But it is within the educational system that the greatest concern with legitimating this inequality is to be found. This alone suggests that the schools are not simply purveyors of education and culture but also ideological centres. The ideology, however, is not an entity that exists in its own right but rather is bound up with the cultural and educational experience that is found within schools. For example, the British educational system has been committed to giving every individual a secondary education commensurate with his age, aptitude and ability; in other words, it is officially devoted to the task of maximising individual talent. To fulfil this task would require more resources than the educational system is ever likely to possess and so ways have to be found to solve the problem that this poses. Intelligence testing in the past has accomplished this function for it was used to determine officially what individuals were capable of achieving. At the same time a greater value was placed upon certain accomplishments as opposed to others which was clearly reflected in the pattern of resource allocation. Intelligence testing, therefore, served a dual purpose: on the one hand it separated students into categories which would enable them better to receive an education that was deemed appropriate for them, while on the other hand it could be used to justify patterns of educational and cultural experiences that were intimately related to inequality.

Although one of the major criticisms of intelligence tests is directed at their inherent cultural biases, with the consequence that they discriminate heavily in favour of middle-class children and against working-class children, they have replaced a straightforward class allocation of educational resources. But they have done so in a way that cushions the interaction between class cultures. Only selected members of the working class will enter the grammar schools and follow the official path that leads to political literacy and perhaps even political power. These selected individuals are not necessarily going to be indoctrinated into different partisan loyalties (although many will find it difficult to resist the pressures to change), but both directly (if they go as far as attending Oxbridge), and indirectly (in terms of skill acquisition), they are entering different political worlds from their parents. The price they pay for this is an inevitable change in their political consciousness and one which pushes them towards the middle-class mores that dominate their new social context. Of course much of this enculturation will take place informally but it does so within the structures that are created by the formal processes of differentiation.

Besides intelligence testing, which has usually determined entry into one type of school or another, externally controlled examinations (especially general certificates of education) have performed similar political functions. The examinations are stepping stones (the 11+, ordinary level G.C.E.s, and advanced level G.C.E.s) that determine entry into the educational élite. In performing this academic task they thin out the number of working-class adolescents who are making their way up the educational ladder.[52] But — and this is a point that will be elaborated upon shortly — they are a two-edged political sword, which is true of many features of the educational system. The secondary modern schools were initially supposed to have an experimental curriculum that would provide a different kind of secondary education, one that was better suited than the traditional curriculum to the abilities and aptitudes of its pupils. No one was fooled into believing that the secondary moderns could offer an education that gave as much prestige and control of scarce resources as that available in the grammar and public schools. Some years after their creation, in an attempt to upgrade their schools' status, secondary modern pupils were permitted to sit general certificates of education. For the pupils concerned this made deep inroads into the experimental curriculum, for their education now had to be geared to the demands of an externally controlled examination. But the increasing examination successes of these pupils cast considerable doubt upon the validity of the 11+ for the general certificate of education was originally considered to be beyond the abilities of secondary modern students. Thus their examination success was another weapon to be used against selective secondary education. Of equal interest, and a much less explored topic, is the impact this had on the secondary modern schools. The examinations increased the range of techniques for refining working-class pupils and further divided them culturally. It was a significant step in the drift towards basing inequality on meritocratic rather than class criteria.

Up to the present two main factors have prevented the British educational system from successfully legitimating inequality in meritocratic terms. The first is the retention of a powerful and prestigious private sector which selects its pupils overwhelmingly from those who can afford to pay the fees. The second is the time it is taking to destroy the 11+ examination, which has discriminated so heavily against the interests of the working class. These two facets of the present system result in class-based recruitment patterns into the schools and the class-related links to the occupational structure. It is not that changing these features will automatically create educational institutions that are favourably disposed towards the interests of the working class, but without such changes there can be no progress in this direction. One of the contemporary struggles is the move towards comprehensive education which is intended to eradicate these central vestiges of its class basis.

In two respects our view of the political functions of education are similar to the part that political socialisation occupies in the systems model. First, our understanding of political education and the part accorded political socialisation in Easton's model both have an underlying objective — to regulate the distribution of power in society. Second, both stress the importance of discovering how particular societies try to achieve this objective. In all other respects, however, the differences are critical. We do not see the central goal as building diffuse support for the polity but rather as legitimating inequality. In both cases it is possible to ignore how this is accomplished (as is true of the political socialisation of literature) but this is a theme to which this book will constantly return. Although it could have chosen otherwise, the political socialisation literature has defined the *political* aspects of support too narrowly and the same problem could apply to the legitimation of inequality. What is needed instead is a broader focus on the political connotations of all aspects of building support or legitimating inequality. In the United Kingdom, for example, workers' support for the current government's 'voluntary' prices and incomes policy is of the utmost significance, just as inequality in access to educational resources has an impact upon both the development of the individual's political consciousness and the character of the political system.

In the systems model of the polity, political socialisation was conceived of as an input into the political system and this tends to de-emphasise its relationship to both the wider societal values and structures. Our view of political education is totally the opposite: the political functions of formal education reflect ideological themes in the wider society, and they are fulfilled by trying to integrate educational institutions with other structures. This is a broad view of the process of political education and one which stresses its controlled, even directed nature. Obviously a considerable amount of political education is implicit and takes place within institutions (above all the family) which cannot be readily manipulated but what transpires within these institutions will generally fall within the parameters established by those who control the state. Where it does not it is usually ineffectual as a political force and if effectual indicative of a divided regime.

Hess and Torney comment: 'These children [referring to some of those with lower I.Q.s and/or lower social status] are graduating from grammar school incompletely socialized into the political community.'[53] By this they mean that these children are not politically literate and as such are unlikely to participate in the political process. Their incomplete socialisation is dependent upon the notion that the complete citizen is a participant. If the societal goal is a participatory citizenry, and there is something more than a token commitment to it, then this is a fair judgement. But if the aim is to create political inequality, and our interpretation of the evidence suggests this is a realistic view of political socialisation goals in the United States, then these individuals are not incompletely socialised. Besides providing a better explanation of the evidence, our understanding of political education de-emphasises such notions as 'incomplete', 'partial' or 'inadequate' socialisation. One may want to disapprove of behaviour (either because it fails to conform to established mores or what we think the mores should be) but this is different from the claim that the behaviour is lacking something. We see behaviour as the product of a complex series of interactions between the individual and his environment, and this is where attention needs to be focused, rather than judgement passed on the individual's political behaviour.

The proponents of the systems model have seen it as a framework for comparative analysis. Political socialisation was a function that all political systems performed and in each case the goal was to build diffuse support.[54] We have posed a different function for political education (to legitimate inequality) with the implication that if this is successful the end result will also be political stability. We do not suggest, however, that we have a framework for comparative analysis. Much of the comparative work in political socialisation has meant applying a slogan ('political socialisation builds diffuse support') to different cultural contexts, and we would not want to replace one slogan with another. As should be clear from our discussion of political education in

Britain, *how* the socialisation process is structured is as important
as the final product. The socialising agents make sense only when
related to wider social structures and it is impossible to see the
function they perform as a mere input into the political system.
In Britain the processes of political education reflect the class
basis of society, although increasingly there is interaction between
class and meritocratic criteria in the distribution of scarce
resources. What we want to know about other societies is how
they distribute scarce resources, including political resources, and
what ideological themes they employ to justify this pattern of
resource allocation as opposed to other possible patterns. The
fact that the end product is also very likely to be inequality pales
somewhat against these demands.

One of the central features of political education is its
ideological nature, that is, it is not a neutral process of citizen
training for it attempts to inculcate *particular* values and attitudes. In this respect we concur with Miliband in criticising the
prevailing political socialisation literature for ignoring the ideological biases that are built into the learning process.[55] However — and this is a point that we return to in some detail in
the following chapter — we are convinced that this is a precarious
process of indoctrination. Social structures are not static so there
is a changing relationship between political education and more
general societal pressures. The chapter on the shifting ideological
basis of higher education also illustrates this point.[56] This can
result in a bitter questioning of the contemporary relevance of
formal education. At the same time the legitimations of inequality
are something that élites cannot take for granted, and we have
seen a concerted attack upon intelligence testing. It was always
doubtful if many parents (particularly parents of children who
were classified as 'failures') accepted them as making either meaningful or just judgements. Although the relationship between the
British class structure and formal education has been carefully
managed, it is a tense interaction. The economy has required the
training of certain skills which has meant that the schools have
sponsored limited amounts of social mobility. The stresses upon
the social control mechanisms of formal education are thereby
increased, and the fact that the schools have managed to fulfil
this task without inadvertently ushering in the revolution is no
proof that the tension is absent. In grander terms, the controlling
and liberating impulses of education are both found within our
educational institutions, and the key to the history of British education is the way in which the precarious balance between the two
has been managed. Our view of the political functions of education

does not flow from an optimistic interpretation of the power structure of British society, as Chapter 3 will show, but where others see order and control, we are convinced that there is in fact growing vacillation and potential chaos, although not necessarily much change.

The political socialisation literature has assumed that the individual political learning process is integrated (learning experiences harmonise with one another to produce a well-rounded political personality), and that the sum of those individualised personalities is a stable political order. We have claimed that the individual learning process is fraught with tension, and although the individual may end up with a stable political personality, it is a precarious stability that can be overthrown by a change in his circumstances. The vague recognition that perhaps some patterns of political socialisation are a threat to the smooth functioning of the political order (thus the references to incomplete socialisation) is overshadowed by the concept of a balanced citizenry in which differentially socialised individuals inter-relate in a harmonious fashion with their fellow men. Even the calls for the introduction of a more radically oriented civics education are usually founded on the belief that this will improve the quality of the present political order and not undermine it. It is our contention that political socialisation processes are ultimately the product of power relationships; what harmony may result from differential patterns of socialisation is an imposed harmony which works in the political interests of the minority and against those of the majority. Finally, although we have a wider view of political learning than the political socialisation theorists — one which sees much of its character being shaped by social and economic structures and processes — ironically this has led us to evaluate more cautiously the direction and extent of its influence.

The Inevitability of Politics

Up to now the state has not controlled the nature of political education in Britain in a direct or explicit sense. It has maintained John Stuart Mill's distinction between 'state education' and the 'enforcement of education by the state' and opted for the latter.[57] Although the state has provided education, it has not used the educational institutions to perpetuate a closed definition of what is politically acceptable. This is unnecessary when nearly all citizens are supportive of the regime and numerous societal institutions harmonise to reinforce that support. Furthermore the indirect political consequences of formal education are considerable: the interaction of the class structure and the educational system, the content of schooling and the bearing this has upon obtaining conceptual skills, the informal inculcation of cultural values, political role socialisation — in particular the distribution of pupils along an active–passive continuum — and in a few cases structural links between the political élite and educational institutions. We are not claiming that schools are the major force for political education in this society. Quite the contrary, for we see the socialisation process as a series of interdependent although not necessarily integrated experiences. It is because of this that we are more than sceptical of trying to bring about social change through educational reform. Without changing the fundamental relationship between the class structure and the educational system, classroom-based reforms are like Canute trying to will back the waves. Unfortunately, unlike Canute, many are blind to the absurdity of this.

Our understanding of the political impact of formal education is also critical of those who would separate schooling as a variable and measure its influence in isolation from other social forces. The influence of schools is measured not simply by their bearing upon known attitudes or behaviour, but also what success they have in preventing alternative patterns of behaviour or attitudes from emerging. In contemporary Britain the individual's educational experience is heavily dependent upon the social intake of the school he attends, while the type of school attended has a close relationship to the varying channels into the job market. We are not thinking of causal relationships between independent and dependent variables, but the gradual accumulation of varying life experiences which slowly mould the shape of individual behaviour.

Defining the schools in specific terms (their civics curriculum has been the favourite definition of those interested in political education) and then ascertaining their impact upon designated attitudes has invariably shown the limitations of their influence. Besides totally contradicting the character of our model of political education, this overlooks the most important political function of formal schooling: its legitimation of inequality. Regardless of how successful educational institutions may be at creating socio-political patterns of behaviour (and we have characterised them as reinforcing agents), their primary function is to provide the ideology which justifies these particular patterns as opposed to others. Therefore it is not only a question of what they create but whether they can successfully legitimate what is created. We see this as a precarious process and one which is forever changing its shape and form. On the one hand there is the inherent tension between education as an agent of social control and as a force for individual liberation, and on the other hand the need to readjust schooling to changing societal goals. So besides a permanent internal tension within the educational process perpetual short-run stresses and strains will emerge. One of the central questions is in whose eyes the patterns of inequality are viewed as being just? Whereas the privileged may feel that all is well with the world, the underprivileged are likely to be less enamoured with their lot and they are a constant source of potential opposition to the prevailing educational system.

Chapter 3

Education and the Hegemony of the British Ruling Class

The Cultural Assumptions of the Ruling-Class Model

Power in British society is not shared equally amongst either individuals or the groups that make up the social fabric. The disagreements are considerable as to how inequitable the power distribution is and while some see small differentials others believe that power in contemporary British society is as unequally distributed as ever. The relationship between perceptions of inequality and a moral evaluation of it is far from simple. For some the moral outrage at the injustices of inegalitarianism knows few bounds, while others are prepared to justify gross inequalities or voice their concern at the steady erosion of power differentials. Another group accepts inequality as either inevitable or desirable but would wish to see it based upon new, invariably more meritocratic, foundations. The purpose of this chapter is to evaluate the case that a morally reprehensible inegalitarianism still exists in Britain. We are analysing this perspective in preference to the others because it is one that is widely supported, because it has a strong theoretical and empirical basis, and because it challenges some of our own assumptions about how the distribution of power in contemporary British society is perpetuated.

Most variants of the inegalitarian view of British society make the exercise of power dependent upon economic variables, that is, the ownership and/or control of the means of production, and patterns of wealth and income distributions. As important as these factors may be, it is not the intention of this chapter to deal with them but rather to examine the cultural forces which buttress inequality. Although economic forces may be viewed as the ultimate determinants of the character of society, in recent years increasing attention has been paid to the influence of cultural power. For example, those who believe that Britain is dominated by a ruling class stress that although the power of this class is dependent upon its control or ownership of the means of production, this economic power is reinforced by the cultural hegemony of the ruling class. This chapter, therefore, examines the assumptions underlying an expanding segment of the ruling-class model, and to undermine these would be to cast doubts upon the model's overall validity.

Various concepts have been used to label the powerful. As Giddens notes: 'No field of sociology has been more subject to vagaries of usage and to nebulous and shifting conceptualisations. Terms are legion: "ruling class", "upper class", "governing class", "political class", "elite", "power elite", and "leadership group" vie with each other for supremacy in the literature.'[1] Each term suggests that not only is power acquired by particular means but also that those who hold power have different degrees of internal cohesion. The terms also imply contrasting power ratios between the 'powerful' and the 'less powerful'. 'Establishment', 'ruling class' and 'power elite' all conjure up images of contrasting intensities and forms of inequality. In this chapter we will confine most of our attention to those who believe that Britain is dominated by a ruling class. Their work is the most sophisticated in theoretical terms for it attempts to relate the study of power to the British class structure. When it comes to ascertaining the cultural forces that help to perpetuate inequalities of power the differences between the various theorists with this perspective are not as pronounced as in other respects. Opinion is sharply divided between those who argue that power is dependent upon the ownership of the means of production and those who are more inclined to stress control of the major bureaucratic organisations (whether these be located in the corporate, political or military spheres). All sides, however, recognise that those who hold power will try to establish their cultural hegemony and the ways of achieving this are relatively similar regardless of what the actual basis of power may be.

Three cultural themes central to the ruling-class model will be examined in this chapter. No matter how the ruling class is defined

if it is to be an effective ruling class then it has first to
maintain its cohesiveness and consciousness. This will not be
achieved by merely occupying an economic role or controlling
bureaucratic structures. In fact nearly all theorists consider the
identity of their ruling groups to be dependent upon a variety
of cultural forces. Those who control power also need to legitimate
this control, and the second theme is thus the process of legitimation or how the powerful in British society attempt to establish
their cultural hegemony. The third theme examines the consciousness of the British working class, for if the ruling class has indeed
established a cultural hegemony then this must have dire consequences for working-class consciousness.

In keeping with the spirit of this book the main focus will
be upon the part played by formal education within these cultural
themes. This is only a partial view, for culture embraces many
forces, but education has been given pride of place in the creation
and perpetuation of the cultural hegemony of the ruling class;
although partial, it covers the cultural force that most ruling-class
theorists consider to be most influential. This chapter examines
a specific class view of British society. The focus is more upon
testing an established theory rather than using data to create
new perspectives as we do in later chapters.

The Cohesion and Consciousness of the Ruling Class

The narrower the understanding of the ruling class the easier it
is to account for its cohesion and consciousness. Aaronovitch has
noted that 'finance capital is not some "lobby" outside the political
system, but is built into its foundation. The finance capitalists
are in truth the ruling class.'[2] The continuing homogeneity of
this ruling class is secured by the ability of its members to hand
on their posts of power and prestige to their offspring when the
appropriate time arrives, and Aaronovitch carries this feudal view
of Britain one step further, for the willing lackeys, without whom
the finance capitalists would find it difficult to govern, are also
recruited on a class basis. In this respect he stresses the importance
of the higher ranks of the civil service: 'They come mostly from
the fringes of those families — the poor relations, one might say;
and this is indicated by the difference in school and club to which
the top civil servants belong as compared with the directors, say,
of the big banks, insurance companies, or Ministers of the Crown.'[3]
At the same time Aaronovitch recognised the necessity for these
two factions — finance capitalists and higher civil servants — to

work in harmony with one another: 'But while they have in this sense a separate existence, viewed overall the Administrative Class and especially the Permanent Heads must be considered as part of the political and executive brain of the ruling class — their loyalty being guaranteed by training, selection and family background.'[4] So, although he commences with a view of the ruling class which would make its cohesion and consciousness dependent upon family replenishment he ends up by stressing the importance of élite recruitment and socialisation patterns.

The emphasis upon élite recruitment and socialisation patterns is necessitated by the fact that most theorists view the ruling class as composed of a number of factions, although in the final analysis all the factions are bound by a common relationship to the means of production. Bottomore writes,

> It is not surprising, therefore, that the elite groups — business leaders, higher civil servants, a large part of the political leadership — continue to be recruited largely from the upper class and the upper levels of the middle class in these societies. The upper class still perpetuates itself by passing on wealth, educational privileges, and occupational chances, and these things ensure the continuing concentration of property ownership, prestige and power in a few hands.[5]

For Bottomore the élite groups form a ruling class because they are recruited overwhelmingly from similar class backgrounds. Ruling-class homogeneity is maintained by the fact that its various factions partake of the same class advantages, material or cultural.

It is hard to disagree with Guttsman's claim: 'There exists today in Britain a "ruling class" if we mean by it a group which provides the majority of those who occupy positions of power, and who, in their turn, can materially assist *their* sons to reach similar positions.'[6] But the more interesting cases enter the ruling class from other family backgrounds, and this eventuality is another reason why socialisation processes are believed to ensure cohesiveness and consciousness. By selecting for entry into the ruling class only those working-class individuals who have experienced a lengthy process of anticipatory socialisation the disruptive potential of recruiting from more diverse family backgrounds is minimised. In a typically uncompromising statement Rex writes, 'The fact is that even the worker's child who makes it to Oxbridge and from there to Whitehall has already undergone a pattern of anticipatory socialization, which ensures that his background makes *no* difference.'[7]

How do recruitment and socialisation processes protect the ruling class against internal factionalism? This is the one field in which British élite studies have proliferated and most of the findings agree on the main trends.[8] Until comparatively recently most members of the British ruling class have been recruited from a narrow band of the class scale (upper- and upper-middle-class families) and have experienced the dubious benefits of a public school education.[9] This pattern has been changing slowly. The erosion is markedly less pronounced in some areas (for example, the City) than in others (for example, the civil service). The trend is towards a more meritocratic ruling class which is recruited from a somewhat wider range of the social spectrum (although still heavily biased against women and individuals from unskilled working-class families) and is dominated by university graduates, especially those from Oxbridge. It is ironic that these changes, which have resulted in the opening up of most élite groups, have had the opposite effect upon the parliamentary Labour Party. As time passes the party is recruiting fewer M.P.s with working-class origins, and although background characteristics still distinguish the M.P.s of the two main parties, increasingly they converge so that to become a member of parliament — regardless of party persuasion — means to join another of the liberal professions.[10]

Crewe has claimed: 'But to establish the common but unrepresentative social antecedents of British elite groups is only part of the story. It does not show that these groups possess Meisel's three "C's" — consciousness, conspiracy or coherence — which form the necessary conditions for something akin to a "ruling class" or "power elite" to be said to exist.'[11] He maintains that even if élites are drawn from the same backgrounds this does not *guarantee* their integration. But we would argue that this is more likely than if they were drawn from widely different backgrounds. One also has to keep in mind the socialising experiences that are associated with these recruitment patterns. In spite of what fissures may appear amongst potential recruits before entry into an élite group, the distinctiveness of their work-centred socialisation patterns is pronounced. These experiences do not guarantee internal consciousness or coherence but they distinguish the individuals exposed to them from the vast bulk of the population. Furthermore some studies illustrate the homogenising pressures that occur within the ruling-class stratum.[12] Work-centred rituals and job performance styles, as well as patterns of social interaction (for example club memberships) can help to cement the internal bonds and further delineate the élite groups from the citizenry at large.

Although Crewe has presented only part of the argument, there is enough evidence to suggest that his implied conclusion — that it is more meaningful to talk of differing élite factions rather than élite groups that are integrated into a wider ruling class — is indeed correct. Due to the widening of the recruitment boundaries the élite groups cannot be described as a ruling class because of their restricted class origins. As Bottomore writes,

> If changes in the recruitment of the elite result in its members being drawn in substantial numbers from several social classes and strata, the social bonds which unite the members can no longer arise merely from the similarities of social origin, but are likely to be formed principally by the occupation itself and the educational experience which leads up to it. In this case the higher civil servants may become more conscious of themselves as an occupational elite, rather than as members of a traditional social class. . . .[13]

And presumably what could be true for the higher civil servants could also be true for other élite groups. The potential for élite conflict is increased by the differential erosion of class-based recruitment patterns. This can lead to contrasting kinds of individuals being drawn into the various élites so that potentially élite groups share *neither* common class backgrounds *nor* common anticipatory socialising experiences.[14]

Even if members of an élite group are drawn from similar social backgrounds there is no certainty that they have shared similar socialisation experiences. In fact few of the ruling-class theorists are interested in socialisation experiences for they believe that entry into the ruling class is dependent upon the steady accumulation of class advantages rather than exposure to special learning processes. Of course part of the class advantage is a special learning experience but once this is considered seriously then broad generalisations become increasingly tenuous because a wide class perspective gives way to the peculiarities of *family-based* socialisation styles. Even that *bête noire* the public school is not the all-embracing institution we have been led to believe. Although Wakeford refers to public schools as 'total' institutions, he goes on to describe contrasting ways of adapting to them, and significantly has concluded that 'conformity' is not the predominant mode of adjustment but 'colonisation', which consists of an ambivalence towards the formal rules and regulations combined with an indifference towards the schools' goals.[15] This does not lessen the social barriers between public schoolboys and other school-students, for, although individual reactions to a public school education may differ, there is not a pattern of shared experiences between public school pupils and their peers in the state schools. In fact quite the contrary, for even though the public school has its rebels they are reacting, albeit in a different manner, to an educational environment which they share with the public school conformists. Certainly Wakeford's data suggests that the broad generalisation Weinberg is prepared to make is unwarranted: 'It is no wonder that the English elite is known for its caution in administration, as well as lack of entrepreneurial *brio*, for the prefect system is ideally suited to produce other-directed men who will make excellent recruits for bureaucracies.'[16] All public school pupils, in fact nearly all English schoolchildren, have to come to terms with the prefect system, but they will do so in very different ways with very different consequences for their future behaviour.

When studies of the social backgrounds of élite groups reveal that many of their members are drawn from either upper-class or upper-middle-class families this is invariably interpreted as a measure of not only the maintenance of class power but also the perpetuation of traditional patterns of behaviour — like father like son. Conversely when individuals from working-class families enter élite groups the assumption is that the influence of their working-class origins has been obliterated long ago by the forces of anticipatory socialisation. Obviously these individuals are in contrasting social situations, and as a consequence one would expect their patterns of behaviour to vary, but whether this justifies diametrically opposite conclusions regarding the socialising influence of the family is another matter. For working-class adolescents it is the educational system, the grammar schools and the universities, which provide the route into élite groups. These institutions, including Oxbridge, are far from being either 'total' or 'closed', and just as responses to the much more tightly knit public schools differ, so one can expect even more diverse reactions to the pressures of what it means to be socially mobile via the educational system. Educationally sponsored social mobility may cause a break with ones class origins, although the extent of this and the forms it can take will vary, but this is a long way from demonstrating that the individual is turned into a well-rounded member of an integrated ruling class.[17] The increase of meritocratic pressures upon élite selection may in the long run assist élite homogeneity but it will accomplish this only by opening up some of the more traditional channels of élite entry, and modifying their associated value biases, that have favoured members of the privileged classes in the past. It is not that the new criteria will exclude those classes which have made up élite groups in the past, but that the range of competition has changed along with the methods of recruitment. For example, all the evidence points to a bridging of the gap between the public schools and the prestigious direct grant grammar schools, brought about by a joint fear of the move towards comprehensive education, and more significantly in this context, by an increasing emphasis upon academic standards as measured by the examination success of their pupils.

Socialisation processes are much more likely to create several élite identities rather than a single ruling-class identity. Some theorists have suggested that the modern propensity for certain individuals to move readily from one élite group to the next is one indication of the integration of élite groups, but as Giddens has pointed out, 'A man may hold several directorships, but may wield effective power in none of them.'[18] We would suggest that it is the social and moral integration of élite groups, established and reinforced over periods of time by their internal socialisation processes, that makes it difficult for 'outsiders' to gain institutional power in the face of opposition from 'insiders'. Exceptions to the norm can be found, but this appears to be the age of career specialisation, and even in the case of the exceptions one would want to know what constraints established personnel place upon the outsiders in their exercise of institutional power.[19]

Cultural forces may not support the concept of a ruling class, but it is evident that they influence quite significantly the social and skill composition of élite groups. This is well illustrated by the higher civil servants, of whom Bottomore has written, 'Recruitment to public offices by competitive examination, or on the basis of educational qualifications only brings about a real equality of opportunity if those of equal ability have equal chances of preparing themselves for the public service, by obtaining the necessary diplomas or the necessary training for the entrance examinations.'[20] In fact the problem goes some way beyond this for significant cultural biases are built into the selection procedures, and in order to achieve equality of opportunity these as well as access to educational resources have to be changed. The alternative is to establish not only equality of educational opportunity but also identical educational experiences to neutralise the prevailing cultural biases, which is both undesirable and unrealistic.

The Victorian reforms of the civil service replaced nepotism with subjective administrative values that over time assumed the status of objective standards.[21] Administration was an art rather than a science and was best fulfilled by those whose education stimulated within the individual a combination of effortless superiority and cultured scepticism.[22] Those responsible for recruitment felt that the qualities they sought were most likely to be found in public schoolboys who had read either classics or history at Oxbridge. Under Method 1, entry into the old administrative class of the civil service was by a rigorous written examination in subjects of the candidate's own choice which has been supplemented (since the 1920s) by an interview. Kelsall has shown that the interview was biased against working-class candidates, for a number of them who performed well in the written examination were eliminated as a result of their interview.[23] Perhaps the interview tests qualities that are overlooked in a written examination; blending the two might result in better recruits. This may be so, but it is equally true that the interviews were socially selective, and as the interview situations stimulate personal judgements, it is hard to believe that this selectivity is not a consequence of the prejudices of the interviewers.

Over time the higher civil service has become an Oxbridge, as opposed to a public school élite, and this change has led to the entry of a larger number of recruits with working-class backgrounds. Meritocratic exclusiveness has replaced social exclusiveness, and until recently so great has been the Oxbridge hold over the recruitment channels that graduates from other universities have persuaded themselves that it is not worth their while to enter the supposedly 'open' competition. In addition, since 1945 the lower echelons of the higher civil service have been broadened, both socially and educationally, by internal promotions. Kelsall, however, has suggested that in the future this may not be so influential a factor, for internal promotions are levelling off and better educated individuals with middle-class backgrounds are being promoted.[24] What is equally significant is that the present method of entry (Method 2) also appears to be biased against working-class recruits. Since 1948 Method 2, by which internal and external candidates are recruited to the post of administrative trainee, has gradually replaced Method 1. Method 2, more popularly known as the country house selection method, relies more upon extensive observation and interviewing of the candidates than written examinations; although this has resulted in an increase in the number of female recruits, the number of men with working-class origins is declining. This is further evidence of the cultural biases of interviews and has led Kelsall to conclude that 'although the position remains very uncertain one would guess that the higher civil service of the future might well be significantly more homogeneous in social and educational background than was the case in, say 1950 or 1967, with all that this implies'.[25] And even more pungently Balogh has claimed that 'a new type of favouritism, if not nepotism, has been obviously infiltrating into the system'.[26]

It is difficult to pinpoint precisely why interview situations should be detrimental to the interests of the working-class applicants. It could be a question of accent, dress and mannerisms, which would suggest the maintenance of subtle forms of social snobbery. Sampson repeatedly refers to the importance of language styles in keeping the well-oiled Whitehall machine functioning and this may mean a closer affinity from the initial point of contact between those whose class and educational backgrounds facilitate easy communication.[27] These differences suggest that at least as far as applicants are concerned, anticipatory socialisation pressures have not succeeded in obliterating all distinctions between the various social groups. Of course observation and interview may weed out those with the worse 'blemishes'!

Although the cultural evidence suggests it is more realistic to talk of élite factions rather than a ruling class, other criteria can be employed to imply the opposite. Bottomore has claimed that 'the upper class in Britain has been able to resist with considerable success the attack upon its economic interests, and that in the sense of having the power to defend its interests it has maintained itself during the present century as a ruling class'.[28] In other words the patterns of power are demonstrated by policy outcomes. This is a dangerous line of argument because policy may be the consequence of all kinds of pressures besides internal power distributions. In fact one of the striking features of the contemporary world is how states with *allegedly* contrasting patterns of internal power adopt very similar policy options. In parallel vein Poulantzas has recognised that factions are to be found in the ruling class but the differences that may divide them are contained by the overall hegemony of the monopoly capitalist faction.[29] But his position is dependent upon class forces ultimately rectifying apparent changes in consciousness that have occurred through an erosion of those class forces. For example, he writes of the working class that 'it continues to be a distinct class, which also (and chiefly) means we can reasonably hope that it will not eternally continue — where it still does — to be social–democratic and that socialism's prospects therefore remain *intact* in Europe'.[30] So workers (regardless of all the pressures to change their consciousness) are still potential revolutionaries while élite factions (regardless of different recruitment patterns, socialisation experiences and functions) are still bound by a ruling-class hegemony. Poulantzas can scarcely be surprised if some of us are amazed not so much by his optimism but by his naïvety.

To ignore the subtleties of cultural forces in the creation
of the ruling-class's cohesion and consciousness is a perilous
course to take. It invariably results in the adoption of vague
and untenable statements which are incapable of disguising the
consequences of cultural differentiation. It represents a retreat
into a higher level of generalisations, which is a way of avoiding
rather than facing difficult questions. For as Poulantzas says
of 'facts': 'They prove nothing, for the simple reason that they
can be reinterpreted ad infinitum in any way one chooses.'[31]
So there is no problem, since the 'facts' can always be made
to fit the theory, and presumably as long as one deems ones
own theory to be superior to opposing theories (and it is hard
to conceive of anyone believing otherwise) then the theory need
never be abandoned.

Formal Education and Cultural Hegemony

Those who look to cultural forces to explain the domination of
the ruling class over other members of society invariably commence
with Marx's famous statement: 'The ideas of the ruling class are
in every epoch the ruling ideas: i.e. the class, which is the ruling
material force of society, is at the same time its ruling intellectual
force.'[32] Gramsci, who has done most to develop this theme,
divided the state into political society and civil society[33] ('in the
sense that one might say that state = political society and civil
society'[34]) and believed that in normal times the control of the
ruling class was achieved through the perpetuation of its cultural
hegemony over the institutions of civil society. Although civil
society is part of the state in an ideological sense, it can consist
of private institutions. It is only when the bourgeois state is faced
with intense internal dissension that the forces of political society
come to the fore and the power of the ruling class is maintained
by force. It is obvious that this is also applicable to allegedly
socialist societies; in the Soviet Union, for example, the family
has progressed from being an outmoded bourgeois manifestation
to a bulwark of socialism as the security of the regime has increased.

Althusser has referred to the institutions of civil society that
perpetuate the hegemony of the ruling class as 'ideological state
apparatuses' and has maintained that to his knowledge, 'no class
can hold state power over a long period without at the same
time exercising its hegemony over and in the State Ideological
Apparatuses'.[35] He argues that formal education, whether it be
controlled privately or publicly, is the key component of the state

ideological apparatus, and goes on to say: 'This is why I believe that I am justified in advancing the following thesis, however precarious it is. I believe that the ideological state apparatus which has been installed in the *dominant* position in mature capitalist social formations as a result of a violent political and ideological class struggle against the old dominant ideological state apparatus, is the *educational ideological apparatus*.'[36] Raymond Williams is even more self-assured: 'The educational institutions are usually the main agencies of the transmission of an effective dominant culture...'[37]

What facets of the British educational system could substantiate the above claim? British schools have been infamous for segregating their pupils along class lines: public schools provide an élite education for the offspring of the upper class as well as the more affluent members of the middle class; grammar schools educate the middle class along with segments of the working class; while the secondary moderns cater for the rest of the working class. Even with the changeover to comprehensive secondary education some have doubted if this pattern will be greatly disturbed.[38] The content of education within the different kinds of schools has been distinctive; it is geared to develop contrasting horizons and to add the appropriate cultural dimensions to fit those horizons. In the words of Miliband the function of education is to confirm a class destiny.[39] Education is a sponsor of social mobility but the price working-class adolescents have to pay for upward mobility is acculturation into middle-class mores. The upward mobility route is an exercise in de-acculturation of the past accompanied by anticipatory socialisation for the future. A strong norm persists that education and politics should be kept apart, which has the advantage of disguising the schools' political functions thus making it difficult to expose them. Many simply do not believe that what is outwardly an educational process is indeed also an exercise in political and cultural indoctrination.

In spite of the persuasiveness of these arguments various problems need to be resolved. Let us consider the concept of hegemony. Anderson has written that 'The power structure of English society today can be most accurately described as an immensely elastic and all-embracing hegemonic order'.[40] If the hegemony is all-embracing presumably there is no opposition to the power structure of English society or that opposition is negligible and irrelevant. So vague and broad is his interpretation of hegemony that the suspicion prevails that opposition which is not directed at the immediate downfall of corporate capitalism is merely bourgeois reformism.

Most theorists who believe that a ruling class has established its cultural hegemony in Britain agree, unlike Anderson, that it is possible to escape its tentacles. But none the less the power ratio is grossly unbalanced: 'For indoctrination to occur it is not necessary that there should be monopolistic control and the prohibition of opposition: it is only necessary that ideological competition should be so unequal as to give a crushing advantage to one side against the other.'[41] This raises the question of what constitutes a crushing advantage, especially when those who perceive a capitalist hegemony are inclined to argue that most changes are a consequence of concessions on the part of the ruling class and serve only to cement, rather than undermine its power. Williams has argued that internal inconsistencies are permitted as long as they do not go beyond the limits 'of the central effective and dominant definitions' but he provides no clear idea as to what those definitions may be.[42] Suspicions are further aroused by Miliband's claim that Conservative Party leaders do not compromise their principles to anywhere near the same extent as Labour Party leaders.[43] To many commentators one of the main trends in British politics has been the ideological convergence of the two largest contemporary parties. What Miliband appears to be saying is that Tory vacillation, compromise, weakness and incompetence are skilful tactical manoeuvres in a grand strategy aimed at ensuring the perpetuation of a ruling-class hegemony. On the other hand the same weaknesses on the part of the Labour Party reflect yet another betrayal of its deeply buried socialist principles.

In spite of this portrayal of the massive dominance of the economic and cultural power of capitalism many Marxists still maintain that the revolution is coming — and for some it is just around the corner. But if the ruling class is as powerful as we are frequently led to believe then it is hard to understand why it should have to make concessions, let alone fear its own downfall. Parkin has shown considerable interest in explaining working-class resistance to the dominant culture. He has written: 'manual workers do not vote Conservative *because* they are deferential, or *because* they conceive of themselves as middle class; rather they have a deferential *and* a middle class *and* a Conservative outlook when they are isolated from structural positions which provide an alternative normative system from that of the dominant institutional orders of society.'[44] The structural conditions which enable workers to escape the dominant ideology are based upon community and work. Traditional working-class communities which are usually centred on one dominant industry have evolved a powerful infrastructure which the individual can depend upon in his dealings with the outside world. In less traditional working-class communities the work situation is the defence against the might of the capitalist hegemony. This is one of the reasons why the reaction to the embourgeoisement thesis was so hostile, for it suggested a decline in the salience of the industrial setting for workers which would lead to a greater exposure of workers to the dominant ideology in a home-centred society.[45]

Both the concept of hegemony and Parkin's claim that those workers who can best resist it are embedded within an equally dominant subculture imply a similar view of the learning process. In each case powerful institutions transmit consistent messages that overwhelm alternative sources of information. Either the hegemony of the ruling class incorporates all opposition or the countervailing forces are limited in number, confined to specific issue areas, and certainly nowhere as powerful as those forces which communicate the dominant ideology. In parallel vein it is the comparative totality of the learning context in Parkin's model that enables some British workers to create and sustain viable alternatives to the mainstream society. In both cases we are presented with a simple transmission model of the learning process in which institutions determine ideology and workers internalise the values and attitudes consistent with this ideology and behave accordingly, which in one case is labelled false consciousness and in the other true consciousness.

This view of the learning process is dependent upon a restricted understanding of what forces shape behaviour and a denial of the idea that individuals interpret the messages they receive from the environment. Although Miliband and Parkin differ somewhat on the strength and scope of the dominant ideology (with Parkin seeing more islands of resistance than Miliband), they are both in substantial agreement as to the institutions from which it emanates: 'Examples of such institutions would include the Established Church, the public schools and ancient universities, the elites of the military establishment, the press and the mass media, the monarchy and the aristocracy, and finally and most importantly, the institutional complex of private property and capitalist enterprise which dominates the economic sector — the post-war innovations in public ownership notwithstanding.'[46] All these are secondary, as opposed to primary, socialising agents and in this respect the difference between the proponents of the ruling-class model and most of the political socialisation literature is remarkable; whereas the former has concentrated almost exclusively upon the secondary agents, the latter has paid most attention to the primary agents. The political socialisation studies have stressed the centrality of the childhood years in shaping behaviour and how the basic values are acquired in an indirect and personalised manner within a non-political setting (that is, the family) whereas the ruling-class theorists have gone to considerable lengths to demonstrate the ideological direction of the learning process with the boundaries controlled by class forces. This is a good example of two partial approaches to an important problem, both reflecting differing ideological positions and neither aware of (or wishing to admit to) their partiality.

Without greater precision as to the scope of the hegemonic order, what precisely constitutes opposition to it, and a more tenable learning theory to explain that opposition, then the concept of hegemony will remain another example of those high level generalisations which have been devised to avoid, rather than answer, difficult questions. At present the concept of hegemony can be used to incorporate conveniently all the facts without explaining any of them.

Our objections to the way the British educational system has been included in the hegemonic order are much more specific. When considering the influence of macro-institutional forces like the educational system care needs to be taken in deciding what variables are to be included in the definition. The educational system includes an enormous variety of ingredients: the different institutions, the various personnel, the curricula, the rituals and the examinations, to name just a few of the most important. The ruling class theorists — and Miliband is especially guilty in this respect — have tended either to treat it as a totally integrated entity (as a coherent system) or to be highly selective as to the aspects they feel are worth examining without any criteria as to what governs their choice. The situation is particularly complex in Britain where so much of the control over formal education is localised, even at the discretion of the individual headmaster or headmistress.[47]

Parry claims that 'educational theories and reforms inevitably have political implications since part of any education is to fit a person out as a member of a body politic whether as a member of a ruling class, a quiescent subject of an administrative state, or a fully-participating citizen in some idealized democracy'.[48] Parry is claiming, perfectly correctly, that in spite of a myth to the contrary, politics and education are interwoven. Although they may be linked, this is not quite the same thing as saying that education is *only* about politics and *nothing else* which is a mistake that some have made in their eagerness to correct the established mythology.[49] In *The Long Revolution* Williams refers to three interlocking purposes of education: the training of a social character, the teaching of skills and 'education for culture'.[50] We doubt whether these purposes interlock quite as neatly as Williams implies and on the contrary would argue that the history of British education illustrates the continuous *potential* for conflict between them. Education is both a force for individual liberty as well as an instrument of social control and what many nation-states including Britain have attempted is to minimise the former and to maximise the latter. But permanent success cannot be guaranteed and structures and processes developed in one age may be inappropriate to another. Skilful élites will naturally adapt formal education to the changing conditions, but this assumes that élites in Britain have been skilful and that the potential for conflict can always be managed. Both assumptions are dubious.[51]

One example of a challenge to the hegemonic order, emerging within the educational system, has been the growth of student protest. This has been interpreted in contrasting ways by Miliband and Rex. Whereas the former has devalued this protest in 'rightist' terms, the latter has written '...it may well be that in the long run the class system is not able to contain the consequences of the expansion of the system of higher education'.[52] Rex has also referred to the cultural challenge to dominant values that has emerged within the institutions of higher education.[53] He may be overstating the case but the central point is that with the growth of political and cultural opposition to dominant values within higher education it is difficult to view educational institutions as compliant tools, as both Miliband and Rex have been inclined to do on several occasions. In this respect, there may be a distinction between higher and other educational levels, but universities as well as secondary schools are part of the educational system.

The final, and perhaps most significant criticism, is that the schools, let alone the universities, do not succeed in imparting values which are consistent with those which one would imagine to emanate from institutions dominated by a capitalist ruling class. It is not that the schools are the seedbeds of the future revolution — apathy, vandalism and a restless nihilism are the modes adopted by the working class for expressing its opposition rather than the posing of political alternatives.[54] But this raises the question of the precise state of working-class consciousness and it is to this that we must now turn.

Working-Class Consciousness

If there is a hegemonic order buttressing the power of the ruling class, what are its implications for working-class consciousness? Superficially one would have thought that if dominant values were as pervasive as we are often led to believe then the working class would be seduced into showing positive support for the established society. Some of the political socialisation research has claimed that a value consensus pervades British society which is not founded on class domination but upon differing class contributions.[55] But few ruling class theorists are prepared to accept that there is either a 'natural' or a class-based consensus, which is certainly a viable interpretation of contemporary realities, but it needs to be matched by an equal willingness to ascertain what this implies for the concept of hegemony.

Marx believed that the bourgeois state created the conditions within which the working class could develop a revolutionary consciousness. None the less the workers needed the revolution to destroy the final taints of bourgeois society: 'not only because the ruling class cannot be overthrown in any other way, but also because the class *overthrowing* it can only in a revolution succeed in ridding *itself* of all of the muck of ages and become fitted to found society anew'.[56] Gramsci's work was a recognition of the immense difficulty of overthrowing the bourgeois state due to its exercise of cultural as well as economic power. It was the cultural hegemony of the ruling class which undermined working-class consciousness, so postponing, perhaps indefinitely, the day of the revolution. To prevent this erosion of consciousness the workers had to develop structures in capitalist society within which they could exercise their own hegemony, in preparation for the time when this could be extended to the rest of the society.[57] This has most definitely not taken place in Britain, and although contemporarily this may be changing, a decline in the radicalism of the British working class has occurred but not to the point where it is possible to talk of mass support for the *status quo*.

Working-class consciousness in Britain assumes different forms. It is still of great political significance that approximately one third of manual workers vote regularly for the Conservative Party. The other two thirds, who vote mainly for the Labour Party, are not entirely distinctive in their attitudes but it is amongst them that remnants of working-class opposition to the *status quo* are most likely to be found.[58] Whereas members of the middle class see the social structure as an ordered hierarchy the working class retains a conflict view of society, with a strong perception of a gap between 'them' and 'us'.[59] When it comes to doing something about that 'gap' most workers define their interests as a corporate class and push for a redistribution of economic resources within the parameters of a capitalist society.[60] Following Parkin's notion of community-based resistance to dominant values, pockets of opposition to the ruling class may still prevail, but it should be stressed that they are few in number and limited in scope, and the opposition to dominant values is measured partially by the strong local appeal of the Labour Party — a dubious measure of opposition.

Mann notes that 'there is little truth in the claims of some Marxists that the working class is systematically and successfully indoctrinated with the values of the ruling class.'[61] Although he accepts that dominant values are to be found in British society, they are not so powerful as to lull the working class into a state of false consciousness. The power of the ruling class depends upon a fatalistic acceptance by the worker of his lot in life; he is aware of his exploitation but has not developed his consciousness beyond the point of pragmatic adjustment to inequality.[62] To Mann this suggests that the potential for building a revolutionary working-class movement still exists. In Gramscian fashion he stresses the need for structures within which socialism can be learned; structures which will interpret to the worker over a long period of time the meaning of his work experience.[63] In the meantime, however, the most potent structure for the worker is his trade union which, at least in Britain, has rarely gone beyond defining the demands of the working class in accommodationist terms.

Another important theme is that working-class consciousness remains remarkably unsullied and it is working-class leaders — especially the trade unions and the Labour Party — who must shoulder the responsibility for the continuing power of the ruling class.[64] How reformist working-class leaders have been able to hold on to their posts in view of the allegedly revolutionary consciousness of the working class remains something of a mystery. A more tenable view is that neither now, nor in the past, have many working-class leaders or workers espoused a revolutionary view of the world. It is more realistic to argue that working-class consciousness in Britain may be shifting in a radical direction. Williams refers to the emergence of alternative and oppositional cultures and Rex has noted a change in working-class styles of protest, as seen in the occupation of factories and attempts to run them along different lines.[65] The state is now intervening in areas which have been left to the forces of civil society in the past, thus merging the domains of civil and political society.[66] This would suggest that those who control the state fear the pressures that are emerging in civil society and intervention is designed to deflate those pressures. This is reflected in the attempt to control prices and wages, both to restrict free collective bargaining and to place constraints upon those who have the power to raise prices.

A number of tentative steps have also been taken in the cultural fields and the universities in particular have experienced new financial and political pressures.[67]

The evidence from the schools illustrates the ability of the British working class to maintain many of its distinctive cultural forms, and because there is no common culture in Britain selective education has encouraged this. It is equally true that there is little political opposition to the *status quo* within the schools but a considerable amount of opposition that assumes other forms. This suggests a retarded or stunted working-class consciousness and Mann has argued that as workers grow older the fatalistic acceptance of their lot in life increases.[68] So that the best the schools can achieve for the ruling class is a compliance which will intensify as long as the structures which interpret reality for the worker remain as they are.

Regardless of how working-class consciousness is evaluated — as supportive of the *status quo*, as defending class interests in corporate terms, as fatalistically accepting dominant values, or as escaping the shackles imposed by a reformist leadership — this evaluation has to come to terms with the fact that the educational system imposes individualistic channels of opportunity upon the working class. Harris has argued that the powerlessness of the working class is softened by the bribe of a meritocratic educational system.[69] He may be factually inaccurate in seeing the British educational system as meritocratic, but he has posed an alternative strategy for the ruling class to maintain its hegemony, one that is dependent upon the manipulation of resources rather than the dominance of cultural values. They are not mutually exclusive strategies but it could prove difficult to use the same institutions in both ways. If the educational system is infused with meritocratic values it cannot legitimise the power of the ruling class except in the same meritocratic terms, but if the ruling class is not a meritocracy, and few have seen the British ruling class in this light, then the possibility for conflict between the values of the schools and those contained in the supposed ruling-class hegemony is very real. At present such conflicts may be unlikely but the need for more short-run tactical manoeuvring changes the odds.

In all societies the educational system has the potential to undermine working-class consciousness. Formal education is used as a mechanism for determining the distribution of scarce resources amongst individuals. Political, economic and social variables decide what pattern of selection will prevail in the educational system but regardless of what the final choices may be it is individuals who are selected and not classes. Given the general trend towards industrialisation the selection biases are increasingly standardised: the price workers may pay for retaining their consciousness, regardless of the kind of society in which they live, is powerlessness. A revolutionary consciousness may be needed to destroy the capitalist ruling class but the socialist society may require a differentiated 'class' structure with its associated consciousnesses if it is to succeed.[70] And this may best be achieved through formal education.

From Cultural Hegemony to Elite Manipulation

In three different areas we have attacked the central assumptions of the ruling-class model. First, we have argued that there is not a united ruling class but at best a number of élite factions. These factions lack the cohesiveness and coherence to serve a well-defined set of class interests. The fact that substantial inequalities persist in British society is not proof of the continuing existence of a ruling class but rather the use of this evidence is an attempt to substantiate an image of society that cannot be proved by commonsense criteria. To further assume that the various factions will unite when society is faced with a crisis is an expression of faith which is impossible to disprove: every time élite fissures rather than ruling class unity are demonstrated it is claimed that the apparent crisis is merely a molehill and not a mountain. Second, we have shown how difficult it is to exercise a cultural hegemony over society. Many socialising institutions, and processes through which the individual acquires his behaviour, are not easily controlled by the state. At the same time those forces within civil society that are amenable to state pressure are invariably complex institutions that perform functions that cannot readily be reconciled with one another. Finally even certain ruling-class theorists accept that the working class show little more than compliance to allegedly dominant values, which we feel raises genuine questions as to precisely how powerful the cultural hegemony of the ruling class might be. As long as societal processes are working smoothly then compliance should enable a ruling class to govern without effective opposition to its interests, but in abnormal circumstances something more than compliance could be required of the working class, and it may not be forthcoming. Furthermore, in a crisis compliance is more likely than support to be transformed into opposition. Whether this occurs or not is an empirical question but the predominance of working-class compliance over working-class support is indicative of a regime that is not fully legitimated.

A realistic view of power in the United Kingdom would show isolated and somewhat inept élites struggling with the problem of manipulating civil and political institutions that are unwieldy, hard to define precisely, have mutually exclusive goals, and are limited in their persuasive powers. These élites face a compliant working class, which with changing objective circumstances may be in the process of moving against the established regime. If no cultural hegemony prevails how do the élite groups perpetuate their power? Some years back Goldthorpe and Lockwood argued that the British working class was increasingly pragmatic in its political allegiances and we would like to extend this by suggesting that it is increasingly pragmatic in its regime allegiances. With the erosion of dominant values, and the power of the institutions from which they emanated, ruling élites have to match the pragmatic instrumentalism of the working class with a pragmatic manipulation of their own. Britain did not experience a thorough bourgeois revolution because the bourgeoisie assumed full citizenship — in civil, political and economic terms — within an aristocratic state. Full citizenship was the basis for the cultural hegemony that bound together the bourgeoisie and the aristocracy. At least in economic terms, it has proved impossible to extend that same full citizenship to the working class, and at the same time it has proved just as impossible to establish over the working class a cultural hegemony which successfully legitimates this inequality. The likelihood of tensions emerging within value systems that attempt to legitimate inequality is always very real as those who are being discriminated against have an objective interest in challenging the value system. The chance that their consciousness will be brought to this realisation is always present. This has not taken place in Britain, but equally significant is the fact that the institutions and processes which in the past have legitimated the inequality of the working class have also preserved a society that is increasingly incapable of holding its own in competition against more dynamic societies. Faced with a crumbling and self-destructive value system, governing élites have had little option but to rely upon 'tactical concessions' to preserve their power.

Miliband has written: 'What value my analysis may have lies, I think, in my attempted demonstrations of the fact that "political socialization" *is* a process performed by institutions, many of which never cease to insist on their "un-ideological", "apolitical", and "neutral" character.'[71] Miliband is essentially correct in this criticism of the political socialisation literature and his approach to the study of political behaviour is far preferable, but it is our contention that to recognise the ideological biases inherent within the political learning process does not negate the need for a sophisticated understanding of that learning process and the societal parameters within which behaviour is acquired. We hope that we have gone a little way towards accomplishing this.

Chapter 4

Political Education: its Emergence as a Curriculum Innovation

A Growing Interest

Many persons have referred to the fact that political education in British schools has been taught mainly in an implicit and indirect fashion.[1] The efficacy of this is challenged by the proponents of political education and their aim is to place the teaching of politics in the curriculum on the same basis as the traditional subjects so that it forms an identifiable part of the weekly if not the daily lessons. The Politics Association, through its mouthpiece, the journal *Teaching Politics*, has been pushing this line since its inception in 1969.[2] The Association's efforts have been reinforced by a series of B.B.C. radio programmes that discussed the pitfalls, and more noticeably, the benefits of political education, and the launching of a research project to set up and monitor school-based courses in political education.[3] The purpose of this chapter is to analyse the pressures behind this drive to place the teaching of politics in schools on a more formal basis. It is of interest to us because of the very explicit understanding of political education its advocates have been forced to evolve. This contrasts vividly with several of our other chapters which draw out the political implications of education from sociological and economic data. Whereas contemporary educational élites have been concerned with the economic implications of the educational system, this chapter examines one response to the present challenge, so much of which is emerging within the educational institutions, to our established *political* values. There is a belief that the educational system, albeit in the long run, can solve what ails us — whether it be economic or political.

It is not the first time that interest in the formal teaching of politics in British schools has blossomed, and the more ardent of the contemporary supporters of the cause would do well to remember this, for the present fervour may wane in much the same way as past bursts of enthusiasm. In all fairness to the more sophisticated members of the movement their awareness of past failures is quite evident. The consensus of opinion is that the present programmes of political education will be more firmly based if they take into account the lessons of the past. The Association for Education in Citizenship, which flourished in the 1930s, promoted much of this earlier enthusiasm. Although its efforts were worthy, they could be criticised for the grandiose nature of their goals (for example, the claim that the individual should recognise his responsibilities as 'a citizen of the world'), the vagueness of their programmes, and their élitist overtones (for example, the statement that the citizen of a democracy requires 'the capacity to choose a good representative and to trust him when chosen'.[4])

What is significant is the failure to consider why the Association for Education in Citizenship did not succeed in increasing the teaching of politics in schools. The assumption is that if only the weaknesses in its approach, such as those referred to above, were eradicated, then success would be more certain. But there may have been more fundamental reasons for this failure: the efficiency of implicit forms of political education was such that explicit forms were superfluous, or the wider political context may have changed so that what appeared as an attractive proposition seemed less relevant in the new circumstances. At the same time, disagreement as to the nature of the ideal democratic citizen, and the possible conflict over the political effect of civics education, may well have diminished support for its goals. What these points suggest is that political education is not simply something on which all reasonable men will agree as long as the specific programmes are properly formulated, but rather it is within itself a political issue because it requires resources to operate, upsets established routines, and may change individual behaviour and thus influence ongoing patterns of social interaction.

One of the important stimulants for the Association for Education in Citizenship was the demise of continental democratic societies such as Germany. The feeling was that judicious programmes of political education could help to stop the rot since the man with political knowledge was naturally a democrat who would seek to fulfil his potential by supporting a democratic society.[5] However, the coming of the Second World War undoubtedly did more to shore up the established order than any programmes of political education, and it became dangerously unpatriotic to challenge the 'national interest'. In the short run, political education lost its significance as the changed context simply made it irrelevant. This provides a convenient entrée into considering the contemporary pressures for political education and whether they are likely to be any more sustaining than past forces.

The New Pressures

Both Derek Heater and Ian Lister have pointed to a number of forces that have led to the revived interest in political education.[6] There are positive changes in the educational system itself. The school-leaving age has been raised from fifteen to sixteen and this has provided extra curriculum space that has to be filled. It is both depressing and potentially exciting that, following the Newsom Report, it has been argued that much of this additional time should be devoted to 'social' education.[7] Depressing in the sense that this could be seen as material suitable for merely filling in a rather inconvenient period of time in the pupil's school life, and potentially exciting if the actual programmes of 'social' education have something meaningful to offer. But the fact that the school-leaving age has been raised is not in itself an argument for formal instruction in politics. There is no reason why the additional year of schooling should not be used to impart any knowledge under the sun. In fact it could be argued that the time would be best spent imparting some of the basic academic skills that so many of our present school-leavers appear to lack.

A second reason has been the lowering of the voting age to eighteen, with the prospect of some school pupils actually having the franchise. The time period between the minimum school-leaving age and the minimum voting age is two years and it could be argued that this places greater pressure upon the schools to provide formal political instruction. Again there is nothing wrong with the logic of this but it does imply that the individual should be (even if he does not need to be) politically knowledgeable before he exercises his franchise. If this is carried to its logical conclusion the implication is that schools should provide very specific bodies of information that relate directly to post-school functions. The list is infinite: marriage, sex education, raising children, opening a bank account, buying a house, and presumably if conscription returns, the rudiments of military training. The schools have already been pushed some way in this direction and consequently political education has to compete with complementary demands. It could be argued that as certain of these bear more immediately and perhaps more pressingly upon the individual they have a prior claim.

A third pressure referred to is the growth of research in the related field of political socialisation. The assumption is that as the political scientists showed an increasing interest in the process of political learning so the educationalists were likewise stimulated into examining what political learning took place in the schools. As with the previous pressures this is a doubled-edged weapon. *Most* of the political socialisation studies have emphasised the importance of family-based, implicit and indirect patterns of political learning as opposed to explicit programmes of formal political instruction.[8] If the educationalists had taken the messages of the political socialisation literature seriously then perhaps they should have poured their time and energy into other fields. This is a dilemma that has been widely recognised but because its implications are so dramatic few have been willing to face up to it seriously.[9] Fourthly, although the list could be extended considerably, references are made to various forms of either political discontent or political alienation on the part of young people.[10] As Lister writes, 'some even think that the legitimating institutions, such as parliament, are threatened by mass ignorance, which leaves people vulnerable to demagogues or to the appeal of extreme, simplistic solutions of political problems'.[11] This is similar to what we have claimed was one of the reasons for the Association for Education in Citizenship's propagation of formal education in the 1930s. As in the 1930s, it is possible to envisage democratic political processes in Britain as under threat and to argue that this can best be met by a vigorous programme of political education. To commence with such assumptions will have a crucial bearing both upon how political education is to be imparted and what its ultimate ends are supposed to be. It is sufficient at this point to note both that political ignorance is not a recent phenomenon and that the spectre of youthful rebellion appears to have faded somewhat in the 1970s. Does the need for political education recede along with it?

These reasons for the expansion of interest in explicit programmes of political education smack very much of *ad hoc*, almost fortuitous, rationalisations. These may be the reasons for the expansion of interest but the precise relationship of the actual programmes of political education to these reasons is rarely spelt out. The raising of the school-leaving age, the extension of the franchise to eighteen-year-olds, the expansion of research in the field of political socialisation, and the emergence of a vibrant youth culture may all in their different ways help to account for the resurgence of interest in political education but they do not provide any meaningful rationale for actual courses in the formal teaching of politics. Without providing such a rationale political education is merely flotsam and jetsam to be pushed aside once the stimulating forces fade away.

From a perusal of the literature we have gleaned four possible rationalisations of explicit political education programmes. It is necessary in order to perpetuate a particular understanding of the discipline of politics; it will assist the individual in developing his political potential and defending his political rights; it is essential if the stability of the polity is to be maintained; and more specifically it is something which no democratic society can afford to be without. Michael Oakeshott has made the clearest statement of the first of these legitimations for political education, although he has not commented on the form that this should take.[12] In true Oakeshottian fashion he has argued that as political activity springs from 'the existing traditions of behaviour themselves' political education should be structured to impart as profound a knowledge as possible of a nation's tradition of political behaviour. In concrete terms it should have a historical dimension, be comparative, and be philosophically founded not with the aim of increasing political activity but in order to remove 'crookedness from our thinking' and to further the more economical use of concepts.[13] Although one may not concur either with Oakeshott's ideas of what shapes political behaviour, or with his views as to the content of political education, at least the two reinforce one another for the former provides an intellectual basis for the latter, and is not simply the product of the wishful thinking of either the ambitious professional or the well-meaning 'concerned' citizen.

Most of the contemporary spokesmen for political education have based their case upon what it does for the individual. Political literacy is the catch-all phrase used to describe the individual characteristics which hopefully will be acquired through the formal teaching of politics. According to Bernard Crick and Ian Lister, 'political literacy must be a compound of knowledge, skills and attitudes, to be developed together, each conditioning the other'.[14] In a nutshell the politically literate individual possesses the knowledge and skills that enable him to be politically effective in relevant situations, but while trying to be effective he respects the procedural values of 'freedom, toleration, fairness, respect for truth and for reasoning'.[15]

The emphasis on the part that political education plays in cementing the established order has been deliberately played down. This is partially a conscious effort to protect the political education research from a powerful body of criticism that has been levelled at the political socialisation literature.[16] Given the fact that its intellectual origins were in systems theory, and that most of the empirical work looked for supportive attitudes amongst school-children, it is not surprising that the political socialisation research was negatively labelled by some social scientists. A further incentive for those involved in promoting political education to avoid a systems orientation label was their policy pretensions. Unlike most of the social scientists working in the field of political socialisation, they have been interested in actually changing what goes on in the classroom, and to have been seen as working for the shoring up of the present society would have been a disastrous image. In spite of this conscious attempt to present another image, certain doubts remain as to the true intentions of those who are advocating political education. We have already suggested that the new wave of interest has been stimulated by apparently high levels of youthful disaffection with the present political order. Although the proponents of political education are willing to admit this, they are coy as to the precise influence this has upon them. Secondly, there is an explicit claim that the politically literate individual is aware of the difficulties that governments face and he eschews simple answers to complex problems. This is a highly convenient state of mind for governments to develop for it could lead to individuals showing forbearance while governments remain incompetent!

Crick and Lister imply that the most significant way in which political education could reaffirm the *status quo* would be by conducting political action according to certain procedural values. 'Freedom, toleration, fairness, respect for truth and for reasoning' are the very values which are supposedly enshrined in Western liberal democracies. Crick further has implied that there is general support for democratic decision-making procedures and that political education should cement this.[17] He has also argued that political participation is not the only way of ensuring that government remains responsible to the people.[18] This is so, but it adds another touch to an image of the democratic citizen: the informed citizen who moulds his action according to the rules.

Of course societies may fail to live up to these procedural values
and then one can expect the politically literate citizen to work
actively for their better fulfilment. But within the Western context
the politically literate citizen is a reformist and not a radical.

In terms of the *political* procedures of Western democracies
many would argue both that they bias the political process in
favour of certain groups and that they are relatively ineffective
at controlling governmental action.[19] Although it is true that Crick
and Heater have suggested that these political procedures are
'sacred', to be fair their main emphasis is upon values that trans-
cend these narrow political confines. But political education will
inevitably have a comparative dimension and it is impossible to
avoid asking where these values are most pronounced, within what
historical framework they emerged, and why they took root. With
a value pattern that is essentially part of the Western tradition
the answers to these questions cannot but help to place societies
like our own in a comparatively favourable light. There may be
nothing wrong with this in the sense that we accept the moral
superiority of a society that attempts to maximise such values
over a society that does not, but it does bias political education
in a certain direction. As most advocates of political education
accept, it is not simply that the individual teacher cannot help
but be biased, but that the very programme of political education
will also have its biases.

Pat White has argued that 'the policy which must be in the
public interest in any human democracy is the ensuring of the
provision of a political education'.[20] This is because she believes
that a human democracy is 'the kind of government the public
ought to have' and that 'a policy in the public interest [in this
case political education] is one which benefits every member of
a given public under the description member of the public'.[21]
On the basis of these assumptions she outlines her actual programme of political education: acquiring values which underlie
the democratic system, learning how political institutions work,
and receiving a liberal education. Most types of societies, whether
they are labelled 'human democracies', 'socialist', 'fascist' or what
have you, are invariably characterised by their governing élites,
if by no one else, as standing for certain intrinsic values that have
to be preserved at all costs. Although those values may differ
from White's legitimation of democracy as being in the public
interest, they will certainly be considered as sufficiently important
to warrant the provision of political education.

Clearly there has been a considerable amount of confusion
as to whether the formal teaching of politics in schools is to be

propagated because politics is a worthwhile subject in its own right, or because it serves other ends — such as making the individual more politically efficacious, or society more stable — or for all three reasons. Not even the traditional school subjects can justify their inclusion in the curriculum solely on the grounds that they have intrinsic qualities of which all should be made aware. Latin and Greek have been included in the curriculum of the public schools because they supposedly develop in the individual certain ways of thinking about problems which will stand him in good stead throughout his life. Recruitment patterns into the higher civil service suggest that some believe that these alleged benefits help to ensure good civil servants. So a subject that may be intrinsically worthwhile to teach also trains the individual mind along certain lines and has vocational implications. However with the subject of politics *the emphasis* of the legitimations has sensitive implications, and there is a world of difference between justifying political education primarily on the basis of a belief in the merits of politics as a discipline as opposed to its societal consequences. This is because a politics course is likely to deal with much more contentious issues than subjects like Latin and Greek. At its best it is not simply a question of equipping the individual for action (by imparting the requisite knowledge and skills), while keeping in mind certain procedural values — it should also make the budding citizen fully aware of an existing power structure with which he has to come to terms. The advocates of political education suggest that the solution to this dilemma lies in becoming a rational activist but others might wish to contend that either apathy or radicalism are more meaningful alternatives.

What Kind of Political Education?

Indirect forms of political education (found for the most part within the history lessons) have always existed in British schools,[22] but what the recent proponents of political education have been calling for is the explicit teaching of politics as a school discipline in its own right. This makes a certain judgement on two central arguments to which we have already had occasion to refer: that the schools are a potent medium of political instruction and that explicit politics teaching is an effective way of imparting the desired messages. In this section of the chapter we will explore the context of these two assumptions by considering the content of some of the proposed political education programmes and the educational environment within which they are supposed to be taught.

What are the alleged advantages of direct as opposed to indirect forms of political education? The widespread belief is that besides increasing the effectiveness of political education the explicit approach will improve the content of politics teaching. Lister argues that it will result in more 'planned, co-ordinated programmes'[23] because specialised politics courses will lead to a more professional training in the discipline of politics within the teacher training colleges and university departments of education. Heater claims that teachers specialising in politics, rather than those without specific politics training, are more likely to concentrate upon political behaviour rather than formal institutions (which allegedly increases the interest of the subject to pupils), to relate the subject to the pupils' own developing political awareness, to characterise the school as a micro-political model, and to introduce more comparative dimensions.[24]

In fact there is already a certain amount of formal politics teaching in British schools, including examination courses leading to a G.C.E. or Certificate of Secondary Education (C.S.E.) at both ordinary and advanced levels. Under prodding from such sources as the Politics Association the character of these courses is changing. Like the American civics programmes the 'British Constitution' courses have been castigated for their 'unrealistic' approach to politics. This criticism incorporated claims that the courses concentrated unduly upon the formal aspects of politics — the prescribed procedures, the institutions and the trivial rituals — rather than the real dynamics of political power. Even without a large expansion of professionally-trained politics teachers these courses have been changing their content which has meant dropping their safe constitutional approach for one which is more prepared to grapple with substantive issues, including an analysis of the socio-economic parameters within which politics occurs.[25] In itself this will be insufficient to satisfy the more ardent supporters of political education. In the first place only a minority of secondary school pupils take formal examination courses, and secondly, these are unlikely to be those pupils who perhaps most require a political education, that is those who leave school at the minimum school-leaving age.

Past programmes of politics teaching have been criticised for their haphazard nature. It is frequently claimed that the aim has been to impart esoteric bits of almost useless information rather than a systematic understanding of politics in Britain.[26] Indeed Crick and Lister have gone so far as to maintain that passing the formal examination in the 'British Constitution' G.C.E. was no guarantee that the individual was politically literate,[27] and in conjunction with Heater (all three are associated with the Politics Association) they have suggested that political education courses should be structured around what they regard as key political concepts. They believe that a knowledge of concepts not only enables one to obtain a better grasp of political reality but also is a useful guide to effective political action, although Crick warns against the danger of teaching political concepts in such a way that it becomes simply an exercise in linguistic analysis.[28] But the question as to what are the key political concepts has given rise to a certain amount of conflict. In 1971 Heater wrote: 'We must return, therefore to the point at which we started and ask whether Politics is a coherent discipline and whether its subject-matter is susceptible to the compilation of general laws... I believe that the subject has sufficient coherence and is capable of sufficient generalisation to be handled by the method of conceptual analysis.'[29] His central framework was composed of six primary concepts: ideas, administration, leadership and decision-making, the role of the individual, techniques of change, and conflict. These basic concepts could be divided into a number of sub-concepts and the hope was that this would provide a coherent strategy for the teacher as well as a comprehensible frame of reference for the pupil.[30]

Crick, while accepting the need for a coherence based upon certain key political concepts, doubts whether Heater's framework provides us with the answer.[31] This is because Heater's language is not drawn 'from everyday life', and Crick believes that the concepts should not be superimposed from 'above' (that is, by political scientists) but should originate from 'below'. But nowhere does he enlighten us on precisely what he means by 'below' and seems to think it sufficient that the concepts should be phrased in less jargonised language to meet this condition. But surely the mere fact that the concepts may be expressed in terms that are more readily understood by pupils does not mean that these concepts have not been issued from on high? In presenting his material on basic concepts Crick has given no indication whatsoever of discussion with teachers, let alone parents or pupils, prior to the formulation of his concepts. In this respect, therefore, the only distinction between Heater and himself seems to be one of terminology. The similarity between them is reinforced by the fact that Crick also believes in a framework centred around certain basic concepts (in his case government, relationships and people) that can be further refined.

In both Crick and Heater's schema political issues provide the material that is to be analysed by their respective conceptual blue-

prints. It is doubtful, however, if an issue-oriented focus will provide a sufficiently contrasting alternative to the present programmes of political education. Some seek forms of political education that will involve the individual in concrete political action
as opposed to learning about politics through the normal methods
of instruction. Crick and Heater are not opposed to such sugges-
tions but they have placed the bulk of their emphasis elsewhere.
By looking for action-oriented schemes these proponents of political education are attempting to meet the criticism raised by Michael
Oakeshott, among others, that it is only through actual participation in politics that truly effective political education (in the sense
of *increasing* political activity) is likely to take place.[32] The most
commonly proposed form of such political education is pupil participation in the politics of the school. In Heater's terms this means
seeing the school as a micro-political organisation. This is one
of the main themes to be found in the literature of the Association
for Education in Citizenship and in a 1936 publication Ernest
Barker wrote of the need to encourage pupil participation in school
societies.[33] The argument was that not only would this give a
certain number of pupils decision-making powers but also it would
impart a sense of the responsibilities that go with holding office.

Contemporarily Harold Entwistle has pushed more strongly
than most for making student participation in the decision-making
processes of the schools an integral part of political education.
As with Barker he sees this as being based upon student control
of school societies, but he is willing to consider its intrusion into
other domains, such as policy areas controlled by teachers, headmasters and governors.[34] Some schools have already taken tentative steps in this direction, but as Entwistle is willing to admit,
the end result is little more than tokenism. Not surprisingly headmasters have been reluctant to relinquish their power, even assuming that their statutory terms of office would allow them to do
this. Entwistle retaliates by claiming that pupil self-government
is not an all-or-nothing issue,[35] and there are areas where school-
students can and should participate. As to precisely what these
areas are he is rather vague, and although he is perfectly correct
in stating that it is not an all-or-nothing issue, it is crucial to
know what is going to be included in the domain of the school-
students. If there is little more than token representation in the
important decision-making areas then that representation is likely
to be entirely ineffectual. In any case pupil representation ensures
that the majority are excluded from actual participation in the
decision-making processes which undermines the justification for
this form of political education. Alternatively if student participa-

tion is restricted to certain areas of decision-making (for example social or recreational activities), then it may be seen as rather a meaningless gesture designed to placate demands for change rather than as a substantive innovation.

Entwistle never raises the question of how the various boundaries that hedge in pupil participation are to be legitimated. Are there certain decision-making areas pupils are to be excluded from because responsibility legally lies elsewhere, and there is nothing the school can do about this? Or is their exclusion to be based upon assessment of the pupil's development — he or she has not yet acquired the experience to tackle such problems? Regardless of what the case may be, if only partial inclusion in the decision-making procedures is granted the reasons for this have to be justified and they may not be reasons readily accepted by all of the excluded — in this case school-students. Official reactions to the student militancy of the 1960s suggest that the widening of participatory channels can be as much an example of élite manipulation trying to control a difficult situation as of a genuine attempt to broaden political education. In Britain and the United States, official bodies recommended that students should be granted a greater voice in the running of the universities through their representation on decision-making committees,[36] but they were thinking essentially in terms of very limited representation and control of only innocuous areas of responsibility. Control of the financial structure of the universities, appointment and dismissal of personnel, and most academic matters were to remain firmly in the hands of the administration and faculty.[37] Perhaps this can be justified but certainly not as an experiment in mass political education. Given the greater constraints upon schools, pupil participation in decision-making processes is likely to be even more circumscribed.

The idea of pupil participation in the policy-making institutions of the school flows out of a traditional British understanding of the school as a harmonious community. Participation is designed to increase the sense of pupil commitment to the community without altering substantially the established power structure. Schools are hierarchical power structures that in the past have not been called upon to legitimise their inegalitarianism but recently there have been small skirmishes instigated by various interested parties — pupils, teachers and parents. When the challenge is pronounced, and apparently 'subverts' the very apex of power within the school, the headmaster, then the wider reaction is indeed extreme.[38]

William Robson, a noted sympathiser of the cause of political education, openly advocates the creation of a stable, hierarchical community. He writes: 'The system of monitors or prefects which exists in most secondary schools promotes a sense of responsibility and of leadership on the part of boys and girls who hold these offices or aspire to them; while the other pupils absorb the notion of authority being exercised by some of "us" as well as by "them" (the teachers), and this is an initiation into self-government.'[39] And how is a sense of identity to be established between those pupils who exercise some of the trappings of power and the others who are waiting in the wings? Robson provides the answers:

> Caps, blazers and other articles of uniform now worn by pupils in a very wide range of schools are not mere attempts by the underprivileged to imitate the exclusiveness of the old school tie. They are primarily intended to serve as an outward and recognizable sign of belonging to a school which is a community; to identify the individual with his fellow-members; and to induce a feeling of corporate pride. All this can have valuable consequences in terms of political education.[40]

Obviously it is important as a form of political education but equally obviously it is a particular type of political education; one which promotes political inequality, supports the principle of representation as opposed to mass participation, and implies that group loyalty is valued above individuality. The recent moves towards 'pupil power', when initiated from above, may in fact be little more than a sophisticated version of this old attempt to legitimise inequality while maintaining community solidarity.

A third approach to political education, and one which is a significant departure from conceptually-based classroom studies and the sponsoring of participation within school societies and policy-making bodies, is to take the pupil out into the local community. Freedman has argued that it is meaningless for political education programmes to create the rational participant if this is not complemented by an open structure of government, otherwise reality may dictate that the courses should promote apathy rather than participation.[41] Freedman continues: 'Political studies should aim to encourage an ability to ask political questions about the phenomena that students observe around them, and a sensitivity to questions of power, especially as it relates to the circumstances of their own lives.'[42] Although this is an interesting approach, Lister has stated that on the basis of his survey of political education courses he has no knowledge of its actual implementation.[43] The main difficulty is self-evident for without careful preparation and a delicate handling of the various problems that are likely to arise, the school could find itself at the centre of a political storm if some of its pupils are intruding into highly sensitive local political issues. And yet without doing this a locally-oriented political education programme may prove to be just as sterile as the older 'British Constitution' courses, with simply a local rather than a national focus.

A variant of this third approach is to bring the political system into the classroom through the use of simulation models. Real life political situations are recreated in the classroom with the pupils playing the parts of the various political actors. This is so far removed from the average school-student's frame of reference that it is difficult to imagine how it could be meaningful to him. Even more pertinent is the limited impact it is likely to have on his political behaviour beyond marginally increasing his political knowledge.

Two central problems which all the approaches to political education have to consider — and rarely do — is their relationship to other aspects of the curriculum and, even more pertinent, how they relate to the structure of their educational environment. Political education can be undermined by the structure of education as well as by what Freedman has called the structure of government. It is widely recognised that the British public schools have been very effective at educating their pupils politically, and that they have accomplished this without resorting to explicit forms of political education.[44] In a very real sense the total educational experience of the public schoolboy is political training. It is effective because it is an integrated experience — public school pupils come from particular class backgrounds, they attend preparatory schools, the curriculum of the public school has been noted for its esoteric qualities, there is an internal power structure that incorporates all the pupils, the rituals create a corporate sense of identity, and finally the public schoolboy has real advantages when it comes to pursuing his career. In comparison to this massive totality the proponents of political education have made feeble claims to the effect that formal instruction in politics needs to be part of a 'general' or 'liberal' education.[45]

The most noticeable and probably most controversial feature of the structure of formal education in Britain is its hierarchical character. This is reflected in differing types of schools and streaming pyramids within the schools. In spite of the fact that this cannot but help to have the most profound impact upon political education, references to it within the relevant literature are surprisingly sparse.[46] The most open attack on the segregation of pupils into different types of schools by an advocate of political education has been made by Robson, who has directed most of his anguish at the special status of the public schools.[47] Robson realised that it is nonsensical to talk of a common citizenship in the face of this educational apartheid. As long as a public school maintains all of its traditional advantages then political education for its pupils has a very different meaning to political education for pupils in the state schools. At the same time the internal structure of the schools can make a mockery of political education. What is the use of attempting to change the political consciousness of pupils in the lower streams of a large comprehensive, for example, when all their other experiences tell them that their life chances are severely restricted? To encourage pupils to be politically active while at the same time educating them for social and economic inferiority makes a nonsense of political education. The political messages will either have no meaning, or if effective (which is unlikely) promote individual alienation.

Those interested in seeing that formal politics courses are expanded in schools should have been in the forefront of advocating a more integrated educational system, rather than standing meekly on the sidelines as has happened. As Derek Heater notes much of the official stimulus for expanding political studies grew out of the raising of the school-leaving age from fifteen to sixteen and the Newsom Report which was concerned with the education of 'less gifted' secondary school pupils.[48] Without taking a positive stand on this issue, political education could be seen as a convenient subject to fill in this rather difficult 'unwanted' final year. The educational convenience of politics has a parallel social convenience for the concentration of apathy, alienation and ignorance is to be found amongst the very group of pupils who are most likely to leave as soon as the law permits.[49] So along with social education, political education could become an adolescent version of 'child-minding'; a subject to pass the time until the pupil moves on to better things, which in the meantime could impart something of use and might not bore or tax pupils as much as the traditional subjects. The reason for reticence was obvious for to advocate structural change is politically sensitive. Some may have felt it was better to avoid such issues in order to maximise the chances of building up a broad-based coalition promoting the cause of political education. This has had the unfortunate consequence, however, of portraying political education as essentially a curriculum innovation (a view strongly reinforced by the content bias of the initial articles in the journal *Teaching Politics*).[50] At the same time it has deflected attention from the fact that the content of education has meaning only when it is placed in an educational

structure. Thanks to the absence of a positive position on this
point, the idealistic goals of political education may be negated
by the harsh realities of the educational context.

There are, therefore, three main approaches to political education: an issue orientation organised according to a conceptual
schema, and in Crick's case, dedicated to furthering certain procedural goals; the attempt to provide practical forms of political
education by stimulating participation within school societies and
school decision-making bodies; and less certainly, using the school
as a basis for community action which will involve pupils in issues
affecting their day-to-day lives. It is our contention that none
of these approaches indicates why the school should be an effective
agent of political education. Certainly direct political education
may have limited pedagogical advantages over the more implicit
forms of political instruction but this is not the same thing as
saying that it can achieve its stated ends. Symmetry is not the
same as effectiveness.

The conceptually-oriented issue approach to political education
is to all intents and purposes a curriculum content innovation;
a different kind of politics course designed to take the place of
'British Constitution'. As such it will compete for its place within
the curriculum alongside the more established school-based subjects. Attempts to increase pupil participation in the decision-making processes of the school rest on the assumption that the school
is a micro-political institution. This may be so but it is a micro-political institution with a well-defined power structure that has been
legitimated by the wider society. Either pupil participation is a
sham (which is invariably the case), or it relates easily and willingly
to the existing power structure (which means fully legitimating
inegalitarianism), or it causes an almighty turmoil when it tries
to extend effective power to school-students. To direct the
pupil to the local community and to the issues therein that intrude
upon his well-being, may be an interesting avenue for political
education to take but it must relate to the internal power structure
and curriculum of the school if it is to be effective. In fact it
is doubtful if this approach to political education is likely to
become widespread until certain of the boundaries that currently
separate school and society are removed, until we have moved
some way towards a de-schooled society. The proponents of political education need to learn why the public schools have been
such successful moulders of character if they are to succeed.
Although the public school offers a well-defined *educational* experience that separates the pupil from the *wider* environment, it has
intimately related its pupils to their particular social context thanks

to its elaborate rituals and esoteric academic experience. In a peculiar sense the public school pupil has always been part of a deschooled society.

Reflections on an Educational Strategy

It is impossible to ascertain the impact of programmes of political education for the simple reason that they are not yet part of the regular curriculum. The programmes that do exist are so few and far between, and geared for the most part to specialised groups of pupils,[51] that they cannot be expected to have a widespread societal impact. They may be important for the individuals exposed to them, although whether they have much bearing upon their political consciousness is another matter. So far we have concentrated on considering some of the assumptions of the proposed political education courses with a view to ascertaining whether they are likely to achieve their proposed goals. It must be clear from the tenor of our analysis that we are more than sceptical. Our objections centre on their failure to challenge the traditional relationship between social class and the British educational system. As we argued in Chapter 1 the British educational system has provided individual channels of mobility for the working class while acting as an instrument of class control.[52] There is nothing in the proposals for political education to suggest that this is likely to be disturbed. In fact, like social education, political education is in danger of being labelled as an attempt to place that class control on a firmer and more subtle basis.

In spite of its probable ineffectiveness at significantly influencing the relationship between class and politics in Britain, the actual drive for political education (as opposed to the probable impact of political education) has interesting political and educational ramifications. It represents a reaffirmation of the traditional faith in the power of formal schooling to mould man and society in a decade of challenge to that faith.[53] This is all the more remarkable when one remembers the restricted definitions of education that have formed the basis of the political education programmes. Besides accepting the potency of formal schooling, the push for political education is a novel attitude to educational change. It runs directly counter to the piecemeal and pragmatic British approach to reform. The proposals are justified by reference to the fulfilment of various goals (some of them not far short of their grandiose predecessors enunciated by the Association for Education in Citizenship during the 1930s) and concrete educational strategies are propounded which it is assured will lead to the accomplishment of these goals. At the same time the movement is bringing out into the open a sensitive and controversial topic — the political biases of formal education. It is asking that the connection between education and politics — which has been swept under the carpet for decades, to the point where some deny that it even exists — be reformulated and placed on a formal footing within the curriculum. The pressure-group tactics mounted to pursue this objective are impressive and the outcome is awaited with considerable interest.

Ironically the very professionalisation of the campaign suggests a number of internal self-doubts and implies that it may end up as a discussion arena for interested parties rather than a viable instrument of change. In its early days the research on political socialisation was justified on the grounds that political socialisation processes were one of the ways in which a polity maintained itself.[54] In other words through an examination of the political socialisation process it was possible to discover the roots of political stability. Over time the assumption that political socialisation performed this function has been challenged and those working in this research area have come increasingly to legitimise their efforts in terms of the need to examine the learning process *per se* rather than its system implications. A narrow professional concern with how political behaviour is acquired has replaced a much wider interest which has tangible policy implications.

Political education appears to be moving in the same direction as political socialisation. As is reflected in the balance of this chapter, most attention has been paid to outlining actual programmes of political education rather than discussing what the end product will be. In fact Lister has shown some petulance at those who continue to worry about ends rather than pursuing the means: 'Already our research makes us feel distant from the preachers and counter-preachers of political education, who are still caught in the rhetorical stage. Often when we listen to the preachers and then observe practice our eyes do not believe our ears. In particular, the problems we have observed in practice do not always coincide with those deduced, cerebrally, by theoreticians'.[55] He is claiming that what is important is to get the show on the road for this is a better way of finding out what problems will arise, and how they should be dealt with, than simply reflecting on the issues at stake. This may be so, but at the same time there is no better way of ensuring professional commitment to political education than actually devoting resources to it. To practise political education means gaining the co-operation of teachers, headmasters, local education officials and perhaps even pupils, parents and local councillors. At the same time the programmes may have been devised by university or college of education personnel with the results monitored by willing graduate students.[56] Once this kind of bandwagon is under way it is difficult to stop it and one only hopes that Lister is correct in his assurance that this is the best way to iron out the problems. Lister appears highly confident of the usefulness of political education and assumes that all that remains to be done is to construct the appropriate programmes and that this is best accomplished by trial and error. Our critique suggests that to be satisfied with the direction of political education means being satisfied with the very limited and somewhat confused goals that have been set for it. This may be sufficient for some but perhaps not for all the cerebral theoreticians.

Another possible indication that political education is turning in on itself is the proliferation of professional activities associated with it. In the push for educational innovation one would expect the foundation of an association, the launching of journals, the publication of textbooks and even the conducting of research projects. The problem is that these can all too easily become ends in themselves rather than a means to an end. The push for the training of specialised politics teachers is probably the clearest example of professional spin-off in the drive for political education. This would require a commitment of considerable economic resources and would have an impact upon teacher-training programmes in both the universities and the colleges of education. It is pertinent to ask who benefits most from this and the answer is obvious — the educationalist.

However, recent developments suggest that even as a campaign for educational change the movement for political education will not take off. On the one hand a considerable amount of internal activity has been generated but this runs up against an environment that is growing increasingly unsympathetic. The recent economic crisis has had a major impact upon educational expansion which has severely hit the teacher-training colleges. While the number of entrants into the colleges is being so stringently monitored it is unlikely that the Department of Education and Science will be willing to back the cause of political education to the point where it becomes a separate component within the colleges attracting students in its own right. In spite of various noises to the effect that it is impossible to base the educational system on manpower needs, there is no doubt that in the future this will have an important bearing upon educational courses.[57] Although political education may have social or even political pay-offs, it is much harder to justify in terms of its economic potential. In addition, as we have already noted, the advocates of political education have been reluctant to stress its societal benefits in order to promote their cause.

Political education is a controversial topic which is likely to prove something of a handicap when the educational mood seems set against further change. The attack upon progressive teaching methods has followed the attack on curriculum innovation which in turn followed the attack upon structural change. The new stress appears to be upon the need to teach the basic skills in the traditional manner. Political education is hardly likely to be considered of overwhelming importance in view of the fact that so many adolescents leave schools without the ability to read, write or calculate fluently. To redirect resources to a peripheral subject like politics would appear to many a blatant misuse of resources in the face of this crisis. So in spite of a great deal of huffing and puffing by the ardent spokesmen for political education they have missed the boat. They have come into the arena at the end of a great wave of educational, including curriculum, innovation and, unfortunately from their point of view, they are likely to be swamped by the growing reaction to the alleged excesses and failings of those innovations.

As a final point a brief reference to the explicit programmes of political education in the United States and the U.S.S.R. may help us to develop a better perspective on the same trend in the United Kingdom. In both the United States and the U.S.S.R. the state relies upon several other agents of political indoctrination besides formal education. Furthermore the schools share their politically educative function within at least an élite consensus on what forms of citizenship should be perpetuated. In a sense the school is a redundant agent of political education for it has a consensus imposed upon it (rather than creating the consensus itself) and it reinforces the messages transmitted by other powerful socialising forces.[58] It is most decidedly not an innovator. If there is a crisis of citizenship in the United Kingdom — caused by such factors as a decline in class deference, the resurgence of nationalism, the emergence of a youth culture, and the visibility of native-born black adolescents who are alienated from the white society — then the experiences of the United States or the Soviet Union would not encourage one to seek a solution in formal political education. The battles have to be decided elsewhere and then, for what it is worth, formal political education will emerge.[59]

Chapter 5

Political Activism Among School-Students

The Context

One of the more interesting features of the past fifteen years of politics in Britain has been the unexpected politicisation of groups previously quiescent. Students, women, homosexuals, prisoners and various types of local community groups are the more obvious examples of fresh faces on the political scene. In many cases these new types of political activism are characterised not only by the unexpected nature of their sudden emergence but also, a related point, by their simultaneous rejection of a prescribed social role. They have frequently assumed a different political role (that is, active rather than passive) and have campaigned for a redefinition of their social role. Clearly these two aspects are inter-related since the social role in question often included the characteristics of passivity and subordination.

The proliferation of these political challenges to the accepted interpretation of certain social roles serves to emphasise the necessary complexity of any analysis dealing with the nature of opposition to *status quo* values. Although it is easy enough to say that these 'challenges' are in fact mere pin-pricks and individually of little political consequence in the long run, this may well be ignoring the possible effects of accumulative politicisation. In this chapter we provide a case study of the emergence of one such group in the educational system, organised school-students, with the intention of demonstrating that political opposition can occur in the most unlikely of places. We will argue that the emergence of autonomous political action by school-students is of considerable significance in that it is an example of a group denying the apparent sociological logic of its situation and seeking to establish its own political identity against what would appear to be all the odds. It provides a clear illustration within the educational system of the need for a more sophisticated approach to the origins of political stress than is currently supplied by other theorists.

The environment in which the budding school-student activist finds himself can fairly be described as unwelcoming — for a variety of historical, legal, sociological and ideological reasons—despite the existence of certain ostensibly supportive factors. What is most puzzling about the politicised school-student, therefore, is not the somewhat chaotic form which his emergence took but rather that he emerged at all. Until recently, the formal teaching of politics in schools was scarcely designed to promote the development of political skills among schoolchildren. It consisted in the main of courses on civics and government which dealt with only the very formal aspects of democratic theory and practice. Small wonder then that Entwistle's general conclusion in 1971 at the end of his review of the state of political education in Britain was that it was quietest, deferential and utopian in approach.[1] To a certain extent the last six years have witnessed something of a reassessment of the purposes of political education. The publication of Derek Heater's book *The Teaching of Politics*[2] in 1969 and the founding of the Politics Association (supported mainly by secondary school teachers) in the same year marked the beginning of a fresh interest in the subject.[3]

The general climate of opinion was also changing. Within the educational field, the Newsom Report's concern with the child of average and below-average ability,[4] the raising of the school-leaving age,[5] an increasing awareness of the need for more 'social education',[6] and the lowering of the voting age to eighteen, have all contributed to an atmosphere in which the question of the political education of the ordinary child has at least some place. In addition, certain political developments, though more difficult to identify, can be said to have aided this revival of interest. In particular, Derek Heater argues that 'complacency has given way to nervous uncertainty concerning the toughness of the nation's political fabric to withstand the wear and tear of current sharply contending forces'.[7] This may be overstating the case, but growing political dissidence cannot but have promoted some unease concerning the general reliance on informal methods of citizenship training.

However despite the fact that these developments have resulted in some curriculum change in the teaching of politics it is too early to be able systematically to assess the impact, if any, of these innovations on school-students given the sporadic and limited manner in which they have been introduced.[8] Certainly they are of no practical relevance to understanding how the school-student activist appeared though they do need to be included in any assessment of his future.[9]

Structural discouragement for any display of self-directed political activity by the school-student is probably most evident in his legal position in the school. Within the confines of the school, as well as outside it, children have very few rights. Teachers standing *in loco parentis*, on the other hand, have very extensive rights including the right to administer corporal punishment to children. Furthermore, the powers of the head teacher in terms of controlling the lives of children within the school mean that in such matters as discipline, uniform, personal appearance generally, freedom of speech, and freedom of association, the word of the head is law against which there is no right of appeal either for the children or for their parents.[10] In short, if children were taught democratic participatory skills they would not lack issues on which these skills could be exercised.

General ideological support for this definition of the politically mute pupil has for a long time existed in the powerful convention that politics should either be kept out of the classroom altogether or, if introduced, should take a 'neutral' or 'balanced' form. The information imparted to pupils, it is maintained, should be apolitical in the sense that they should not be influenced in any particular political direction. To the student of political socialisation, to whom virtually all aspects of the learning process from the pot to the peer group can in certain situations be seen to have political connotations, this is something of an odd idea. However its political currency is such that few would be prepared to challenge it outright. But running parallel to this traditional apolitical norm is another one which favours the notion that, in a low-key way, children should be educated for democracy. When these two norms are brought together the result is not a particularly happy one for teacher or pupil — namely the provision of apolitical pro-democratic information. When one recognises that 'apolitical' means 'not politically partisan' the position is uninspiring to say the least.

Although the general suspicion of politics and politicians 'interfering' in education is beginning to be challenged, it remains a powerful ideological theme. This power was demonstrated not so long ago when the Conservatives organised a conference for sixth-formers in January 1973. Not only that, but there was mention of questionnaires being circulated at the conference designed to collect data on social and political attitudes.[11] The justification for the conference advanced by the Conservatives was that with the lowering of the voting age 'we are faced with a generation many of whom feel politics have no importance'.[12] Others thought their actions less reasonable. In the outcry that ensued, Roy Hattersley led a Labour Party demand for a public enquiry and the National Union of Teachers (N.U.T.) condemned the conference out of hand. In the face of such aroused passions the Conservatives swiftly withdrew and up to the present time no further attempt has been made by any of the major political parties to 'interfere' with the political education of schoolchildren.

However, other non-party groups have been taking up issues whose import for (though not necessarily impact on) the teaching of political education and the political position of the children in the school structure is considerable. These are what can loosely be described as the 'progressive' elements in the educational world who share the common belief that schools, particularly secondary schools, should in some sense become more 'democratic' — though precisely what they mean by 'democratic' varies considerably.

They can by no means be described as a small unified group of politically motivated men, although this conspiratorial thesis has gained some prominence among the responses to the more overt forms of school-student politicisation. On the contrary, a remarkably broad range of educational interests are represented among them. Parent groups such as CASE (Confederation for the Advancement of State Education) are becoming more confident in their ability to confront the teachers over such issues as abolition of corporal punishment. And within the teacher unions splinter groups like Rank and File and STOPP (Society of Teachers Opposed to Physical Punishment) are growing increasingly impatient with the authoritarian attitudes of the union hierarchies. (It is interesting to note that Rank and File supported the demands of the pupil demonstrators in London, May 1972.) Other pressures for change have come from the curriculum innovators. Both the Moral Education and Social Education projects of the Schools Council have often been more concerned with the internal organisation of schools and the sort of relationships which are possible in them than with injecting new materials and new packages into them.[13] Similarly the Humanities Curriculum Project questioned the whole idea of the teacher's role in the classroom by conceiving of him as a 'neutral chairman' assisting the process of discovery learning.[14] In the curriculum field generally there is a growing wave of local battles over the introduction of controversial topics, whether they be sex, drugs, politics or race. As the need increases for courses in secondary education which can equip the school-student to deal with the outstanding social questions of the day, so the doctrine of quietist political education is steadily more out-moded. This has been emphasised by the raising of the school-leaving age to sixteen with attempts at 'social education' for the fifteen to sixteen year olds who are not studying for exams and for whom new activities have had to be constructed.[15]

The growth of the community schools movement has provided some interesting models for the advocates of greater democracy in schools. In Countesthorpe and the other Leicestershire com-munity colleges, for example, issues such as corporal punishment and the personal appearance of pupils have become largely irrele-vant. The discussion concentrates instead on breaking down the barriers between school and community and on issues such as where, if anywhere, the principle of pupil participation and choice stops.[16] Small wonder, then, that the development of community schools is a central plank in the National Union of School Students' (N.U.S.S.) platform.

Outside the state system of education the free school movement has emerged.[17] Like the state-sponsored community schools the free schools, despite their organisational diversity, have a declared anti-authoritarian bias and attempt to gear their teaching arrange-ments to the needs of the children rather more explicitly than do state secondary schools. They appear to aim for as much flexibi-lity and equality between teachers and taught as possible. Despite their structurally fringe position in the educational world their influence on educational thinking is nevertheless considerable— while accepting that there is always a large gap between educa-tional thinking and educational action. A. H. Halsey, national director of the government's educational priority area projects and well-known educationalist, ended a recent review of one of the American free school classics, *The Lives of Children*,[18] with the hope that: 'The emancipating and amiable elements in the free school movement may be quickly and comprehensively absorbed into a radically decentralised State system. If it is not, then our whole society will be impoverished and not only the lives of children.'[19] Free schools thus have a fair amount of sympathetic recognition among the liberal educational establishment, but as always a little help is worth considerably more than a lot of sym-pathy. While it is in theory not that difficult to set up a free school, in practice it requires reasonable resources in order to meet the Department of Education and Science's requirements on premises, attendance and education to qualify as an independent institution.[20] Consequently, given the reliance of free schools on voluntary contributions, charities and dedicated helpers, their significance for any national trend towards greater democracy in schools remains primarily one of example rather than of actual impact.

Behind this somewhat motley collection of pressures for democratisation lie the various developments in educational thought which have come to be labelled as 'progressive'.[21] Theoretically their common concern and hence the common origins of their anti-traditional stance, is the understanding of the child as the centre of the educational and pedagogical process. As Sharp and Green point out:

> The child centred teacher sees him, or herself as engaging in a radical critique of the authoritarian–elitist assumptions of the more formal traditional approaches to education. He does not wish to subordinate the child's individuality to some predefined social requirements or impose 'high culture' upon the child in an arbitrary fashion because these would frustrate the realization of the child's inner potential.[22]

But when it comes to the question of how this common assumption can best be realised in the classroom, the progressives' position is less than monolithic. Some, such as Gagne and D'Arcy, emphasise that individualised learning is *the* natural process and that teaching methods should recognise this fact. Others attack the subject-based curriculum as constituting the core of the problem and suggest that interdisciplinary and integrated schemes of work supply the child with the freedom necessary for his full development.[23] In both cases the implementation of the ideas tends to be associated with organisational changes such as the use of team teaching to allow for greater flexibility in the didactic process. Occasionally the concept of the teacher as an authoritative transmitter of information is explicitly rejected and substituted by the notion of him as an arbitrator (as in Stenhouse's Humanities Curriculum Project).[24]

Despite these differences, it could be assumed that because progressive educationalists are all child-centred in some sense or other, they would support the autonomous political development of school-students. After all, they do talk a great deal about democracy and the supposed contribution of their methods to its emergence, or extension, both in the school itself and society at large.

As the authors of *Education for Democracy* put it: 'We want more education for more people, leading to more democracy. We want an educational system that is varied and flexible enough to develop fully all the different abilities and talents that children possess and want to use.'[25] Unfortunately, what they leave out are the precise links between their ideas and a more democratic political system. While it can be argued that a move away from authority, hierarchy, assessment, selection, streaming and so on represents a move towards what can be formally described as more democratic structures it is by no means the case that the new structures would automatically breed democratic, participating citizens. If this argument is to be advanced, then the nature of the learning process and how individuals relate to one another within these structures must be clearly spelt out. Instead, the progressives tend to rely on a touching faith that the development of the 'whole child' will result in the development of more democratic educational and political systems.

The implications of this approach for the politicisation of school-students is not particularly helpful since it ignores what might be termed the 'sociological continuities' underlying apparent changes in pedagogic methods. In this respect, Ivor Goodson has pointed out how his use of progressive methods at Countesthorpe in some sense 'failed' because the methods were based on a 'prior definition of outcome' and hence did not escape the dominant pedagogic model.[26] This, he argues,

> is unanimously derived from a formal belief in the transmission of knowledge. Implicit in the notion of transmission is a one-way communication, it is to 'pass on, hand on' knowledge *from* the teacher *to* the pupil. I take 'transmission' as characterising any educational incident which sets the learning of knowledge *previously* planned or defined by the teacher as the basic objective.[27]

Thus, although a teacher may be using progressive methods, he is almost certainly still maintaining the traditional role-relationship between teacher and taught. And his enthusiasm for introducing curriculum innovation may well compound the problem. Armstrong rather scathingly writes, 'we have become our own curriculum's ideal pupils; our resources are beautifully designed to satisfy not our pupils' intellectual demands, but our own!'[28] By defining the outcome so rigorously the progressive teacher can become almost uniquely self-centred while at the same time claiming to be child-centred merely because he is using certain methods. He may give the learning situation the trappings of self-determination but retain the substance of teacher control and direction. So long as this remains the case, progressives are effectively going to be more of a hindrance than a help to the emergence of any independent-minded political movement among school students.

The problem with self-determined, as opposed to adult-guided, political action by school-students is that it has the capacity to challenge not only the concrete authority of the school as embodied in its formal rules but also that somewhat more abstract authority contained within the definition of the teacher's role. This role is based on the assumption that it is the teacher with his superior knowledge who has the right to prescribe the direction which the pupil's learning should take; and conversely that the pupil with his inferior knowledge should accept the right of the teacher to make such prescriptions. The notion of the teacher's monopoly of knowledge coupled with his supposed superior mental ability implicitly defines the pupil role as subordinate to and dependent on the teacher role. This natural inter-relationship of the two roles means that a change in one has an immediate and unavoidable ramifications for the other and that teachers are bound to be wary of the politicisation of school-students with its consequent challenge to their self-definition.

It is not entirely surprising, then, that the approach of progressives to the task of educational democratisation has rarely included the question of what role the exploited group (the school-students) can itself play in this process. As Simon Emerson, President of the N.U.S.S. in 1975, puts it,

> The dynamic of change is seen as either coming from the teacher inside the school, or as coming to the teacher from political forces outside the school, with little discussion centering on what school students can do ... Surely school students themselves must be at the centre of the action to help correct the faults and to take part in decision making to initiate change.[29]

To the politically sensitive school-student it could appear that the radical educationalists have such an adult-centred view of the agents in the move toward a democratic educational system that their neglect of the school-students' political development is inevitable. Thus, in their failure to consider in any detail the kind of political education necessary for a democracy the progressive intellectuals have shown themselves to be strangely traditional.

It should be said, however, that exceptions do exist. Leila Berg, Michael Duane and A. S. Neill were all editorial advisers to

Children's Rights, a hard-hitting magazine with little pretence of
cultivating the educational middle-roaders. Its first few issues included such articles as 'Exam resistance — fighting the system',
'Sex books for kids', 'Alternative education' and 'Getting out of
trouble: the Children's Bust Book'.[30] Some of the progressive
educational thinkers then — though not many — are prepared to
implement their writing talents on the shop floor, as it were, and
give those they are trying to help — the school-students — the
ability to help themselves.

Others are somewhat less fastidious in their assessment of the
political impact of the progressives on school pupils. The editors
of 'Black Paper Two' write: 'Our notion that "progressive education" might be in some part to blame for lack of knowledge or
for naïve and destructive political attitudes in its victims has been
seen as common sense by most people.'[31] Permissive education,
lack of discipline, abdication of standards equals delinquency, violence and political unrest — this is the equation advanced by the
Black Papers. They are inclined to see the educational system
as an isolated, self-contained structure where cause and effect occur
uninfluenced, or only marginally so, by wider social considerations.
As a result, they are able to state quite unreservedly that a link
exists between too much freedom in the schools and various social
'maladies', rather than the causal relationship being in the opposite
direction.

As a final comment on the environment in which the school-
student activist is likely to find himself we can look at the direction
which possible innovations in political education are likely to take.
For the most part it is assumed that school-students are being
trained for a future rather than a present political role. This is
clearly shown in the initial statements of 'The Programme for
Political Education', a project sponsored by the Hansard Society
and associated with the Politics Association.[32] It is fairly forthright
on the question of the development of political knowledge and
attitudes but markedly reserved when it comes to how political
skills can best be developed. The stumbling block is the fact that
political skills, like most skills, are best learnt through their practical implementation and experience. The project directors comment, 'Some participation in decision-making in school is essential.
How much is needed, we recognise, is extremely debatable in
theory, and is highly relative in practice.'[33] So although supporting
the notion of 'learning through doing', they are at the same time
hedging their bets. It is interesting also to speculate on what they
mean by 'relative in practice'; relative to the needs of the child
or those of the school's authority structure? The undeniable prob-

lem with teaching political skills through participation is that the exercise if too enthusiastically pursued might 'take off' with the school-students demanding more than the generally rigid school authority structure can supply. It is unlikely that many headmasters would actually sponsor challenges to their authority through 'excessive' pupil participation in decision-making and the encouragement of autonomous political development by pupils. It is much more likely that we will continue to see token school-student representation, with strictly limited power, on decision-making bodies in schools.[34]

The Emergence of Organised School-Students[35]

It is not entirely surprising, therefore, that despite the pressures and gains of the progressives and their ideas on educational democratisation, little practical assistance has been given to school-students to improve their political position in the schools. They have largely been left to help themselves. At the end of the 1975–6 academic year the membership of the N.U.S.S. was an estimated 15,000 — not much in terms of its potential membership but quite a lot in terms of its scratchy beginnings in May 1972. The Schools Action Union (S.A.U.) is defunct — all of its ex-members having been drawn under the N.U.S.S. umbrella. The general policy of N.U.S.S. is now 'community power' — to be achieved in alliance with teachers. (It has never advocated 'pupil power'.) Its political legitimacy is developing, though slowly. It has submitted evidence to the Parliamentary Committee on grants for sixteen- to eighteen-year-olds, liaises with the T.U.C. in the course of its campaigns and is recognised by the National Association of Schoolmasters — though not by the National Union of Teachers. Simon Emerson, President of N.U.S.S. in 1974–5, saw its future as an arduous one with the emphasis on the consolidation of organisational coherence in conjunction with membership expansion. All in all, organised school-students have a much more pragmatic political outlook today than they had a few years ago when the S.A.U. was campaigning to 'smash the dictatorship of the head'. Their beginnings can be traced back to 1968.

Local School-Student Unions and the S.A.U.

In September 1968 *The Times* issued the following sombre warning to the nation: 'Assistant masters in grammar schools have been given a warning that in hundreds of schools "student power" may well be followed by "pupil power" . . . Unless there are some unlikely changes in the schools, the example of student agitation and protest in the universities could spread to all age groups.'[36] Although in today's context this quotation has something of an alarmist ring about it, in 1968, the year when student revolt reached spectacular heights, it was far more acceptable. In France, the May and June events saw school-students heavily committed to the battle. Organised through their Comités d'Action Lycéen (C.A.L.s) they occupied their places of study, fought with the police and were closely involved with the actions which led to a mass strike and factory occupations by ten million workers.

The impact of these events in Britain, linked with the 100,000 strong Vietnam solidarity demonstration in October a few months later in which many school-students took part, was to stimulate the idea among the more politically conscious school-students of organised action on their own behalf. As a result, a scattering of local school-student unions were set up at the end of 1968 and the beginning of the following year. They included the Cardiff Union of School Students with 250 members, the Portsmouth and District Inter-Schools Union (70 members), Swansea Union of Progressive School Students (100 members), the Manchester Union of School Students and several London-based groups including the core of the emergent S.A.U. Many of these groups attended a national conference of school-students in January 1969. The aim was 'the formation of a national organisation encompassing all the groups present'.[37] In this respect the conference was a dismal failure since it ended by deciding that its branches were to be completely autonomous in their organisation and policies — which left very little room for the development of a co-ordinated political force.

In the early days, organisation at the local level reflected this general political immaturity — not surprisingly, of course, given the fact that school-students had no previous experience in this field. After an area committee had been set up, sometimes with the help of a radical left group or a local students' union, highly involved constitutions and sets of aims were drawn up, debated for considerable lengths of time and then often forgotten. Occasionally, this preoccupation with organisational complexity did not entirely stifle the desire for political action. The Cardiff Union, for example, launched a highly successful campaign in defence of the right to have long hair, producing both results and increased membership. This was the exception rather than the rule, however, and many local unions dwindled away within a year of their being set up or else became purely social organisations.

Meanwhile, back at the S.A.U. (which had laid claim to being the national organisation of school students), other problems were encountered. Despite its aspirations for a national presence, it never succeeded in gaining permanent recruits on a large scale. In 1970 it had about 250 members, mainly in London, Birmingham and Manchester. During its short life it remained consistently disorganised, achieving only sporadic local victories on issues such as long hair and school rules. As vanguards go — for so it regarded itself — it was certainly far in advance of any possible support base, attracting only the most politicised and left-wing of school-students. It was not long before even its nominal links with the local school unions were severed, speeding up their transformation into social clubs.

By November 1970 this process of division between a politically strident national leadership and the politically unsophisticated grass-roots movements was more or less complete — certainly when seen in organisational terms. At a conference in that month the simmering factional conflict in the S.A.U., which had so disenchanted many school-students, crystallised into three groups: Maoist, Trotskyist — International Socialists (I.S.) and International Marxist Group (I.M.G.) — and the Labour Party Young Socialists (L.P.Y.S.). From then on, the factional infighting became increasingly bitter. The aim of the S.A.U. at this time was to achieve 'democratic schools in a democratic society' by 'smashing the dictatorship of the head'. Grass-roots support was to be built up by running campaigns, for example around the issue of corporal punishment, and the methods proposed were generally terroristic.

By May 1972, when the N.U.S.S. was formed, the S.A.U. was as far removed as ever from achieving any lasting impact on school-students, despite the fact that the potential discontent was clearly present. This was illustrated by the demonstrations by school pupils in May 1972 which, although called for by the S.A.U., occurred in the customary absence of any S.A.U. organisation such as stewards or route arrangements with the police. Probably more significant to the S.A.U. was the triumph of the Maoists and the expulsion of its I.S., I.M.G. and L.P.Y.S. members.

Given its considerable political ineptitude, therefore, the importance of the S.A.U. to the history of the school-student movement stems mainly from the fact that it was there rather than from what it did. Its degeneration into a small bureaucratised group planning occasional mad actions was accelerated by its isolation from the day-to-day problems in the schools and hence the kinds of issues which could win it support, but none the less it did initiate the idea of political organisation in the schools and provide a lesson on the mistakes to avoid in the future.

The N.U.S.S.

In 1968 the National Union of Students (N.U.S.) set up what was called the 'Scholars Associate Scheme' (S.A.S.) whereby school-students were able to become associate members of the N.U.S. and gain the usual travel concessions. No attempt was made to organise the S.A.S. school-students and they had no access to N.U.S. decision-making bodies. By 1971 the S.A.S. had 12,000 members, mainly sixth-formers since the lower age limit of N.U.S. was sixteen. But it was also clear that at this stage not even the potential of organised school-students was anticipated since their records were arranged alphabetically without reference to school, town or area. This made it at least clerically difficult to mobilise the S.A.S. membership politically.

It seems that appreciation of the S.A.S. potential dawned first on the Young Communist League (Y.C.L.). By 1970 they had decided that the S.A.U. was not going to 'take-off' and develop a mass base, and that the local unions were too unstable and anaemic to develop spontaneously into a national union. In addition, by 1970 the victory of the Broad Left[38] over the right wing in the N.U.S. was consolidated and hence the potential for S.A.S. expansion was politically viable. As a result, joint discussions took place throughout 1971 between the Y.C.L., the Communist Party (C.P.) and the Broad Left in the N.U.S. with the object of forming a schools union: a process which culminated at the N.U.S. Margate conference of November 1971.

The debate at the conference on this issue was polarised around the questions of whether the new organisation should be an independent one, or whether the N.U.S. should take steps to involve school-students in its own substructures. The left wing supported the former position, the right wing the latter, and the left won. Meanwhile attempts to convene regional conferences of the S.A.S. had flopped completely owing, first, to the problems of finding out where members lived and, second, to the fact that the concessionary basis of S.A.S. membership was by no means a guarantee of campaign activism. The N.U.S.S., therefore, had to be started largely from scratch. This was achieved by the use of leafletting campaigns by left-wing school-students backed up by local student unions. For the most part the strategy was a considerable success. During the spring of 1972 over thirty-five area conferences of school-students took place and a national steering committee of area delegates was formed to prepare for a national conference.

The first two conferences of the N.U.S.S. in May and October 1972 were basically an exercise in political feet-finding. In May

1972 the majority of the 12,000 members constituted a silent majority, transferred in bulk from S.A.S. but hard for the area organisations to contact because of the inefficient filing system. The minority of activists were organised in thirty or forty area branches, mostly fifth- and sixth-formers and mostly from grammar or comprehensive schools. The steering committee had yet to establish viable communication with the branches and the central administration was not yet in operation. The question the N.U.S.S. executive faced in 1972, therefore, was what was the best strategy for lifting themselves out of this unenviable position?

The dominant feeling was that it was essential to get the apparatus working properly and to build up a strong base in the schools as a precondition for serious action. The drawback of this position was that it led to an ambiguous response to issues which developed in the meantime and this, in turn, did very little to help N.U.S.S.'s credibility. This problem became very apparent during the school strikes and marches in London in May 1972 with which the S.A.U. was, at least initially, heavily involved. The N.U.S.S. leadership both supported the strikes and at the same time condemned the S.A.U. for acting prematurely — that is, before their organisational base was sufficiently prepared.

By the second conference in October 1972 some of the more obvious of the structural problems had been remedied — local/national communications were more organised as the result of a functioning national office. However, the strategic problem remained very much in evidence, and the conference did very little in the way of finding an answer. Instead, it concentrated on drawing up a huge and intricate constitution which spelt out in immense detail standing orders for school branch meetings, area conferences, area committees, etc. — scarcely the stuff of political mobilisation, as the local unions and S.A.U. had already discovered. This was followed by the election of a President on an 'anti-red' ticket whose term of office was notable for its concern for communicating constitutional niceties to schools' branches but not for finding the key to developing a broad support base.

In the first year of its existence up to the third conference in May 1973, then, the N.U.S.S. had floundered around in much the same way as previous attempts to build a school-students' organisation. It had the initial advantage of a parent union, the N.U.S., and the accompanying travel facilities but relations were becoming somewhat strained — particularly as a result of the N.U.S.S.'s failure to become financially self-sustaining. By the third conference, therefore, it was essential that a new direction be found if the N.U.S.S. was not to go the way of its predecessor. The solution the conference came up with was the use of campaigns. To this end a national campaign organiser was elected and the following campaign issues decided on:

(i) The right to organise and negotiate freely in schools;

(ii) Representation for school-students on democratic schools councils, boards of governors and local education committees;

(iii) Abolition of all confidential non-academic files;

(iv) Grants for all school-students over sixteen;

(v) Fully comprehensive education.

Although the issues could have been more specific for a first campaign, they were at least all educational, non-doctrinaire and easily understandable to the average school-student. Furthermore, rather more diverse recruiting methods were recommended by the national organiser, Simon Emerson, such as rallies, rock concerts, discos and film shows. In other words, the N.U.S.S. was moving away from a strategy which was geared to relatively politically sophisticated school-students (that is, current members and friends), to one based on a much more realistic conception of potential members' needs — social as well as political.

In the last two years the use of campaigns by N.U.S.S. has become standard practice — the most recent one (1977) included the effects of government cuts in educational spending. This naturally provided a joint teacher–pupil issue and also fitted in with N.U.S. policy. The campaigns have so far produced a membership of 15,000 — allowing N.U.S.S. at least to break even financially — so in the more obvious practical terms their value is clear. But just as important has been the beginning of the legitimation of the politically active school-student in the eyes of both the authorities and the school-students themselves. The emergence of a national school-student body, with policies which stress the importance of 'the community', as opposed to a sectarian emphasis on school-students alone, has increased both its respectability and acceptability. This in turn has increased its chances of building the alliances which, as a weak union with such a mobile membership, it so obviously needs. There is, however, as the next section will show, still a long way to go.

The Response

The response to the emergence of the politicised school-student was a varied and not always predictable one. It ranged through horror, amusement and sympathetic concern and stimulated quite bitter exchanges between left- and right-wing educationalists. Some treated it seriously while others regarded it as a source of humour. For the most part the analysis follows the usual political guidelines but the fact that the issue is concerned with age-related authority patterns produces some complications.

Reds Under the Desks

It may be platitudinous to say that nowhere is the Left better organised than in the minds of the Right (and vice versa) but this conspiratorial view of the world does emerge with consistent frequency in even the most respectable of circles. It has the general characteristic of oversimplifying the source of what it regards as dangerous and threatening political opposition — perhaps in order to provide itself with an easy solution should the need ever arise. Thus in July 1969, the alert Mr Patrick Wall, a Conservative Member of Parliament, addressed the following question to the then Secretary of State for Education and Science, Mr Short:

> Is the Minister aware that Trotskyist and Anarchist forces behind some of the recent University unrest are now turning their attention to the secondary schools? Would he not agree that organized attempts to undermine discipline and the authority of teachers and parents can only disrupt our whole educational programme, and will he keep the whole situation under review?[39]

Mr Short was less concerned, however, and replied with the classic liberal formulation: 'It is not illegal to advocate the overthrow of our Parliamentary institutions, and it is a good thing that this is so: that is why they are so strong.'[40] Such self-confidence in the resilience of British institutions when faced with revolutionary pressures is not shared by the Right.

The problem as the Right sees it is that not only are the Left skilful manipulators but that they have in school-students unusually malleable material on which to work their will. Rhodes Boyson, Conservative M.P. and ex-comprehensive school headmaster, puts the infiltration of the teaching profession by 'wreckers', 'grievance mongers' and 'neo-Trotskyist cells' down to the recruitment of teachers *en masse* in recent years with no regard for quality.[41] From this one can only assume that he believes 'right-thinking' to mean 'Right-thinking' and sees a strong correlation between low teaching ability and left-wing views. Commenting on the school-student demonstrations in May 1972, Ronald Butt wrote in *The Times*: 'It is quite clear that we have seen an embryonic attempt to use children as political instruments and that the demonstrations have not been entirely without some encouragement, implicit or explicit from some other teachers.'[42] Similar fears regarding the pervasive influence of left-wing teachers were expressed during the recent enquiry into the William Tyndale School affair. One senior inspector identified Rank and File, a ginger group within the N.U.T., as the main culprit although all the teachers at the school except one denied any connection with this or any other left-wing group.[43] The problem is compounded by the fact that it is not only adults who are doing the manipulating — or at least, not directly. In some cases, the Right argue, they remain at a safe distance while children whom they have indoctrinated do the manipulating for them, using 'front' organisations such as the S.A.U. and N.U.S.S. One headmistress, Madeline McLauchlan of North London Collegiate School, found that a pupil had inadvertently joined N.U.S.S. while obtaining its travel concessions (which can be taken up without actually joining N.U.S.S.). In a letter to *The Times* she wrote: 'Sixth formers need to be on their guard against this kind of political engineering... It is indefensible that young people should be tricked into membership of an organization of whose nature they are unaware until after they have joined.'[44] Once you assume a conspiratorial interpretation of school-student politics, a bureaucratic error can become a calculated manipulative act.

The conspiratorial perspective also means, of course, that the political actions of school-students are basically meaningless since they are no more than a left-wing contrivance worthy of little more than derision. Ronald Butt commented on the 1972 demonstrations: 'If even a thousand children can be brought out like automata to shout slogans which they do not understand, this conditioning must be a matter for concern — if only because of the insult to the personal dignity of the children whose vulnerability and immaturity is exploited.'[45] He then went on to talk about this 'pathetic striking role' and this 'travesty of political protest'. Nor was it only adults who took up this kind of position. One incensed school-student wrote to *The Times*: 'I not only hope that the S.A.U. will be suitably crushed to prevent more sheep — short-sighted and impressionable youngsters hounded on by communist wolves — flocking to its banner, but that some weak-kneed parents will assert some authority over their protegés.'[46] Or perhaps it was a joke.

To some, the ripples of conspiracy could be seen as spreading beyond the immediate vicinity of the hard-core Left to include 'those who sail under the liberal flag'.[47] Ronald Butt argues that the 'political exploitation and conditioning of children merge into extreme forms of support for progressive education to produce an emulsion of attitudes which is the real cause for concern'.[48] Depriving children of the 'proper discipline and guidance to which they are entitled in favour of bogus self-determination creates a seed-bed in which anarchical progress can take root'.[49]

The solutions offered by the Right to the current malaise among school-students as they see it flow logically from their interpretation of the problem. First, it is necessary to remain alert to the build-up of neo-Trotskyist cells among teachers and the corresponding fall in educational standards.[50] Second, firm discipline should be maintained to prevent the beginnings of a slippery slide into anarchism. Certainly, no concessions should be made in the name of liberalism. The headmaster of Emanuel School, Wandsworth, described such a plea for tolerant treatment of the school strikers (May 1972) made by Dr Briault, the Inner London Education Officer, as 'manifest nonsense'. In a letter to parents the headmaster stated that he would suspend any boy who wilfully absented himself from school or, if he were 'a young and foolish boy, and shows signs of contrition', he would cane him[51] — which may or may not be a concession. A third alternative is that recommended by the London Head Teachers Association — that compulsory education be waived for children who are troublemakers.[52]

No Problem

While the Right took the appearance of politics among school-students seriously, two other groups viewed it with varying degrees of amusement, implicitly dismissing the point of attaching any value to it. The popular press were not slow to squeeze the last drop of joke potential out of 'pupil power' as they labelled it. A typical example was a report by the London *Evening News* on a meeting of Manchester school-students headed 'Wots Rong with Skool by the New Militants'.[53] The article was very evocative of the Greyfriars syndrome, including phrases such as 'ranks of pimpled girls in crushed gym slips and scruffy boys in blue blazers', and 'not a pellet whistled through the air'. In similar vein, the *Guardian* ran a report on the 1972 demonstrations, entitled 'School Marchers find Police have the Master Touch'.[54] This use of ridicule against the initial political demands made by previously quiescent minority groups is of course common enough — witness the reaction to the political emergence of students, women's lib and gay lib for instance.

An alternative response, but one which treats the politicised school-student phenomenon with an equal lack of concern, is that of amused disdain — rather more distant in its style than obvious ridicule, but no less effective in its devaluatory impact. A *Sunday Times* article on an S.A.U. demonstration at a London school captured the style well.

> They [the demonstrators] were welcomed by an inquisitive crowd
> of small boys who willingly offered to distribute the small pieces
> of yellow and white paper. Solidarity, however, broke down
> when the Headmaster, Dr Badcock . . . appeared in person.
> To shrill cries of 'Here comes old . . .' the school yard emptied
> as if by magic, leaving the thirteen members of the Schools
> Action Union to deposit their letter of protest and retreat. Dr
> Badcock felt no obligation to read it, and the incident was
> not counted as one of the group's great successes. But it was
> considered only a temporary set back in a movement which
> aims to revolutionize secondary schools — both public and
> State.[55]

Such benevolent patronage is based on the assumption that action by school-students is of little political relevance or moment but nevertheless an interesting subject for the display of journalistic skill. A similar assumption clearly lay behind a letter to the *Guardian* from the headmaster of St Marylebone Grammar School who expressed his pride in his boys' non-response to the S.A.U.-inspired demonstrations. He went on: 'the very large majority . . . treated this particular exercise with the amusement which is the very most it deserves'.[56]

The Sympathisers

Not all the authorities in the educational system itself were quite so damning of the school-student activists as the discussion has perhaps so far suggested. Many headmasters recognised the validity of at least some of their pupils' claims and agreed to the setting up of schools' councils — though often with only token powers. Even in the midst of the 1972 school demonstrations when feelings were running high, the Inner London Chief Education Officer Dr Briault was prepared to write to London headmasters stating that it was necessary for pupils to know 'that if punishments are given, these are not on account of their views or attitudes'.[57]

He argued that it was important to give consideration to the views of pupils and to give them opportunities to participate in decisions which affect them in schools — such as through schools' councils.[58] To the Right, this statement from an educationally authoritative figure must have seemed like the encouragement of a 'seed-bed' for further discontent.

Like the Right, some progressives saw the politicisation of the school as symptomatic of the faults within it — but naturally they disagreed on the nature of the faults. While the Right emphasised the lack of discipline and presence of Trotskyist teachers, the progressives saw the pupils as reacting to too much authority, often inadequate facilities and a basically uninteresting form of education, but as having essentially reformist rather than revolutionary goals. A *Guardian* article noted:

> The S.A.U., along with the Daily Telegraph, believe that in the final resort schools should be made to serve the aims of society. They just happen to believe in different sorts of society. The more thoughtful youngsters on Wednesday's demonstration clearly believed the opposite: that along with the universities, schools can be institutions whose role it is to question the values of society and reform it from within.[59]

Again the insistence is on an educational system which questions its parent society only within strictly defined, non-revolutionary limits. This position appears to rest on any one of four assumptions which go largely unrecognised and unchallenged. First, the development of an independent, enquiring mind can be structured so that it never aspires beyond reformist goals. Second, the political system is so flexible and responsive that, whatever the nature of the demands on it, it can adapt itself to them. Revolution is therefore rendered obsolete and all political change is reformist. Third, the nature of independent thought is such that it always prefers reformism to revolution. Fourth, the qualities of our society are objectively such that once people are taught to think independently it will become obvious that reform is the only change required. Until these assumptions are substantiated by the progressives they are scarcely justified in labelling the S.A.U. and the *Daily Telegraph* as politically motivated and themselves as reformist educationalists with no political axe to grind. Furthermore, given their preoccupation with the relationship between education and democracy one is obliged to assume that they do have, in some sense at least, a 'service' conception of education — that is, it should serve the aims of a democracy.

The Teachers

The notion of the teacher as traditional adult, operating as a substitute authoritative parent, has fairly clear structural backing in the secondary education sector. And even if the more obvious trappings of this authority have been reduced in recent years, for example in the decline in the number of schools using the cane or insisting on uniforms, nevertheless its tight control over the content and direction of the learning process remains intact — as indeed it has to if the demands of the present system are to be adequately met. It is of course no coincidence that most increases in permissiveness and flexibility in adult–child relationships in the school have occurred in the primary sector, an area relatively well protected from the implications of the selection process.

Given the structural position of teachers, it is likely that autonomous political action by school-students, at least initially, should have been seen by most of them as an affront to their authority, a rejection of the guiding hand, an assertion of unstructured independence. If your role is one of a paid mentor, you do not expect those you are leading to start making their own decisions, or not without consulting you first. Not surprisingly, the reaction of the teacher's unions to the attempts of school-students to organise themselves was one of unveiled hostility. The N.U.T., the most left-wing of the teachers' unions, rejected outright an invitation to send a delegate to the first conference of the N.U.S.S. in 1972 and has not subsequently recognised its existence.[60] In other ways the N.U.T. has campaigned for greater democracy in schools — but within certain limits. In 1971 it set up a working party to consider the establishment of school councils elected by the staff that would take over policy-making on the curriculum, school organisation, internal school finance, and parent–teacher relations.[61] Although head-teachers were to be *ex officio* members of such councils, it was nevertheless a significant democratic step — in terms of increased teacher power, that is. Pupil representation naturally went unmentioned and this is a standard illustration of selective radicalism whereby ones immediate group interest dominates any wider consideration. It remains to be seen whether N.U.S.S.'s policy of building political bridges between school-students and teachers can succeed. To do so it will have to overcome a great deal of adult chauvinism strongly anchored in the existing authority structure.

The response of the progressive school teacher to the politicised school-student was confused both by the demands of the adult role and by the tensions within the progressive educational value position, or positions. Even if he was already systematically employing pupil-centred and free-choice methods of teaching, which in the majority of cases was unlikely, he was bound to experience at least some reservations over school-student activism that he did not control — particularly in its early phases when its organisation was so chaotic. In much the same way, some male members of the Left find difficulty in backing women's liberation or gay liberation since although these are 'radical movements' they are also antipathetic to a conservative definition of the male role. To state the obvious, cultural and political radicalism do not always go hand in hand.

Nor did progressive educational thought offer much constructive guidance. As was pointed out above, its failure to establish any efficient connection between educational means and ends leaves its proponents in something of a quandary when school-students themselves decide on their objectives. The focus of the progressives on individual self-fulfilment through individual choice has left them ill-prepared to judge whether an aggregate of individuals, such as the school-student activists, are moving in the right direction. The concept of 'direction' in this context after all presupposes a coherent knowledge of desired social goals as well as individual goals. In the absence, or near absence, of a well-defined set of social objectives the fact that school-students were choosing for themselves their own form of political activity should have been justification in itself to the individual-orientated progressive values. On the other hand, blanket support for pupil self-determination naturally cut across the teacher's adult sense of responsibility for his charges. The progressive school teacher therefore frequently found himself in a fundamentally ambiguous position on this issue.

Conclusions and Prospects

The emergence of the politicised school-student has been, and is, fraught with tensions. The traditional normative opposition to the intrusion of overt politics into the classroom has provided a generally unwelcoming atmosphere scarcely conducive to the growth of political skills among pupils. Indeed according to this view, political action by school-students amounts to educational heresy since it also rejects the traditional idea of educational authority on which the norm itself rests. That is, it rejects the idea that the school necessarily knows what is best for its pupils and replaces it with the notion of development with at least some degree of self-direction and autonomy. And in so far as this cuts across the paternalistic definition of the teacher role as authoritative and all-knowing, political support from many teachers for school-student activists is at present unlikely.

At first sight, the various pressures from the progressive educationalists for more democracy in schools appear to be straightforward support for political activity by school-students. After all, democracy is generally taken to include participation in decision-making by all the members of a particular structure, and the secondary education system is largely made up of school-students. However, this interprets the progressives' position a little too literally since they also talk of education *for* democracy — thereby assuming that some kind of training period is necessary before school-students can become fully-fledged democratic citizens (though it is unclear as to precisely *what* training is required). Training in turn implies that someone other than the school-student knows what direction and form his politicisation should take. The net result is that autonomous school-student action cannot be regarded by the progressives as quite what they have in mind when they talk about school democracy since this activism is by definition beyond their control. On the other hand, the progressives' definition of what exactly they mean by 'more democracy' is both loose and largely unrelated in any detailed fashion to their individual-centred teaching methods. Thus because of these tensions and inadequate linkages in their overall educational value position their reaction to politicised school-students is bound to be, at the very least, confused.

At the same time the specifics of the progressive pedagogy certainly ensure that this confusion will not result in a relinquishing of the various forms of classroom and social control. So long as progressive methods remain based on a hierarchical ordering of the learning process and until this process becomes, as Goodson puts it, 'less a matter of mastering externally presented material' and 'more a case of actively reconstructing knowledge',[62] the control mechanisms will inevitably continue to operate. Indeed Sharp and Green have maintained that 'with child centred progressivism, far wider ranges of the child's attributes become legitimate objects of evaluative scrutiny and explanatory variables in the construction of success and failure', and that progressivism actually enhances the social control possibilities.[63] In this respect, they suggest, 'the radicalism of the "progressive educator" may well be a modern form of conservatism'.[64] Certainly this has been the case so far as the school-student activist is concerned.

The general political climate in which he first found himself was not, then, a particularly helpful one — unlike the situation in France where the development of the C.A.L.s was assisted by a traditionally higher level of overall politicisation as well as the particular issues of the 1968 ferment. Nor, to begin with, did the British school-students have the active support of students in higher education since N.U.S. was still sorting out its internal political problems up to the early 1970s. Going it alone with just occasional and often ineffectual help from groups on the far Left led fairly inevitably to a haphazard organisational growth shot through with glaring inconsistencies between goals and structure. The result was a split between the national and local groups and the clear possibility that both would slowly wither away.

The sponsorship of N.U.S.S. by N.U.S. solved some of the more obvious organisational problems of a school-student movement but still left it in need of finding its own political direction, suited to its own particular needs. To a large extent, the problems have been identified and the process of dealing with them has begun. The inherent political vulnerability of school-students to pressures from teachers and parents has been countered by the N.U.S.S. emphasis on alliances within the context of community power and greater democracy in schools. For example, in its 1976 campaign for democracy in schools it emphasises that 'school students should have a greater say in the running of their schools *along with parents, teachers and non-academic staff*'.[65] Campaigns in general form a vital part of N.U.S.S. attempts both to politicise and to recruit school-students and to attract the support of other educational groups. Thus the 1976 campaign included both specific issues (such as corporal punishment, youth employment, sex discrimination) and broader concerns — in particular the education cuts.[66] Politicisation is designed to flow out of school-student involvement in the campaigns, and the experience gained in carrying out programmes of action.[67]

There is, then, little doubt of the increasing sophistication of the school-student activists. Whereas in 1968 the S.A.U. saw itself as forming part of the vanguard of the revolution, in 1976 the N.U.S.S. unequivocally defines itself as a normal, if weak, trade union operating within a whole series of political constraints. However, whether or not this recognition of the pragmatics of political life will in itself ensure the survival and growth of the N.U.S.S. is a different matter, given its vulnerability. The organisational problems it faces are as considerable as they are obvious. Not only is the potential membership scattered but it is also susceptible to a range of sanctions from authority both inside and outside the school. The headmaster has not only the direct legal powers already mentioned but also the threat of a poor university or job reference if a pupil should step too far out of line. No less relevant sanctions are those which can be operated by those parents unsympathetic to the political activities of their offspring.

The vulnerability of the politicised school-student is matched by his lack of political resources. Any school-student union has to cope with the inevitable fact of a high membership turnover as pupils move through and out of the educational system. A developed organisational base one year can become a political wasteland the next if conscious steps are not taken to provide continuity. Unfortunately, there are few if any institutionalised means in the school structure to ensure such continuity in the politicisation process. David Paterson, 1975–6 President of N.U.S.S., points out that 'campaigning around points isn't as easy as it sounds, especially in schools, where there isn't the same opportunity for debate, questioning and arguing about the system as there is, say, in a university or college. One of the main problems we face is simply getting the issue across to sufficiently large numbers of school students.'[68] School-students do not have union buildings to supply them with a political and organisational base and necessarily have to rely on the vagaries of more informal methods of organising. Nor do they have the guarantee of automatic funds from the local authority as do college students. As a union, the N.U.S.S. is in the unique if unenviable position of being dependent for its funds on subscription from members with no regular source of income.

Apart from the limitations of these obvious political resources school-students also suffer from the absence of a more subtle resource — political skills. N.U.S.S. is well aware of this. David Paterson notes: 'After spending quite a few years in a school system which does their thinking for them, school students develop a notorious apathy and indifference, and it is our job when campaigning to combat this attitude first, by means of argument, posters, leaflets, etc.'[69] There is little doubt then, that the N.U.S.S. recognises the problems confronting it and is doing its best to cope with them.[70]

In tracing and assessing the context and development of school-student politicisation we have sought to show how it is a form of political opposition apparently denying the logic of many aspects of its situation. Certainly the reactions to its emergence illustrate this in that they were often instinctive and laced with various forms of fear, patronage, ridicule, plain incomprehension and confusion. The school-students' movement has highlighted the traditional reluctance to deal rationally with the direct intrusion of politics into the classroom, the stubborn defence of rigid patterns of adult authority, and the failure of the progressive educationalists to provide a coherent perspective that makes sense of this intrusion. Although its own goals are still taking shape, its challenge has exposed the many limitations of those who wield educational power.

Chapter 6

Youth Culture
and Political Discontent

The development of political discontent amongst school-students
is a severe embarrassment not only to the school authorities but
also to those theorists who hold that the school forms part of
a harmonious learning experience producing largely harmonious
results. Ironically, this group includes both bourgeois political
scientists and Marxist sociologists. On the one hand, political socialisation theorists maintain that the school reinforces the learning
of supportive attitudes already begun in the family and on the
other hand, many Marxist sociologists argue that the school is
an instrument of social control perpetuating the hegemony of the
ruling class. Both assume the socialisation experience to be an
integrated process in which the various component parts interlink
without too much difficulty. Yet as we have shown in Chapter
5, political opposition has emerged within the school itself and
among those who should be passing without complaint along the
socialisation conveyor belt — the school-students. It is a clear
example of the inadequacies of integrated models of socialisation
which do not allow for diversity and discontinuity at both the
individual and system levels of analysis.

In seeking an explanation of this discontent in this chapter,
we draw upon the range of research conducted into student unrest

in higher education[1] since very little material of direct relevance to the secondary sector exists.[2] The ideas this research has generated are applied to an analysis of data gathered by a questionnaire survey of school-students' political attitudes. (See Appendix I for the details of the survey.) As well as investigating the school and home environments we will be paying particular attention to the possible role of the youth culture in supporting or promoting anti-school attitudes. Here is a potential source of values which could introduce an element of conflict into the learning experience of the school-student. In providing an alternative reference point at odds with home and school values, the youth culture could make nonsense of integrated socialisation models.

Defining the Discontent

Rather than examine the discontented school-student in isolation a framework which would analytically bind all school-students together was constructed. It was thus possible to consider the social environment of the two groups together. This goal was achieved by creating a classification scheme based on several known and clearly defined elements. The organising concepts for this process were: (a) attitudes toward the school structure, and (b) interest in politics generally. This approach is based on a method of category creation successfully employed by Maykovich and Block in their research into the political attitudes of American adolescents.[3] Both found it useful to construct their classifications on the basis of an individual's *involvement* in politics as well as his attitude towards particular political structures or values.

In order to make the classification a rigorous and (we hope) a discriminating one, attitudes towards two aspects of the school structure were combined. These were the decision-making and the exam function aspects of the school. The relevant questions were:

(i) How much say do you think you should have in the running of your school/college? — more say than at present, about the same say as at present, less say than at present, don't know.

(ii) Do you think that the examination system should be abolished, reformed, or left as it is? — abolished, reformed, left as it is, don't know.

From these two questions the matrix in Table 6.1 was constructed, creating three types of attitude combinations — support, discontent, apathy.

The primary concern in this category creation was to isolate an inwardly consistent core of potential radicalism. To be labelled as discontented, therefore, an individual had to exhibit a radical attitude on both questions whereas the same consistency was not

TABLE 6.1   Constructing the Classification: Stage I

	Exam system		
Say in School	*Reformed/Abolished*	*Left as it is*	*Don't know*
More	Discontent	Support	Apathy
Same/Less	Support	Support	Apathy
Don't know	Apathy	Apathy	Apathy

required for a respondent to be categorised as supportive. Apathy was defined as a 'don't know' answer to either or both questions.

To measure an individual's general involvement in politics the question was asked: How much interest do you have in politics generally? — a great deal, quite a lot, not very much, none at all. When this political interest factor is combined with the school attitude factor the matrix in Table 6.2 results (the 'political interest' categories are collapsed to form simply 'high' and 'low' interest).

TABLE 6.2   Constructing the Classification: Stage II

	School attitude		
Political interest	*Support*	*Apathy*	*Discontent*
High	Support	Apathy	Rebellion
Low	Acquiescence	Apathy	Hostility

The distribution of respondents within this classification of what we shall from now on call *school orientation* is contained in Table 6.3.

This approach to the definition of discontent contrasts sharply with the many analyses which employ a behavioural measurement

TABLE 6.3 Distribution of School Orientation Categories

	Support	Acquiescence	Apathy	Hostility	Rebellion	All
%	19	35	7	25	15	100
N	174	342	73	239	142	970

Note: The failure of 20 individuals to respond to one of the three items used in the classification creation leaves us with a working sample of 970.

of rebellion — such as participation in a demonstration or sit-in — where the group being studied can rarely be related to other students except in terms of the behaviour/non-behaviour distinction. This limitation is often compounded by a tendency to equate discontented behaviour with a radical political orientation and inaction with attitudes supportive of the *status quo*. Even if this assumption is not overtly present its inclusion is difficult to avoid once the 'active' group has been separated out and the examination of its various socio-psychological characteristics begun. A reliance on the behavioural definition of discontent may therefore easily oversimplify the situation and disguise the extent of underlying forms of political opposition.

To test out the validity of the classification as a measurement of school discontent it was cross tabulated with attitude towards school discipline (Table 6.4).[4] Moving from the support to the

TABLE 6.4 School Orientation by Attitude to School Discipline (%)

	Discipline (%)						
Orientation	Far too strict	A little too strict	Just right	Not strict enough	Don't know	All	N
Support	4	17	61	18	0	100	172
Acquiescence	5	17	67	10	1	100	340
Apathy	8	22	62	3	6	101	73
Hostility	10	41	43	5	2	101	236
Rebellion	18	39	33	6	3	99	142
All	8	27	54	9	2	100	963

Chi-square = 135.0159 with 16 d.f. $p < 0.001$

rebellion category, the disenchantment with school discipline increases significantly. This is particularly important since the overall level of discontent with school discipline is not that high and the discriminating power of the classification has to be considerable to produce such differences. We now turn to the exploration of these attitudinal groups under the major headings of the home, school and youth culture.

The Home

The relevance of experiences in the home situation to the development of political attitudes in children and adolescents has been strongly emphasised by many political socialisation theorists. In particular writers such as Greenstein, Easton and Hess were influenced by the theories of Freud and Erikson regarding the primary importance of the earlier years and hence the family in the shaping of political attitudes.[5] For the most part they operated with a simple transmission model of the socialisation process whereby general orientations were transferred from parent to child. The research carried out within this tradition seemed to indicate the presence of fairly straightforward linkages between the social character of the home environment and the political attitudes of the children. While the middle-class children of Greenstein's sample, for example, exhibited favourable attitudes towards the presidency, the rural working-class children surveyed by Jaros were 'dramatically less favourably inclined toward political objects'.[6] More recent research into the political attitudes of black children also fits this pattern in that most of them are both disaffected and socially disadvantaged.[7]

Political socialisation theory is quite incapable as it stands of dealing with the recent phenomenon of widespread unrest in higher education bearing in mind that the majority of university students are middle class. In fact, the explanation of student unrest which stresses the importance of the family background moves in completely the opposite direction and argues that it is precisely the middle-class parents, or certain sub-groups of them, who have been most successful in producing politically radical offspring. Flacks in particular maintains that in the American case broad cultural changes were taking place which involved the emergence of what he called 'humanistic sub-cultures'.[8] A decline was occurring in the power of mainstream American values and goals and at the same time:

Moving parallel to the line of conventional middle class values and families which carry them, there appears to be emerging an alternative value system embodied in certain types of families. These variant families, intentionally or not, create dispositions in their children toward radical social action. This is result not revolt.[9]

The difference between parents and children, he argues, is that while the parents espouse radical values in an abstract way, these same values have become embodied as personality traits in the new generation. Hence the radical students are not 'converts' to a 'deviant' adaptation but individuals who have been socialised into a developing cultural tradition. Their radicalism is the natural 'acting out' of the political expectations instilled in them by their parents.

Other variations on this explanatory theme point to the mechanisms of the interaction between parents and children as a reinforcing agent in the development of a politically militant disposition. The family environment is described as 'permissive', 'democratic' or 'individuating' — meaning that the child becomes accustomed to taking part in family decision-making. Broad participatory expectations result and the individual seeks to operationalise them in whatever decision-making structure he subsequently finds himself. Should the structure not be responsive to these expectations then frustration combines with radical attitudes to produce political discontent.[10]

To explore the possible relevance of this argument to school-student discontent we first cross-tabulated father's social class with school orientation (Table 6.5).[11] Although a statistically significant relationship exists, its direction is not immediately obvious. The upper-middle-class school-students have the highest proportion in both the 'support' and the 'rebellion' categories. The structure of their discontent is markedly different from that of the working class, for whereas the latter are the most hostile the upper-middle-class school-student is three times as likely to be rebellious. The corollary of this example of low affect among the working class, well documented elsewhere,[12] is that it has twice as many in the apathy category as any other class. The lower-middle-class school-student is also less positive than his middle- or upper-class peer in his pro- or anti-school commitment. But whereas the working-class school-student is correspondingly more hostile or apathetic the lower-middle-class pupil tends to be more acquiescent. The higher the social class of the school-student, therefore, the more likely he is to find

TABLE 6.5   Father's Social Class by School Orientation (%)

Social class	Support	Acquiescence	Apathy	Hostility	Rebellion	All	N
			Orientation				
Upper middle class	22	33	2	22	22	101	190
Middle class	21	33	7	24	15	100	303
Lower middle class	13	44	6	22	15	100	135
Working class	16	35	15	27	7	100	190
All	19	35	7	24	15	100	818

Chi-square = 45.0118 with 12 d.f. $p < 0.0001$

himself in one of the high interest categories of 'support' or 'rebellion', and vice versa.

Although the social class composition of the home environment does not have much of a bearing on school radicalism it may be that the 'permissive family socialisation' content of the Flacks argument has an independent effect of its own. Democratic child-rearing practices may produce potentially discontented school-students quite independently of class factors. To investigate this possibility school orientation was cross tabulated with the answers to a question on family decision-making (Table 6.6).[13]

Although the chi-square computation for this table indicates a significant association to be present, it does not in any way corroborate the ideas of the 'permissive family' thesis. If this were the case then it could be expected that disproportionate numbers of hostile and rebellious respondents would be present in the 'nearly always ask for my ideas' category. As it is, the bulk of the correlation is clearly caused by the association between apathy and family decision-making. The apathetic individual is far less likely than any other orientation group to have been involved in family decisions.

An earlier and much less widely supported explanation of student unrest presented the student militant as an adolescent in rebellion against all kinds of authority, including those of parents and university. In this context the home environment becomes a constraint against which the individual struggles, just as he struggles against what he sees as the injustices of the educational struc-

TABLE 6.6 School Orientation by Family Decision-Making (%)

Orientation	Family decision-making				
	Nearly always ask for my ideas	Sometimes ask for my ideas	Just tell me what they've decided	All	N
Support	56	33	10	99	165
Acquiescence	47	43	10	100	327
Apathy	25	59	16	100	68
Hostility	48	44	8	100	229
Rebellion	50	36	14	100	139
All	48	42	10	100	928

Chi-square = 24.1596 with 8 d.f. $p < 0.005$

ture. It is all part of the same generational rebellion process whereby, as Katz and Sandford put it, 'the time between 17 and 21 is often one of nagging self-doubt, of intense conflict in relations with other people, of painful and sometimes rebellious struggles for independence from one's parents, of an uneasy search for one's eventual occupational and sexual roles'.[14]

If this 'overflow effect' from rebellion against parents to rebellion against political authority is a characteristic present in the school-students of our survey then we could expect that the discontented will get on less well with their parents than the supportive (Table 6.7).[15]

In strict percentage terms this may be the case, but the differences are so small that statistical significance barely exists between orientation and mother relationship and not at all between orientation and father relationship. Part of the problem is undoubtedly the good family relationships enjoyed by such a high proportion of the sample rendering the testing of the 'adolescence rebellion' hypothesis rather academic.

The relevance of the home environment to discontent in the schools is therefore a very ambiguous one. Neither of the two major home environment hypotheses emerging from the research into university student discontent, the 'permissive family' and 'adolescence rebellion' theses, provide any useful insights in this respect. While statistically significant relationships exist between school

TABLE 6.7   School Orientation by Relationship with Parents (%)

| Orientation | Relationship with father | | | | Relationship with mother | | | |
	Very well/ Quite well	Not very well/ Not at all	All	N	Very well/ Quite well	Not very well/ Not at all	All	N
Support	91	9	100	163	96	4	100	168
Acquiescence	90	10	100	313	94	6	100	330
Apathy	94	6	100	67	97	3	100	70
Hostility	85	15	100	222	89	11	100	232
Rebellion	86	14	100	131	93	7	100	138
All	89	11	100	896	93	7	100	938

Chi-square = 6.8299 with 4 d.f.   Chi-square = 10.3908 with 4 d.f.
p not significant $p < 0.05$

orientation and a number of background factors, the direction of these relationships are not consistent with the idea of distinct home experiences for the pro- and anti-school school-students often share common background experiences as do the hostile and acquiescent — leaving the apathetic as the single most distinctive category with the most theoretical consistency. It is after all the apathetic individual whose social class background is disproportionately working class and who is by far the least involved in family decision-making — although still getting on very well with his parents. What these findings presumably mean is that the political 'affect' or 'intensity' element in the orientation classification is more sensitive to the home experience than is the direction of the attitude. This would obviously explain why the 'support–rebellion' and 'acquiescence–hostility' pairing has occurred. The school environment is now examined to see whether experience of this can be shown to have an impact on the development of discontent.

The School

Considerable research has been conducted demonstrating the broader political ramifications of the British educational system.[16] However, while the conclusions of the research at this macro-level are well established, the details of the process of differential political role socialisation are not. One oft-quoted but rarely tested idea is the school equivalent of the permissive family socialisation theory. Almond and Verba argue that the role an individual plays within the school can be considered training for the performance of a political role. If he participates in school decisions he will probably be able to participate in political decisions as well.[17] The greater assumption of responsibilities and authoritative positions by public and grammar school pupils, as compared to their less fortunate secondary modern contemporaries, is held to develop the kinds of skills necessary for a future politically active role. But apart from Abramson's findings which give mixed support to this thesis, very little work has been done to investigate it.[18] It is in any case only indirectly relevant to the concern here since it begs the question of what direction this activity–passivity orientation takes: does the individual accept or reject the school structure?

Nor does the research into student revolt in higher education supply any specific avenues of investigation in this context. There is, admittedly, support for the importance of the immediate structural environment of the university as a means of explaining student discontent but it is scarcely directly applicable to our investigation. Its major tenet is that increasing institutional size and bureaucratic complexity produces situations in which the student comes to feel alone, alienated and frustrated and that this frustration is manifested in political discontent.[19] Clearly it is not possible to test this thesis directly since it depends largely on sophisticated measures of institutional characteristics which cannot be replicated in the case of secondary school and technical college structures. Nevertheless the general idea of specific institutional experiences contributing to the development of radical attitudes towards the school can be investigated in a number of ways.

Individual School and School Type

The cross-tabulation of the individual institution with school orientation produces massive differences (Table 6.8). The grammar schools are arranged in order of both their accepted status in the locality and, correspondingly, the degree to which they embody the traditional credo of the grammar school. The steady decline in the support for the school as one moves from Uptown Grammar (the most traditional) to Downtown Grammar (the least traditional) is matched by a rise in the level of hostility towards the

TABLE 6.8 School by School Orientation (%)

School	Orientation						
	Support	Acquiescence	Apathy	Hostility	Rebellion	All	N
Public	27	32	5	21	15	100	146
Uptown Grammar	39	39	2	9	12	101	51
Middletown Boys Grammar	27	19	1	22	32	101	97
Middletown Girls Grammar	11	27	4	35	23	100	109
Downtown Grammar	7	11	5	50	27	100	44
Comprehensive	21	36	0	21	23	101	53
Technical college	13	43	12	24	7	99	470
All	18	35	7	25	15	100	970

Chi-square = 64.2062 with 24 d.f. $p < 0.0001$

school. A similar decline also takes place in the level of acquiescence, with Middletown Boys Grammar and Middletown Girls Grammar changing positions. Although in the case of the rebellion category Middletown Boys Grammar rather than Downtown Grammar has the highest percentage, it can be argued that within the more liberal grammar schools the development of discontent is rendered possible by a less rigid insistence on discipline and conformity.

One problem with this argument is that easily the most liberal institution in the sample, the comprehensive school, has a far higher level of school support and acquiescence than Downtown Grammar — although not as high as that of Uptown Grammar. Speculatively, it could be ventured that the kind of concessionary liberalism engaged in by the Middletown Boys Grammar and Downtown Grammar schools serves only to stimulate discontent beyond the levels present in the more fully liberal comprehensive. Limited reforms may act as an aggravating factor by raising expectations which they cannot fulfil.

The structures of the public school and the technical college are so different from those of the other institutions that comparisons along, say, the liberal–non-liberal continuum are virtually impossible. The public school has a more embracing control structure than any other institution by virtue of its being a boarding school yet at the same time is more progressive than Uptown Grammar, for example, in its encouragement of diversified leisure activities such as unsupervised film making. Whatever dissent develops is nevertheless unlikely to be present in a majority of the public school pupils, as it is in Middletown Boys Grammar, Middletown Girls Grammar and Downtown Grammar, given the pervasive nature of public school control mechanisms. Unlike day school-students, their experiences are limited mainly to the school which supplies them with values which cannot easily be challenged by vacation experiences or the youth culture. It is therefore somewhat surprising to find the levels of hostility and rebellion so much higher at the public school than at Uptown Grammar.[20]

The pattern of responses from the technical college is less difficult to assess. Most of the students there undoubtedly have a predominantly instrumental attitude towards their education and are not particularly bothered about their 'political' position in the college so long as they leave with the desired qualifications. Their tendency towards rebellion is consequently minimal (7 per cent). But so also is their contribution to the support category (12 per cent). Further analysis of their educational experience supplied additional insights into these figures (Table 6.9).[21] The high proportion of technical college students from secondary modern schools (76 per cent) combines with its relatively high working-class composition (40 per cent) to encourage high percentages in the low affect, or low intensity, categories of acquiescence and hostility.

TABLE 6.9 Pre-Technical College School by School Orientation (%)

Pre-college school	Orientation						
	Support	Acquiescence	Apathy	Hostility	Rebellion	All	N
Secondary modern	11	46	13	23	7	100	336
Grammar	14	40	9	29	9	101	58
Public	48	20	12	12	8	100	25
Comprehensive	4	48	9	30	9	100	23
All	13	44	12	24	7	100	442

Chi-square = 34.3281 with 12 d.f. $p < 0.001$

Although the ex-pupils of grammar schools and comprehensives also have similar orientations these could be the result of self-selection or an accord with the dominant instrumental ethos of the college.

The individual school experience is clearly of considerable importance in the development of school orientation but less obvious is the relationship between school type and orientation. This examination of the data has produced some insights in this respect but has also left some question marks.

Position in the School Structure

Two aspects of how the experience of different parts of the school structure can lead to different school orientations are considered: course studied and positions of responsibility held.

The research on discontent in the higher education sector showed that the radicals were disproportionately likely to be students in the liberal arts or social sciences.[22] For the purposes of assessing the relationship between course and school orientation the sample is split into two: secondary schools and technical college (Table 6.10).

The findings in the secondary schools fit the model of the liberal arts man and the conservative scientist perfectly. The pupil studying a subject in the arts is twice as likely as a scientist to be hostile or rebellious towards the school. Moreover, the pupil taking a combination of the two lies in between in terms of his allegiance to the school, although probably more influenced by the arts than the science course. The influence of courses in the technical college is less clear-cut, even though a statistically significant relationship is present.[23] The only noticeable difference is between the craftsmen and the other two categories. The craftsmen are predictably lower on the 'high affect' orientations of support and rebellion, as is usually the case with lower status groups. But apart from this, the experience of different status courses does not appear to be a formative one with regard to school orientation.

The second aspect of school structure considered is that of positions of responsibility within the school. How does this particular experience relate to school orientation? Are the discontented 'withdrawers' from the formal roles the school has to offer or are they participants? Table 6.11[24] supplies the answer (technical college students are excluded because few such roles are offered

TABLE 6.10 Course by School Orientation (%)

(*a*) Secondary schools

Course	Orientation					All	N
	Support	Acquiescence	Apathy	Hostility	Rebellion		
Arts	19	20	5	28	27	100	207
Science	27	44	3	15	11	100	115
Arts and science	23	26	1	26	24	100	147
All	22	28	3	25	22	100	469

Chi-square = 38.7836 with 8 d.f. $p < 0.0001$

(*b*) Technical college

Course	Orientation					All	N
	Support	Acquiescence	Apathy	Hostility	Rebellion		
Craftsman courses	7	47	16	26	4	100	144
Technician courses	16	37	12	22	13	100	128
White collar (O.N.C., O.N.D., H.N.C.)	17	45	10	22	6	100	188
All	14	43	12	24	7	100	460

Chi-square = 20.3078 with 8 d.f. $p < 0.01$

them). The distinction between 'disciplinary' and 'social activity' types of responsibility was introduced in the expectation that those school-students with anti-school orientations might have 'withdrawn' into social activities within the school rather than taken on the more obviously school authoritative role of prefect. This could have been an alternative to complete alienation from the school and non-participation in any school activity. However, not only is there no statistically significant relationship between responsibility type and school orientation, but also those pupils with social activity responsibilities are the ones most likely to be supportive or acquiescent. So, if anything, the converse of

TABLE 6.11 Responsibility Type by School Orientation (%)

Responsibility type	Orientation						
	Support	Acquiescence	Apathy	Hostility	Rebellion	All	N
Disciplinary	21	29	3	29	18	100	180
Social activity	30	36	6	12	16	100	50
Both	21	24	2	27	25	99	84
None	23	24	3	24	27	101	97
All	22	28	3	25	21	99	411

Chi-square = 13.5321 with 12 d.f.   p not significant

the 'withdrawal hypothesis' is more accurate. Apart from this minor association, responsibilities do not appear to be linked to orientation. Certainly the notion of increased responsibility leading to more positive attitudes towards decision-making structures does not find any backing in this data. For the most positive categories, support and rebellion, are more than adequately represented (compared to their average presence) in the 'no responsibility' category.

The 'multiversity explanation' of discontent in the universities argued that various characteristics of the students' immediate structural environment were responsible for this rebellion. Transferring that argument to the secondary sector the question has been posed as to what distinctive experiences within the school structure there are with regard to the emergence of different school orientations. The data supplies an ambiguous answer. At the general level, individual schools differ markedly in the levels of pro- or anti-school feeling present among their pupils. Yet when an attempt was made to provide a link in terms of common school structures to explain these variations difficulties were encountered. Some connections can be made along the liberal–non-liberal axis but they are not that convincing. At the more specific structural level, the students of arts subjects (as expected) exhibit by far the most radical attitude towards the school. But there is no parallel relationship between school orientation and perhaps the most obviously 'political' aspect of the pupil's structural position — the decision-making posts open to him.

The Youth Culture

Although both the home and university environment were assumed to have exclusive causal rights in the matter of student unrest, it was not long before compromises were made — particularly on the part of the family socialisation theorists. As early as 1967 Flacks was arguing that 'children raised in the humanistic sub-cultures are potential recruits to a wide variety of student deviant, bohemian and drug-cultures'[25] — thereby suggesting that the influence of non-family subcultural agents is considerable. Perhaps even more important, later in the same article he maintains that there is an increasing diversity of recruits to the radical movement: 'they come from widely diverse backgrounds, even from conservative and conventional parents. Protest appeals to an increasingly broader spectrum of students. The movement is spreading to the dominant culture'.[26] By the early 1970s it had become clear that Flacks' foresight was justified. Research conducted over the past five years indicates that the previously established relationship between type of family background and student activism has disappeared.[27] Student unrest has become less an activity carried out by a socio-economic élite and more a generally accepted form of behaviour with broad roots in the student culture.

The principal attempt to account for this change is associated with the concept of counter-culture.[28] To appreciate the full significance of the theoretical shift in the treatment of student revolt contained in the emergence of this concept it is first necessary briefly to provide it with an historical context.

At the risk of oversimplification it can be said that the early and mid-sixties saw the growth of two quite separate but parallel student subcultures which can be called 'hippie' and 'radical'. The hippie subculture was, in the Mertonian sense, essentially retreatist, characterised by a concern with the self and interpersonal relationships, hedonism and opposition to the puritan work ethic, and was often associated with the use of drugs. It was therefore a direct successor to the 'bohemianism' of the 1950s, particularly in its non-political stance. The radical subculture, on the other hand, addressed itself to the problem of political change, and saw political activism on behalf of others as more important than a personalised search for truth or identity. Drug-taking was therefore far less of an integral part of the radical's life-style than it was of the hippie's.

Because of the differences in their outlooks it is not surprising that friction between the two groups was frequent — hippies being labelled as 'self-indulgent freaks' by radicals and radicals as 'game-playing politicos' by hippies. In his research into the differences between the two groups Keniston came to the conclusion that the sociological bases for these differences were considerable:

> But having worked for several years with a group of undergraduates who are intensely repudiative of American culture, I am inclined to see most student protest not as a manifestation of alienation [by which he means the hippie subculture], but rather of commitment to the very values the alienated students reject . . . the activist seems determined to implement and live out his parents' values whereas the alienated student is determined to repudiate them and find alternative values . . . Thus, on the whole, alienation as I have studied it, and the current phenomenon of student protest seem to me quite distinct, if not opposed, phenomena.[29]

In terms of their rejection of the structure of society the differences are clear. Whereas the radicals focused on a rejection of specific parts of the political structure (for example, the position of students in the university power structure, national government policy), the hippies concentrated on the rejection of broad cultural norms (for example, the idea that leisure has to be earned through hard work).

In the light of this, the counter-culture approach to student discontent argues that a *rapprochement* and overlap between these two groups has occurred to the extent that they have merged to produce an alternative culture with a self-sustaining identity of its own. Far from being opposing groups, the argument runs, they are now mutually reinforcing in their political and cultural opposition to the *status quo*. So much so, in fact, that together they exercise a powerful and independent influence on the development of radicalism in higher education dominating other socialisation sources such as the home or university structures.

One problem with counter-culture theory, however, is that it has evolved separately from that youth culture theory is geared to pre-university adolescents. For our purposes we need to consider the research conducted into the youth culture characteristics of adolescent anti-school groups. The primary concern in this respect is: how separate from the surrounding youth culture is the anti-school group or groups? The literature supplies a highly ambiguous answer. The main points of conflict centre on (a) the separateness of youth culture from adult culture, and, (b) the homogeneity of youth culture. Clearly these two questions are inter-related since overlap between adult and youth cultures could well affect the homogeneity of the latter, though not necessarily. In any case, there is little agreement on the answers. In his seminal work, *The Adolescent Society*, Coleman argues that adolescents are 'cut off' from adult society and consequently that 'our society has within its midst a set of small teenage societies, which focus teenage interest and attitudes on things far removed from adult responsibilities, and which may develop standards that lead away from those goals established by the larger society'.[30] Stenhouse goes further and while emphasising the gulf between adult and adolescent cultures he also excludes Coleman's idea of subdivisions within the adolescent culture: 'Teenage culture, the shared understandings within which the adolescent discusses and reflects upon adult problems, is in its way a kind of protest flung by those who consider themselves to be grown up at a society which denies them full adult status.'[31] He therefore presents the reader with two distinct and monolithic cultural modes, incorporating little diversity.

Needless to say this rather simplistic conception of youth culture has been seriously attacked from several angles. Murdock and Phelps argue:

it is misleading to maintain that there is one single set of more or less homogeneous activities, symbols and meanings which can be called a 'youth culture'. By treating age as the predominant dimension of stratification, previous researchers have directed attention away from the continuing importance of sex and social class position in determining adolescents' access to various role sets and cultural milieux.[32]

Referring to the United States of the late 1950s, Bernard points out that while teenage culture of the early teens is on the whole a lower-middle-class phenomenon in which girls are equally involved as boys, that of the later teens tends to be an upper-middle-class phenomenon in which young men outnumber young women by half.[33] Different levels of purchasing power among different socio-economic groups of different ages ensures that these divisions within the youth culture become visible.

Also attacked is the idea that adult and youth cultures are isolated from one another. It is pointed out that values characteristic of certain types of youth cultures are common to parts of adult culture. For example the hedonism, inability to defer gratification, and expressive orientation of the bohemian elements in the youth culture are also present in the working-class adult world.[34] As Berger suggests, it would appear that 'adolescent rebel-

lion takes on ideological supports from existing deviant traditions'.[35] When combined with the notion of a heterogeneous youth
culture this 'adult overlap' idea produces a far more complex model
than Stenhouse apparently envisaged. Indeed it severely questions
whether 'youth culture' is a particularly useful concept, for
it presupposes that the different youth subcultures have an underlying cultural unity which is distinctively non-adult.

The findings on the characteristics of the anti-school pupil bear
out the need for a flexible model of youth culture. Polk and Halferty develop the idea of a scale whereby a delinquent, anti-school
subculture is at the other end to that of the system-committed
subculture.[36] The delinquent youth withdraws from the school
in terms of both his studies and participation in school activities,
since he is not interested in the adult-sponsored success offered
by the school. Sugarman advances a similar thesis when he argues
that there are two dominant adolescent life-styles available to the
school-student: first, that of the official 'pupil' role, involving
acceptance of the values and norms held by the school; second,
the 'teenager' role with values and norms in important ways opposed to much of adult society.[37] Unfavourable attitudes towards
the school, he finds, tend to go along with high teenage commitment.[38]

Data already presented in this chapter questions whether this
American approach to anti-school culture is applicable to the British context. It has been shown that little difference exists between
the pro- and anti-school groups in terms of the holding of formal
roles in the school. Prefects and society officers are equally present
in both groups — that is, school-based activities do not act to
cement favourable postures towards the school. The question to
be addressed now is how far all or part of the youth culture
outside the school is associated with anti-school feeling.

In this respect, the Murdock and Phelps study suggests that
merely equating teenage commitment with an anti-school orientation is oversimplifying the problem. They argue that there are
two 'major cultural constellations pupils may use in order to define
and articulate their disengagement from school' — the 'street culture' and the 'pop media culture'.[39] The street culture they see
as working class, inner urban, with male-dominated values (for
example, those of the footballer or fighter) and the pop media
culture as middle class, geared to the expression of emotional
and physical capacities, whose main medium is that of pop records
and certain magazines. Although the publication of these ideas
came too late for them to be tested out in detail in the survey,

nevertheless the data does allow for the notion of diversity in the youth culture to be investigated in some depth.

To do this the sample was first split into two fairly obvious cultural groups: the secondary schools, dominated by the grammar schools and the middle class, and the technical college, with its preponderance of ex-secondary modern pupils, an instrumental educational ethos and a relatively high working-class composition. These two groups are compared to see whether there is any indication of differential youth culture support for latent discontent in the school and college. The working assumption is that the secondary schools and technical college have different types of youth culture environments. The analysis has two main aspects: (a) attitudes towards predominant symbols of youth culture, and (b) wider youth culture values.

Salient Youth Culture Symbols

Controlling for the secondary school–technical college split, school orientation was cross-tabulated with attitude towards four salient aspects of youth culture (salient in the early 1970s, that is): 'way out' clothes, long hair, 'underground' newspapers (for example, *Oz*, *Rolling Stone*, *Ink*, *It*) and 'progressive' pop music (Table 6.12).[40] These are all fairly obvious symbols of youth culture and will provide an initial indication of whether orientation groups are differentially linked to it.

In the case of the secondary schools, the relationship between latent discontent and the various youth culture symbols is clear. The percentage of respondents approving of these symbols consistently increases as one moves from the 'support' category to the 'rebellion' category: in addition, the relationships are all statistically significant. However the results for the technical college are less convincing. Although the direction of the percentage differences is the same — that is, greater approval for the youth culture factors among the hostile and rebellious — nevertheless the differences are not only far smaller than in the case of the secondary schools but also, with the exception of underground newspapers, not statistically significant. However at the same time it is noticeable that the overall level of approval is consistently higher in the technical college subsample. It may well be that the contact of the college students with the broad youth culture is so general, given the fact that they have all 'left school' (though not education), as to blur the relationship between school orientation and youth culture attitude. It is unlikely

that the technical college could ever desire or get the kind
of allegiance or commitment that the secondary schools often
require of their pupils. The exclusive hold of the schools on
its members has little parallel in the technical college where
part-time courses, block release courses, and vocationally-oriented
students ensure that the non-education world of the student
is not far away.

Although Table 6.12 displays the relationship between orientation and single youth culture symbols it does not deal with
the coherence of this association over the four symbols. In other
words, it may not be the same individuals in, for example, all
four of the rebellion categories. To test out the consistency of
attitudes, the average score of each respondent was computed for
the four youth culture questions and a composite youth culture
attitude created. This was then cross-tabulated with school orientation — again controlling for the school–technical college division
(Table 6.13). The secondary schools' figures demonstrate fairly
conclusively that there is a genuine coherence in the relationship
between discontent and the several youth culture characteristics.
Also present is the dim reflection of this association in the
technical college percentages.

In terms of attitudes towards these four youth culture symbols,
then, the schools and the technical college do not appear to have
distinct youth culture environments. They appear instead to share
a common environment in terms of the particular symbols examined here, with the hostile and rebellious groups in the secondary schools being disproportionately favourable towards this
environment when compared to their fellow school-students. The
question now arises as to whether this appearance is reinforced
when assessed in terms of particular social values often associated
with the more deviant types of youth subcultures.

Youth Culture Values

The counter-culture explanation of student revolt maintained that
discontent in the universities was fostered and supported by an
overlap between political and social values antagonistic to the
status quo. In applying this conception to the latent discontent
of this survey, the first question examined is: how developed is
the dissatisfaction with the school structure? In Mertonian terms
is it rejection alone, or is rejection in the context of at least some
notion of alternative political horizons? To investigate this, school
orientation was cross-tabulated with the replies to the question:

TABLE 6.12   School Orientation by Attitude towards
Youth Culture Symbols (%)

(*a*) Secondary schools

	Youth culture symbols – % approving			
Orientation	'Way-out' clothes	Long hair	'Underground' newspapers	'Progressive' pop music
Support	20	26	21	46
Acquiescence	19	31	32	64
Apathy	33	47	40	64
Hostility	38	58	53	76
Rebellion	38	51	63	75
All	29	42	42	65
p	<0.001	<0.0001	<0.0001	<0.0001

(*b*) Technical college

	Youth culture symbols – % approving			
	'Way-out' clothes	Long hair	'Underground' newspapers	'Progressive' pop music
Support	30	36	38	64
Acquiescence	30	44	40	59
Apathy	37	50	39	61
Hostility	37	50	57	62
Rebellion	36	44	62	85
All	33	45	45	63
p	Not significant	Not significant	<0.005	Not significant

'Do you think there is a system of government, actual or ideal, superior to the British system?' (Table 6.14). The pattern here demonstrates quite clearly that the latent discontent is associated with the acceptance of alternative political perspectives at the regime level of government — more so in the case of the schools than the technical college. When questioned on the nature of these

TABLE 6.13   School Orientation by Composite
Youth Culture Attitude (%)

(*a*) Secondary schools

	Composite youth culture attitude			
Orientation	Approve	Indifferent	Disapprove	All
Support	27	57	15	99
Acquiescence	45	51	5	101
Apathy	50	36	14	100
Hostility	71	25	4	100
Rebellion	66	32	2	100
All	52	41	6	99

Chi-square = 66.6566 with 8 d.f. $p < 0.0001$

(*b*) Technical college

	Composite youth culture attitude			
Orientation	Approve	Indifferent	Disapprove	All
Support	52	40	8	100
Acquiescence	53	44	4	101
Apathy	52	41	7	100
Hostility	64	31	5	100
Rebellion	71	23	6	100
All	56	38	5	99

Chi-square = 10.2421 with 8 d.f.   p not significant

alternatives the majority of respondents described various types of 'pure' democracy. Communism also received frequent mention but again with the emphasis on 'pure' — presumably indicating a dislike of existing models.

Two of the predominant cultural values of the bohemian or 'hippie' elements in the youth culture are rejection of the impor-

TABLE 6.14   School Orientation by Alternative
System of Government (%)

(*a*) Secondary schools

Orientation	Alternative system of government		
	Yes	*No*	*All*
Support	31	69	100
Acquiescence	34	66	100
Apathy	8	92	100
Hostility	43	57	100
Rebellion	52	48	100
All	39	61	100

Chi-square = 15.9612 with 4 d.f. $p < 0.005$

(*b*) Technical college

Orientation	Alternative system of government		
	Yes	*No*	*All*
Support	33	67	100
Acquiescence	22	78	100
Apathy	22	78	100
Hostility	31	69	100
Rebellion	47	53	100
All	28	72	100

Chi-square = 10.1569 with 4 d.f. $p < 0.05$

tance of possessions and success. To see what overlap exists in the sample between political and cultural opposition to the *status quo*, school orientation was cross-tabulated with attitudes toward these two factors (Table 6.15).[41] The results indicate that it is in the matter of broader youth culture values, rather than in the mere symbols of youth culture membership, that

TABLE 6.15 School Orientation by Deviant Cultural Values (%)

(*a*) Secondary schools

Orientation	Deviant cultural values	
	Anti-materialism	*Anti-success*
Support	29	34
Acquiescence	29	34
Apathy	44	27
Hostility	32	49
Rebellion	47	55
All	35	42
p	<0.005	<0.05

(*b*) Technical college

Orientation	Deviant cultural values	
	Anti-materialism	*Anti-success*
Support	24	32
Acquiescence	23	23
Apathy	33	17
Hostility	25	21
Rebellion	28	38
All	25	24
p	Not significant	<0.05

school and technical college differ most markedly. On the counts of both anti-materialism and anti-success the schools score considerably higher than the technical college. Furthermore the faint relationship previously observed in the technical college between discontent and commitment to certain youth culture symbols now practically disappears when we turn our attention to youth culture values. Certainly the significant correlation between anti-success and orientation in the technical college is not caused by such a relationship. In the case of the secondary schools, however, there is strong evidence to support the idea that the hostile and rebellious school-students are culturally as well as politically radical. In other words, their commitment to a more deviant type of youth culture extends beyond approval of its symbols to support for its values.

Of the three aspects of the social environment explored in this chapter — the home, school and youth culture — it is the youth culture which has been shown to have the most consistent relationship with school orientation. However it is also apparent that the secondary school and technical college members of the sample have different types of youth culture experience. For the school-student, the youth culture probably represents an alternative to school, or adult-dominated values, and is therefore associated with anti-school orientations. For the technical college student, the distinction between the educational and adult world is far more blurred, primarily because many of them no doubt see themselves as already part of adult society. Furthermore, although the school and technical college students had similar general qualities at the level of attitudes towards youth culture symbols, substantial differences emerged when the analysis was changed to the level of youth culture values.

The End of Harmony

The neat socialisation models of political scientists and Marxist sociologists alike have assumed an integrated learning experience with basically stable implications for British society as a whole. In previous chapters we have argued that this is very much an over-simplification of a complex process — that tensions and conflicts coexist with harmony and continuity; that political opposition can occur in the most unlikely of places; and that alternative conceptions of what the political order should look like are constantly evolving, albeit in a piecemeal fashion.

The explanations of student unrest are illustrations of how such complexities can develop. First, within the family, the instilling of 'democratic' expectations in children can lead to tensions once they move into universities too authoritarian to accommodate these expectations. At the same time, characteristics of the universities such as their size and bureaucratic complexity can also result in alienation and discontent. Applying these kinds of arguments to our secondary sector data we have found, however, that the home environment has no influence upon the emergence of discontent, though it is related to apathy. (The apathetic individual is more likely to be working class and to have had little experience of participation in family decision-making.) Second, different schools do contain markedly different levels of hostile and rebellious students but precisely why this should be so is unclear.

The more recent research into student revolt has emphasised the role of the counter-culture as a supplier of alternative values and promoter of student discontent and as such it was clearly pertinent to our investigation of possible conflicts in the socialisation process. Unfortunately, much of the literature appears to have been written more by sympathetic propagandists than by impartial social scientists (whatever they may be) and has presented the counter-culture both as more coherent than it in fact is and as the new orthodoxy which lesser subcultures can only fall short of. Hence Musgrove regretfully writes,

> But there is also a bogus accretion [to the counter-culture] which takes two main forms: derelict, conventionally delinquent and mainly ill-educated lower-class inadequates, on the one hand; and, on the other, well-heeled with-it middle class and aristocratic week-enders who wear the gear, learn the language, and smoke a joint. The former are spurious, disqualified essentially because they are simply destructive; the latter because they follow and aspire to success in orderly, structured conventional careers.[42]

He also bridles fiercely at the idea that the counter-culture is a youth culture since this would bracket it with the 'mods' and 'rockers', football hooligans and juvenile delinquents. He continues: 'The delinquent breaks the rules but accepts their legitimacy. The counter-culture questions the legitimacy of the rules and the concept of legitimacy itself.'[43] It is therefore a qualitatively different phenomenon.

Or is it? The counter-culture theorists frequently present it as the only viable alternative to 'straight' society and, at least implicitly, downgrade the oppositional potential of other subcultural forms. In fact as Hargreaves and Whyte have shown in their classic studies of 'delinquent' subcultures,[44] these other forms have a highly developed sense of their identity and legitimacy even though they may not be able to articulate it as fluently as the mainly middle-class members of the counter-culture. Furthermore it is probably a far more secure identity than that of the increasingly diffused and fragmented counter-culture.[45]

In searching for the origins of social conflict, we should therefore remain sensitive to the diversity of oppositional forms. To point to the attempts of the counter-culture to change as well as oppose mainstream society, (as a measure of its cultural distinctiveness), is also to point to the reasons why it is cracking up under the strain. Its internal divisions are becoming more pronounced as its commitment to change increases. Furthermore a subculture does not have to seek actively to change society either to be seen as in opposition to or in conflict with it. It may be that the mainstream society is defining the opposition and forcing the conflict upon the subculture. In such circumstances the middle-class counter-culture may be the first to evaporate.

Despite its exaggerated sense of self-importance, counter-culture theory has demonstrated the possibility of overlap between political and cultural opposition to the *status quo*. Our evidence indicates a strong association of this kind between school discontent and deviant youth culture symbols and values. However, what should be stressed is that the association is mainly restricted to the predominantly middle-class secondary school and that discontent in the more working-class and lower-middle-class technical college does not have the same kind of cultural support. On the other hand, the technical college student may of course have a different kind of cultural support for which we have not tested, perhaps along the lines of Murdock and Phelp's notion of street culture, but this remains a question open to further research.

This chapter has shown that the integrated model vastly underestimates the possibilities for conflict in the socialisation process. It has also revealed some of the complexity associated with those possibilities. In particular we have argued that the umbrella concept of youth culture is a misleading description of a variety of possible subcultures, some of which contain both 'adolescent' and 'adult' members. In addition, different youth subcultures may well give support to different types of anti-school groups — probably differentiated along class lines. The potential sources of conflict are therefore many and varied, which further increases the strain placed on the control mechanisms of the school to ensure compliance among its pupils.

Chapter 7

Elite Ideologies in Conflict: the Case of Higher Education

Writing in 1961, A. H. Halsey argued that the 'pedagogy of cultivation', or higher education as the cultivation of a chosen few for a distinctive life-style as a status group, has persisted in England as a core element of 'ideology, planning and decision making at the highest levels'.[1] The university is portrayed here as a critical cementing agent in the maintenance of élite solidarity and consciousness. Seven years later, post-Robbins, post massive university expansion, he reiterates this point of view and describes the 'historical continuity . . . of de facto control of elitist institutions [i.e. the universities] by likeminded members of the elite'.[2] This, he observes, demonstrates in turn 'the extraordinary stability of the British system of elite recruitment to positions of political, industrial or bureaucratic power'.[3] What we intend to do in this chapter is to show that at the ideological level Halsey is completely wrong. Far from there being an élite consensus on the purposes of higher education, there is in fact a severe élite conflict between positions with such substantial and opposing structural roots that they cannot be reconciled.

The three groups primarily involved in this ideological conflict are the universities, on the one hand, and the Department of Education and Science (D.E.S.) and the government, on the other, with the University Grants Committee (U.G.C.) sandwiched between. Obviously this oversimplifies the situation in that other groups and individuals have contributed to and been drawn into the conflict. However it is our contention that their contributions are subordinate to the two major ideological positions emanating from the D.E.S. and the universities. It is these positions which have supplied the bulk of the normative themes employed in the conflict. Concepts such as 'academic freedom', 'pursuit of truth', 'manpower planning' and 'social relevance' can all be shown to have their origins in distinctive sets of educational values each with its supportive political context. Naturally, in arranging separate values into systems of ideas the problem of 'reading history backwards' arises: are we imposing a spurious order on what are fundamentally discrete ideas? Faced with this same question, Mannheim maintained that 'the aim of the analysis on this level is the reconstruction of the systematic theoretical basis underlying the single judgements of the individual'[4] — which really does not get us very far. The only practical test is whether, as a result of this systematisation, we are capable of greater insights into social phenomena than we were before. Specifically, in the case of our two higher education ideologies the test is whether we can establish the points of articulation between them in a way which enables us to assess the significance of the élite fragmentation we claim they represent. In terms of the ideas already advanced in previous chapters, our interest here is in the legitimations offered for inequality by the different élite ideologies rather than in the processes by which these inequalities are created — while accepting that the two are inter-related.

The University Ideal

The 'university ideal' is not and never was a single, coherent conceptualisation with a practical, institutional manifestation. Rather, as Betteridge points out, it is 'an abstraction which never had any reality', an ideal which has 'shifted with the passage of time and under the pressure of its concrete realisations'.[5] Nevertheless it does have a fairly limited number of component parts. These have at different times been arranged in differing orders of priority producing heated arguments from the proponents of the various alternatives. However — and this point is critical — what we will argue is that regardless of the priorities adopted, the intended political function of the university ideal, implied or explicit, remains the same: that is, the maintenance of a particular kind of socio-cultural élite.

Sir Sydney Caine, Director of the London School of Economics from 1957 to 1967, writes that in his view there is a

> permanence of four basic elements in the varying pattern of university activity in different historical periods, which may be labelled scholarship, training, research and mind-building; or spelled out a little more fully, the acquisition of existing knowledge for its own sake, study as a preparation for particular professions or vocations, additions to knowledge and the cultivation of habits of logical thought, intellectual curiosity and moral leadership.[6]

This neutral statement of the university ideal focuses on its individual elements without any consideration of how they relate either to one another or to their institutional or social context. Once this latter step is taken priority decisions soon follow. Thus Bruce Truscot in *Redbrick University* adamantly maintains that the primary aim of the university is the search after knowledge for the sake of its intrinsic value and that all else is subordinate to this particular institutional objective.[7] He continues: 'A university without research would be nothing but a super secondary school.'[8] Dent provides support for this position when he writes that 'the scholars of the Middle Ages, had the question been pressed upon them, would have declared with united voice that the pre-eminent function of the university was to *advance* knowledge'.[9] Green, on the other hand, quotes a sixteenth-century scholar Roger Ascham as saying: 'I know that universities be instituted only that the realm may be served with preachers, lawyers and physicians.'[10] More confusion still if one reads Sir Charles Grant Robertson's *The British Universities*: he is convinced that if the men of the Middle Ages were inspired by one passionate conviction

> it was that membership in a university was *membership in a society*, that a course of university study is not merely the process of acquiring knowledge, but a life, that praying together and playing together are as important as working together, that examinations are tests of character as well as of capacity, and that a degree is a solemn admission to the full brotherhood of your fellow guildsmen.[11]

In other words, the 'community of scholars' is an end in itself, rather than merely a means to particular personal or academic goals.

Without wishing to labour the point, it is apparent that there is no universally agreed convention as to how all the constituent parts of the traditional university ideal are meant to fit together. Model One arranges the concepts so that the commonly accepted relationships are apparent.

MODEL ONE   The Traditional University Ideal and its Cultural, Social, Economic and Political Functions

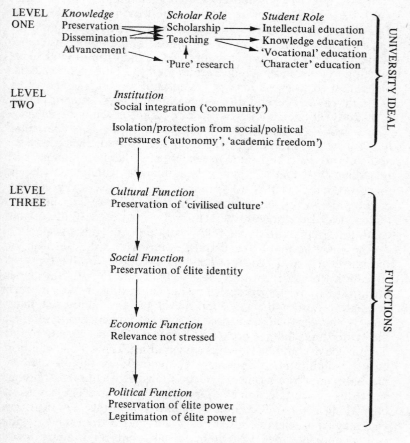

However, what is interesting about the disagreement is that it is confined almost exclusively to Level One of the model. As one moves to the institutional context of the ideal, and hence closer to its cultural, social and political functions, so the disagreement declines. This is not accidental for while an élite ideology may indulge in the luxury of dispute and division at the level of inter-role relationships, it is scarcely going to do so when it comes to the question of relating the aggregated effect of these roles to the preservation of élite power.

Nowhere, therefore, does one find the preservation of civilised culture challenged as being part and parcel of the traditional university ideal. The most effective vehicle for the 'conservation of the most highly prized beliefs and skills in the cultural heritage', as Halsey puts it,[12] is the closely-knit community where social control can be exercised in the most subtle and total of fashions. This enables the process of cultural transmission to occur smoothly and efficiently. At the same time this mode of cultural transference unavoidably (and conveniently for the elite) performs a vital social function by cementing an élite group identity. Thus, Dobrée combines the two when he defines the cultural task of the university as 'the creation, generation by generation in a continuous flow, of a body of men and women who share a sense of civilized values, who feel responsible for developing them, who are *united by their culture*, and who by the simple pressure of their existence and outlook will form and be enlightened public opinion.'[13] It is assumed, of course, that only a minority can participate in this process for, as T. S. Eliot puts it, 'it is an essential condition of the preservation of the quality of the culture of the minority, that it should continue to be a minority culture'.[14] Without this condition, there is no chance of any 'continuity of consciousness'.[15]

The integration of the cultural with the social function of the university ideal has important ramifications for the types of education contained within the student role. First, and most obviously, it must include 'character education' which in turn breaks down into the development of (a) the 'cultivated man' (that is, the personalised aspect of cultural transmission), and (b) the leadership qualities necessary to ensure the perpetuation and dominance of a minority culture. Second, the critical contribution of a broad cultural education to the maintenance of élite identity inevitably invites a suspicion of its opposite, vocational training, since this has certain non-élite, technical overtones. The suspicion has a long history. Raymond Williams notes how new learning emerging from scientific discovery was excluded from 'liberal education' and interpreted 'in terms of its technical training for a particular class of men'.[16] He contrasts this with the position of disciplines such as classical linguistics which, although originally vocational, 'had acquired a separate traditional dignity'.[17] Probably more important is the fact that this 'dignity' is the sign of the élite culture's stamp of approval. Therefore it is not vocationalism *per se* to which the university ideal objects, but the non-élite class culture which it may represent. Hence directly vocational disciplines, such as law and medicine, are accepted since their place in the power structure which the élite culture dominates is recognised and assured. They in no way represent a possible threat to the established order, culturally or politically, whereas the 'new', applied, scientific and technological disciplines may do.

Although the university ideal may be an unreal abstraction in that it means different things to different people, yet its socio-cultural function is potent enough. As an example of educational ideology it undoubtedly lacks a certain logical beauty in that views differ on how its constituent ideas should inter-relate. But from the point of view of our analysis, it does not matter since they all rest on a common understanding of élite culture, and the need for its preservation and transmission.

The socio-cultural function of the university ideal is the bridging concept between the ideal as an educational and as a political ideology. By providing the élite both with the identity and the means for cultural dominance, it is making a substantial and very practical contribution to the preservation of élite power. Coupled with this is its legitimation of the élite through its particular justification of the inequalities on which this interpretation of élite power rests.

This legitimating aspect of the university ideal has the obvious initial advantage of being couched in educational and cultural terms which serve to obscure the very potent political function the ideal is performing. In addition, the most relevant concepts have acquired an 'absolute' status and validity which until recently rendered them safe from attack by isolating them from the normal hurly-burly of political argument. Thus ideas such as 'the pursuit of knowledge' and the 'preservation of civilised values' were cloaked in a kind of religious dignity so that to question them was to commit educational heresy. But although the high status of many of the component ideas lent the university ideal a well-protected legitimacy, this status did not in itself legitimise inequality. After all, why should not everyone, rather than just a small minority, engage in 'the pursuit of knowledge' and 'the preservation of civilised values'? The answer to this question can be found in the assumption implicit in the university ideal regarding the uncivilised nature of the populace as a whole and the care which has to be taken to ensure that the universities are protected from its influence. To open the gates of the universities to the masses would unavoidably result in the dilution and extinction of the higher cultural values. The universities must therefore remain the property and domain of the minority if civilised society is to continue. They are the aristocrats of the educational system, naturally ordained with the right of cultural preservation and dominance. But as aristocrats, their rights are closely linked to their duties towards society. In the Burkean conception of aristocracy, they are the mighty oaks of England, ruling yet at the same time serving — though this service is, of course, strongly paternalistic. The idea of the universities exercising their social responsibility by imposing their values upon it — for example, 'by focusing the community's intellectual conscience', as Sir Walter Moberly puts it[18] — is the natural legitimating concomitant of the assumption that the majority of the people are lacking in the higher status cultural values. To put it another way, inequality is right because élite people care.

In this analysis of the primary constituents of the traditional university ideal we have focused on the dominant ideology in the universities. This is not to deny that other secondary themes have coexisted with this ideology and indeed opposed it. The older civic colleges, like 'the godless institution in Gower Street', had their roots in traditions which were in certain respects quite different. They tended to be more unequivocally research oriented (following the example of German universities), more localised in their student intake, more reformist and more likely to have links with local industry.[19] But in no way can it be said that they, and the ideas they embodied, represented a substantial challenge to the traditional ideal. This is illustrated by the fact that later civic universities such as Reading, Southampton and Exeter, all explicitly aimed at establishing traditional collegiate institutions. Furthermore, as we discuss below, when the massive expansion of higher education commenced in the late 1950s, its direction was very much influenced at least at the outset by traditional university values.

The Developing Challenge

On 20 January 1967, Mr Crosland, Secretary of State for Education and Science, opened a speech on the binary policy at Lancaster University by saying:

> A severely practical reason for this policy and the system of higher education that goes with it is that the system already existed. I did not invent it; it had been developing steadily since the turn of the century or earlier. Alongside the universities we had the training colleges under local authority or denomina-

tional control; and we had a strong and growing sector of higher education in further education.[20]

To a large extent he was spelling out what the universities had almost entirely missed: that the structural source for the challenge to their dominant ideology was under their very noses in the relationship which had developed between the D.E.S. and the Further Education (F.E.) sector. To a degree they may be forgiven for not recognising the emergence of the threat. Up to 1963 they were cocooned in a cosy relationship with the U.G.C. and the Treasury, and it was only after that date when their financing became the responsibility of the D.E.S. that they were directly exposed to its ideas. In addition, their own ideology fostered a certain complacency containing as it did assumptions regarding the universities' automatically privileged and protected status in society. Its long-established dominance had rendered it flaccid and ill-equipped for self-justification, let alone outright conflict with an alternative ideology.

The ideological challenge to the university ideal is based on the idea that education is fundamentally an economic resource which should be employed in a way which maximises its contribution to the development of Britain as an industrial nation. Contrary to the apparent belief of universities, as exhibited in their hurt and surprised reactions to recent government statements on manpower planning in higher education,[21] it is not a new idea. Probably the seminal document of much of the post-war developments in technical and scientific education was the Percy Report of 1945, set up 'to consider the needs of higher technological education and the respective contributions to be made by universities and technical colleges'.[22] It concluded that:

The annual intake into the industries of the country of men trained by Universities and Technical Colleges has been, and still is, insufficient both in quantity and quality... In particular, the experience of war has shown the greatest deficiency in British industry is the shortage of scientists and technologists who can also administer and organise, and apply the results of research to development.[23]

In succeeding years this statement was to be echoed time and time again as the attack on traditional conceptions of education developed.

It rests on the assumption that Britain as a nation is in direct competition with other countries and that every effort has to be made to ensure that she does not lag behind in the race — otherwise we will all suffer. Thus in the 1956 White Paper on Technical Education, a watershed in the development of technical education, the introduction points out the dangers of being outpaced in the production of suitably qualified manpower by the United States, Western Europe and the Soviet Union, and an appendix provided detailed supportive evidence for the warning.[24] In this context, education is forced to take on a 'national responsibility', it has to be responsive to 'social need', it must ensure that what it does is 'socially relevant'.

Once it is assumed that economic goals are necessarily paramount, all else naturally becomes subordinate to and dependent upon these goals. The search for knowledge and its maintenance, for example, can no longer be accorded an absolute status but must be measured by the yardstick of social relevance. Likewise its transmission in the type of courses taught must be closely intermeshed with the needs of the economy. The monolithic structure of these ideas means that to deviate from them is to be at best socially irresponsible and at worst downright unpatriotic. Hence in summing up what it regards as the attitude of the general public towards education, the 1956 White Paper comments: 'The management of full employment, with its much greater need for a responsible attitude to work and its challenge to greater output per man as the only way further to raise living standards, has brought a *sense of our dependence on education as the key to advance.*'[25] Without an educational system appropriate to our economic needs, therefore, we are doomed.

That the initial expansion of this approach to education took place in the technical colleges was no accident. The twin traditions of vocational teaching and links with local industry ensured a sympathetic response by the colleges themselves to an economic conception of education — although the growth of this conception was by no means an easy and straightforward one. A major reason for this was the legacy of what Cotgrove has called the apathetic and hostile 'attitude of industry towards the application of science to the production process',[26] resulting in the slow growth and low status of technical education. 'There is no evidence', writes Cotgrove, 'of any pressure by industry before the 1930s for any extension of technical education.' Indeed, 'there is evidence of distinct apathy in many industries towards the technical education of their workers' as well as towards research and development.[27] Given this historical antipathy to vocational education, the technical colleges were bound to welcome with particular enthusiasm an educational ideology which promised them release from the status doldrums to which they had been confined for so long.

However, the government's (or more accurately the Ministry of Education's) acceptance of this new ideology was by no means a swift one. Since most of the higher echelon of government administration in the 1950s were Oxbridge graduates[28] they had inevitably been exposed to the quintessence of the traditional university ideal with its inherent opposition to the applied sciences and the more narrowly vocational disciplines of the arts and social sciences. Indeed Halsey has argued that 'the British case is instructive as one in which the medieval and aristocratic traditions of the universities have hitherto acted as a powerful brake against movement towards the technological society'.[29] As an initial compromise the government responded selectively to demands for more qualified manpower by attempting to conduct the necessary educational expansion within the orbit and control of the universities rather than the technical colleges. In this respect it is notable that the recommendations of the 1946 Barlow Report on the increases necessary in the numbers of graduate scientists were met[30] whereas those of the Percy Report on technical college expansion were largely neglected for ten years.[31]

By the mid-1950s, however, the economic pressures which were to result in the erosion of the university-dominated ideology of education in Ministry of Education circles, were mounting. In 1954, a Parliamentary and Scientific Committee memorandum pointed to Britain's lamentable record in producing appropriately qualified people compared to the United States — for example, while 40,000 engineers were wanted every year, only 25,000 were produced.[32] At the same time, there was a growing awareness of Soviet successes in this field of education.[33] Somewhat belatedly, it was becoming clear that the universities alone could not be expected to cope with the problem, even had they wanted to, and that the development of the technical colleges on a much larger scale was essential. This course of action was reinforced by two other factors: first, the type of qualified manpower required was comprehensive in its range — that is, it included craftsmen and technicians, as well as scientists and technologists — and second, the technical colleges were under more direct Ministry of Education control, via the local authorities, than were the universities.

The ideological shift within the Ministry of Education towards a predominantly economic view of education was manifested in a number of ways in the years following the publication of the 1956 White Paper. Considerable effort was made by the Ministry to improve both the organisational and prestige position of the technical colleges. The White Paper itself announced a £70 million building programme for the colleges: this was followed shortly by their reorganisation into local colleges, area colleges, regional colleges and colleges of advanced technology (C.A.T.s).[34] More advanced courses approaching university degree standard were continually introduced and encouraged — for example, the Higher National Diploma and the Diploma in Technology. *Education in 1958*, the annual report of the Ministry of Education, stressed that 'new courses were required, equal in standard to university courses and comprising comparable amounts of academic study, but *different in kind*'.[35]

This idea that the technical colleges were creating an area of higher education (the advanced F.E. courses, for example) which was an alternative to rather than a subordinate of the university sector comes through strongly in Ministry of Education reports of the late 1950s. *Education in 1958*, for instance, referring to the newly created C.A.T.s, commented:

> The main justification for their existence, however, will lie not in their ability to copy the universities but in their success in marking out a distinctive place in the educational system. For this purpose, their principal instrument is their *intimate link with industry*... They [the government] are convinced that the more strictly academic approach of most universities and the close association with industry that characterises the colleges of advanced technology can form a stimulating *complement to each other* to the national advantage.[36]

And what exactly is meant by 'the national advantage'? The Report leaves us in little doubt: 'One thing is certain: neither the colleges nor the universities (unless they were to be dominated numerically by their technological faculties)[37] could alone produce the number of technologists which this country so urgently requires'.[38]

As the idea of education as the servant of the economy gained ground in the Ministry so the prestige accorded to the technical colleges increased. Their traditional ties with industry naturally became the object of considerable attention since these could help improve the efficiency of the links between education and the economy. Thus the Willis Jackson Committee recommended in 1957 that 'there must be a much greater interchange of staff and ideas [between colleges and industry] and it must be a commonplace for individuals to move from one domain to the other and back again, or for them to be fully recognised members of one and both at the same time'.[39] Similarly, the 1962 White Paper *Industrial*

Training: Government Proposals listed the weaknesses in the arrangements for training in industry and said: 'The Government has therefore decided that the time has come to strengthen and improve the *existing partnership* between industry, the Government and the education authorities in the provision of industrial training.'[40] To this end, regional boards were to be set up with the majority of representatives provided by employers and the trade unions but also with 'appropriate educational representation'.[41] Both these examples should be seen in the context of increasing amounts of space devoted to further education in the Ministry of Education's annual reports, steadily expanding sophistication and detail in its planning of this sector, and a whole series of reports on technical colleges, their courses and supportive organisations (advisory boards, for example).[42]

The significance attached to these developments, and in particular to the links with industry, by the Ministry of Education is made abundantly clear in its annual report of 1963 where it comments on the Robbins Report on Higher Education[43] in these terms: 'Perhaps even more far-reaching [than Robbins] in its implications for the educational system as a whole was the Industrial Training Bill, which was introduced in Parliament in November to give effect to the proposals outlined in the White Paper of 1962.'[44] If the proponents and protectors of the traditional university ideal had taken this statement seriously they would surely have been better prepared for the attack on their ideology which was shortly to emerge.

The new ideology of education made its first major political appearance at Woolwich Polytechnic on 27 April 1965 in a speech by Mr Crosland, then Secretary of State for Education, in which he announced the setting up of degree awarding polytechnics.[45] The speech is in effect a condensed statement of the ideological developments we have discussed above. Mr Crosland first set the scene by referring to the 'twin traditions which have created our present higher education institutions'[46] — the autonomous sector, the universities and the public sector, 'represented by the leading technical colleges and the colleges of education'.[47] He then identified four basic reasons for the continuation of this dual system. First, 'in Britain, as elsewhere, there is an ever-increasing need and demand for vocational, professional and industrially-based courses in higher education'.[48] Second, 'if the universities have a "class" monopoly of degree-giving, and if every college which achieves high standards moves automatically into the university club, then the residual public sector becomes a permanent poor relation perpetually deprived of its brightest ornaments, and with a permanently and openly inferior status'.[49] In other words, the autonomous and public sectors must remain 'separate and different but equal in status'. Third, 'it is desirable in itself that a substantial part of the higher education system should be under social control, and directly responsive to social needs'.[50] Fourth, 'we live in a highly competitive world in which the accent is more and more on professional and technical expertise. We shall not survive in this world if we in Britain alone down-grade the non-university professional and technical sector'.[51] As these four themes were increasingly evident in the documents produced by the Ministry of Education (after 1963 the D.E.S.) in the decade preceding Crosland's speech, his statements can be seen as the logical expression at the overtly political level of an emergent ideology of education. In the following year, 1966, it gained further official support with the publication of the White Paper *A Plan for Polytechnics*.[52]

With the increasing awareness in the Ministry of Education and the technical colleges of the economic need for manpower qualified at degree level, the encroachment on to the university preserve had become only a matter of time — as had the inevitable ensuing ideological conflict. Crosland left the universities in little doubt that this conflict was likely to be a bitter one when he said in his Woolwich speech: 'Let us now move away from our snobbish caste-ridden hierarchical obsession with university status.'[53] How prepared for this conflict were the universities?

We Can Handle Them

The myth that the Robbins Report[54] of 1963 inaugurated university expansion is not only widely prevalent but also wrong. In fact in 1956 the U.G.C., basing its calculations on birth-rates and an increasing proportion of the seventeen and over age group staying on at school, advised the Chancellor of the Exchequer that student demand would double from the then current figure of 85,000 places to 168,000 by 1968.[55] In 1959, the U.G.C. subsequently recalculated that the number of places required by the late sixties might be 200,000[56] (Robbins estimated that 197,000 places would be needed by 1967–8). Between 1958 and 1961, seven new universities were founded — Sussex, York, East Anglia, Essex, Kent, Warwick and Lancaster. In other words, the universities had already entered a period of change well before the new educational ideology had fully crystallised. To what extent had this prepared the traditional university ideal to meet the challenge of a changing society?

The Niblett Report on Halls of Residence (1957)[57] was pub-

lished at a time when the demand for these changes were first
becoming apparent and provides an insight into the initial response
to this need. It leaves us in little doubt of its reliance on traditional
ideas. The specific question it is addressing itself to concerns the
role to be played by the halls of residence in a university expansion
programme and this naturally raises the central concepts of 'community', 'character training' and 'cultural transmission'. Halls of
residence, the Report argues, are essential to the production of
'graduates who possess, as well as their specialised knowledge,
a wide range of interests, initiative, consideration for others, a
strong sense of personal integrity and a willingness to take responsibility'[58] (that is, leaders). Such a mode of living assists the process
of 'moral tutoring' and 'provides a natural way of bringing students
into touch with members of staff, and it is these contacts with
more richly stored and mature minds, as well as with other students, that are among the most educative agents in a hall of residence'.[59] The Report could scarcely be more paternalistic.

It is also quite blatant about the function of the university
as a means of controlling entry into the élite by inculcating the
appropriate values into the raw university material increasingly
coming from a non-university background. The problem as the
Niblett Report sees it is that these élite applicants

do not see it [the university] also as a society where knowledge
is advanced and a whole range of intellectual values revealed
through a way of life — a society whose standards they must
themselves embody if they are properly to have a university
education. To accept the idea that university standards should
*influence their whole personality, their range of interests and their
social being, requires a revolution of mind and attitude.*[60]

Such a revolution, Niblett argues, is particularly difficult if these
students are living at home since 'in many cases there was a real
disharmony between the leisure interests which the students' home
and neighbourhood afforded'[61] and the university culture. Far
better for them to accept the warm embrace of the hall of residence
where cultural controls could be maximised.

The strength of this notion of managing a fresh influx into
the élite by the use of traditional means of socialisation is demonstrated by the fact that four of the seven new universities founded
between 1958 and 1961 set up collegiate systems of residence.
Indeed the University of York board was quite explicit about
its intentions and 'claimed that for the undergraduates of the present age, often lacking in family background conducive to studious

habits and cultural interests pursued in common, residence is a part of the benefits of a university education whose value can scarcely be overstressed'.[62]

Yet at the same time as these traditional mechanisms were being called upon to handle and assimilate the social intruders, limited recognition was also being given to the idea of university responsiveness to 'national needs' as defined by the government. In 1946 the terms of reference of the U.G.C. had been changed and the following addition made: 'and to assist, in consultation with the universities and other bodies concerned, the preparation and execution of such plans for the development of the universities as may from time to time be required in order to ensure that they are fully adequate to national needs'.[63] This responsiveness had been demonstrated, according to the U.G.C., in their preparedness to implement the recommendations of a series of reports on new courses in science and technology, medicine, dentistry, veterinary science, agriculture and forestry, etc.[64] In practice, then, the traditional idea of the universities defining for themselves what their social responsibilities were, was being eroded by the realities of public funding. As the U.G.C. put it: 'They [the universities] are not shirking their responsibilities; they appreciate that liberty must be limited in order to be possessed'.[65] Nevertheless it is significant that in the same report the U.G.C. opposed the 'uncritical acceptance' of demands on the universities and stated that 'individual universities should have the last word in deciding whether to undertake a particular activity'.[66]

In an interesting if confused metaphor Sir Robert Aitken, former chairman of the Committee of Vice-Chancellors and Principals (C.V.C.P.), wrote that 'Robbins, like the Flood, is a watershed in history'.[67] We have already pointed out that the process of expansion was well under way before the Committee on Higher Education was set up and it is more accurate to see it as the result rather than the cause of that expansion. But in the words of the U.G.C., 'what their Report did do was to establish, publicly and authoritatively, the principles which should govern the scale and pattern of higher education in this country'.[68] It was both a precise and statistical affirmation of the need for an expansion already in progress, and an ideological statement as to the form this expansion should take. It is the latter that we are primarily interested in, to see whether it was, to use Sir Robert's phraseology, an ideological watershed.

Of the four aims of higher education laid down by Robbins, only one, 'instruction in skills', can be seen as incongruous with the traditional university ideal. The others are familiar enough:

the education of 'not mere specialists but rather cultivated men and women', the advancement of learning and 'the transmission of a common culture and common standards of citizenship'.[69] Robbins saw these as the prime responsibility of the university for which special provision should be made: for example, the ratio of teachers to students in the universities should be more favourable than in other institutions of higher education that do not have 'in the same measure the duty to preserve and advance knowledge'.[70] It naturally followed from this assumption of university privilege that Robbins should recommend a 'unitary' system of higher education with universities at its apex after which the lesser forms of higher education would aspire. At the same time he argued that certain of the C.A.T.s should be given university status. (This would effectively 'cream off' the top tier of the technical colleges — a critical point which we will return to later in discussing the capacity of the polytechnics to establish an alternative identity to that of the universities.) All this is consistent with maintaining and protecting the existing mode of élite recruitment and socialisation — and to this extent perfectly predictable. But what of the new educational ideology? How aware of this is Robbins?

Although the Report recognises the importance of higher education's contribution to Britain's competitive position in the world,[71] it does so with certain reservations. In a section entitled 'Education as an Investment', it discusses the concept of human capital while adding the caveat: 'provided we always remember that the goal is not productivity as such, but the good life that productivity makes possible'.[72] (Precisely what the 'good life' is we are not told.) Later on, a further rebuff for an economic view of education appears with the statement that educational investment cannot be 'measured adequately by the same yardstick as investment in coal or electricity'.[73] What education can do, apparently, is to create a certain milieu of 'general adaptability' and 'increased capacity for technological advance'.[74] It is with vague phrases such as these that the Robbins Report deals with a topic of which it is clearly suspicious. It is aware of the new ideology but unsure of the appropriate response.

Where it feels on safer ground is in its treatment of the concept of 'academic freedom' and it is here that we find a classic statement of the normative theme subsequently much used as a defence against the encroachments of manpower planning. Robbins argues that effective machinery for the running of the universities can only be achieved if a nice balance is kept between two necessities: 'the necessity of freedom for academic institutions, and the necessity that they should serve the nation's needs'.[75] The Report continues: 'We are convinced also that such freedom is a necessary condition of the highest efficiency and the proper progress of academic institutions, and that encroachments upon their liberty, in the supposed interests of greater efficiency, would in fact diminish their efficiency and stultify their development.'[76] The fact that the Robbins Report felt it necessary to devote a chapter to the subject of academic freedom, to reassert its value and to spell out its relationship to the idea of national needs is, we feel, highly significant.

Although the notion of 'university autonomy' is today a much debated issue, its position within the traditional university ideal was assumed rather than overemphasised. After all, given the role of the university as the preserver of élite values and producer of élite people, conflict between one section of the élite (the government) and another section of the élite (the universities) was quite simply not a part of the traditional ideal model. Rather, the model assumed (and as late as 1968 Halsey argued was still the case[77]), élite homogeneity based on élite consensus. The élite could be expected to look after its own. In this context the concept of university autonomy is necessary only as a legitimation of the objective, apolitical role of the university (thus disguising its élite socialisation function) rather than as a description of the desired reality. However, once a split between the universities and another section of the élite occurs then the idea of university autonomy becomes a critical part of their ideological defence and the frequency of its use a measurement of the extent of their insecurity. Part of the significance of Robbins, therefore, lies in the indications it gives of the beginnings of élite fragmentation.

Equally important is its contribution, oddly enough, to the undermining of the traditional university ideal despite the general reiteration of this ideal throughout the Report. Where the crucial departure occurs is in the oft-quoted principle of 'social demand': that higher education should be available to all those qualified to receive it.[78] In so far as the Committee on Higher Education was set up to examine the question of an expansion already under way, some such statement of this nature was inevitable. It is perhaps surprising that it was presented in such authoritative, principled and categorical terms given the fact that it conflicts so totally with the traditional university ideal pervading the remainder of the Report. For how is it possible to reconcile a basic principle of mass higher education with an ideal which rests securely on an assumption of education for the minority? How can the traditional university function of élite culture transmission be applied to the vastly expanded university population envisaged by Robbins?[79] While it may have made some sense in 1957 for Niblett to recommend the absorption of new members of the élite using traditional methods before the full extent of the projected expansion was appreciated, it can scarcely be said to do so six years later. Elites are just not that large.

Two explanations are possible for this ideological incongruity within the Report. First, it may be that the Committee was unaware that the university ideal is a fundamentally aristocratic conception scarcely capable of successful integration with the meritocratic concept of 'higher education for all those appropriately qualified'. It may have thought that taking culture to the masses, or more accurately vice versa, was a worthwhile end in itself while forgetting the potent role the university plays in cementing élite identity. Certainly there is a great deal in the Report reminiscent of Moses bringing down the tablets from Mount Sinai. Second, the Committee may have recognised the incongruity but also realised that there was little it could do about it. On the one hand, the doctrine of 'equality of opportunity' in higher education was a powerful political theme reinforced by economic demands for more graduates and, on the other, the Committee's natural inclination was obviously to see itself as the protector and perpetuator of the traditional ideal.

For whatever reason, the Robbins Report is undoubtedly a watershed — though not in the sense that Sir Robert Aitken used the term. Given that university expansion was well under way before the Robbins Committee was constituted, along projections that the Report did little to change, its main significance lies in the insights it provides into the reaction of the old university ideology to the challenge to its authority. Furthermore, its eloquent and sonorous conceit did little to impress decision-makers and many of its more important recommendations were subsequently ignored: a unitary system of higher education was *not* introduced, the colleges of education were *not* placed under the aegis of the universities, and a separate minister for higher education with direct access to the cabinet was *not* created.[80] The accepted recommendations were largely concerned with overall rates of expansion that were in line with previous policy decisions, and the raising to university status of the C.A.T.s. Even at this early stage in the burgeoning ideological conflict, therefore, it was apparent that the political weight of the university ideal was not all that it might be.

The perpetuation of the Robbins myth in the face of much of the evidence is an interesting example of an authoritative statement fulfilling a societal need for ideological legitimation of a course of action despite the gap between the myth and the reality. While in one respect the Report was little more than ideological candyfloss, in that it did not initiate or direct higher education development in the 1960s, in another it provided an essential, if erroneous, impression that order underlay an unprecedented change in higher education policy. It legitimated what it did not control.

The Challenge Shapes Up

With the transfer of financial responsibility for the universities from the Treasury to the newly created D.E.S. in 1964, it could have been expected that the clash between the two educational ideologies would become more overt. As our later analysis of the U.G.C.'s changing role will demonstrate, conflict there certainly was. However, an important constraining factor in this situation was the problems encountered by the Department in attempting to work out the operational constituents of its new ideology. The primary characteristics we have identified so far — that is, the contribution of education to economic growth in the face of international competition, links with industry, prestige for vocational courses, and social control over education — provided some policies (for example, the Industrial Training Boards and separate development for the polytechnics) but left the major question of how best to link the educational system to the economy unanswered.

While the principle of social demand guiding higher education development in the early 1960s effectively undermined the minority tenet of the traditional university ideal, it was also not particularly useful to any manpower planning approach to education. Indeed the two are often seen as contradictory. There is no natural 'fit' between social, or more accurately individual, demand for higher education and demands of the economy for certain types of qualified manpower — unless, of course, one assumes the individual to be perfectly rational, guided solely in his decisions by economic criteria, with perfect information regarding the opportunities for maximising his economic goals, and the best paid occupations to be those which are necessary for economic growth (to oversimplify). In the absence of such a situation, the difficulty the D.E.S. faced was in knowing what types of vocational courses to promote, and to what degree, in its educational policies. Manpower forecasting was then, and still is, in its infancy and precise identification of the occupational requirements of economic growth impossible.[81]

(It was believed that trends in the demand for service occupations such as medicine and teaching were easier to measure though the recent and unexpected massive cuts in teacher training severely question this idea.)[82] In the face of this, the solution adopted by the D.E.S. was the general and largely undiscriminating encouragement of courses in science and technology, in all sectors of education.

A major structural promoter of the theme 'more means good when it comes to science and technology' was the Committee on Manpower Resources for Science and Technology under the chairmanship of Sir Willis Jackson, formed in 1965. This Committee produced a series of reports in the late sixties which, taken together, can be seen as championing with some success the idea that one of the major weaknesses of the British educational system is its failure to train and keep the quantities of scientists and technologists necessary for an expanding economy. In particular, the Dainton Report (1968)[83] demonstrated 'the drift from science' in the schools, the Jones Report (1967)[84] showed that there was a net 'brain drain' of engineers, scientists and technologists from our shores and the Swann Report (1968)[85] argued that postgraduate courses tended to produce individuals geared more to academic study than work in industry. For these problems to be solved, the reports maintained, the universities would have to change their ways and their treatment of scientists, engineers and technologists. They should: (a) reconsider their entry requirements in order to increase the flow of candidates into the sciences and experiment with new courses to render them more attractive (Dainton); (b) appreciate that, 'if scientists were brought up to believe (and trained by curricula which recognised) that manufacturing industry was an honourable occupation on which depended the economic strength and prosperity of the community, more would choose to enter it as a career',[86] and be less likely to seek academic jobs abroad (Jones); and (c) review their methods of postgraduate training with a view to orienting it less towards academic research and more towards industry (Swann).

The assumption which guided the Jackson Committee was that a causal relationship links the output by the educational system of scientists and technologists and the rate of economic growth. As it happens, an O.E.C.D. report on this subject, *Gaps in Technology between Member Countries* (1968),[87] severely questions whether this is in fact so. It demonstrates that the United Kingdom is training 40 per cent more technologists in relation to the size of the age group than the United States, and a higher proportion of pure scientists than any O.E.C.D. country except the United

States. Yet the U.K. economy is still lagging. Commenting on these figures, the U.G.C. stated that they 'called into question the rationale of seeking to influence student preference and the justification for imposing severer competition for university places on some subject choices than on others'.[88] Indeed — but what such a statement ignored was the increasingly secure ideological base within the D.E.S. for such policies regardless of external evidence against them. Not only did the 'science and technology' theme have secure roots in the now influential technical college tradition, but also combined for a while with an emerging 'quantitative and objective planning' theme in forming an ideological bridge between education and the economy.

The first major structural confirmation of this new ideological component was the establishment in 1966 of the planning branch in the Department. This represented a move away from the use of external advisory committees, such as Robbins focusing on particular areas of education, and had instead the aim of examining relationships between different elements of educational policy and of attempting to develop an overall view.[89] The method to be used in choosing between alternative patterns of development was the examination of 'the quantitative implications of policy in terms of money, manpower and other scarce resources'.[90] The branch's immediate terms of reference were to include 'the distribution of students in higher education between universities, colleges of education, polytechnics and other technical colleges; the educational implications of manpower studies; and a review in cost–benefit terms of provision for the 15–18 age group in schools and elsewhere'.[91]

Although the Jackson Committee had already introduced the notion of manpower forecasting, this was both limited in its application (to engineers and doctors, for example) and excluded the question of the costs of the implementation of policy. Manpower forecasting alone, therefore, did not allow for choices between policies on the basis of limited resources. The system that did provide this capacity, that of output budgeting, was subsequently formally discussed in *Educational Planning Paper No 1*[92] and *Educational Planning Paper No. 2.*[93] Its aims were defined as 'being to analyse expenditure by the purpose for which it is to be spent and to relate it to the results achieved'.[94] Within this general budgeting system the D.E.S. also developed the human capital approach to further and higher education planning — a cost–benefit analysis where expenditure on education is treated as a form of investment from which benefits accrue in the future, both to individuals receiving the education and to society as a whole.[95]

While private rates of return could, according to this model, provide evidence in connection with 'social' or, more accurately, individual demand projections, it is undoubtedly the economic benefits to society, or the social rates of return, which are regarded as most relevant to the resource problems of central government.[96]

The D.E.S. is thus moving towards, and apparently searching for, a completely economic approach to higher education both in terms of the goals pursued and the means used. Although it claims that its planning methods supply a choice of policies, one suspects that its links with the Unit for Manpower Studies in the Department of Employment (which has the policy implications of its findings discussed by government departments collectively)[97] severely limit the amount of choice available. Not that the D.E.S. would or could admit such pre-emptive bias, since its approach is by definition — its definition — value free. Unlike the traditional university ideal it does not explicitly root its view of higher education in what it regards as high status values (such as the pursuit of knowledge) but in some kind of objective, measurable reality. It just happens that this reality is economic.

So also is the inequality it seeks to create and legitimise. In the heady first years of university expansion, it appeared for a while that the aristocratic minority principle was banished for ever. The translation of the equality of opportunity doctrine from the secondary to the higher education sector seemed assured in the form of the general acceptance of the 'social demand' principle as enshrined in the Robbins Report. So far as higher education was concerned, social and political inequalities would therefore be based on merit and merit alone. However, with the onset of the economic recession, the increased pressure on government to employ its resources more economically, the transparent limitations of the indiscriminate production of scientists, technologists and engineers, and the emergence of the human capital approach to educational planning in the D.E.S. as an operational support for its economic ideology of education, the chances of survival of the social demand principle steadily diminished. There is little room for individual preference in an ideology dominated by the requirements of the economy. Once priority is accorded to economic demands it is only a question of time before the logic of the position dictates that a politician, in this case Lord Crowther Hunt addressing a conference on the implications of low economic growth for higher education, makes this kind of statement:

It simply will not do to allow universities and polytechnics *to produce whatever people they fancy or to relate the number*

*and kind of places they provide to the applications that come
forward. . . We* need to estimate our likely future needs for
different broad categories of trained manpower deriving from
the experience of some of our industrial competitors and from
their views on the different propositions and types of trained
manpower they now have and are planning for.[98]

It follows that from the individual's point of view, the opportunity
structure in higher education will be organised in accordance with
society's economic needs, as defined by the D.E.S., and that his
choice of course will consequently be limited and, implicitly at
least, directed. Furthermore, given the fact that the numbers in
a manpower élite, as in any other, are limited, we can expect
the reintroduction of some kind of economic minority principle.

Whereas the legitimation of the inequality inherent in the traditional university ideal is aided by its inclusion of certain 'absolute'
ideas, such as the preservation of civilised values, that of the new
ideology rests on its claim to incorporate objectively necessary
goals, such as economic growth, which can be both identified
and achieved employing 'scientific methods'. Its goal definition
is in much the same category as the statement 'What is good
for British Leyland is good for the country' in the sense that
it is, after all, only aiming for what is clearly the best for everyone.
This 'inevitable' quality of the ideology is reinforced by its use
of the 'impartial' sciences of economics and statistics in the construction of educational policy. In this way, it legitimises itself
by claiming to be value-free and non-ideological. The difficulty
with this claim is that certain educational goals are more quantifiable than others. How do you quantify the cultural benefits of
education, for example? The research problems raised by such
a question ensure that the economic focus of the ideology is reinforced by its methodological component, naturally suited as this
is to the answering of economic, quantifiable questions.

With the emergence of the human capital approach to educational planning, a reassessment of the importance attached to the
production of scientists and technologists gradually took place as
economic needs began to be interpreted in broader and more sophisticated manpower terms. An early signal of this was the replacement
of the Willis Jackson Committee in 1968 with the Committee
on Manpower Resources — removing the previous emphasis on
science and technology. This is not to deny that concern with
the latter remained a powerful part of the D.E.S. ideology but
rather to argue that it was increasingly being placed in the context
of a broader view of manpower requirements. In other words,

the ideology was expanding its definition of 'vocational'. More recently, this trend has been evidenced by D.E.S. encouragement of more general courses which allow for greater flexibility both in higher education itself and for the individual who may well be faced with a changing occupational structure. Examples of these are the Diploma in Higher Education and certain innovatory courses sponsored by the Council for National Academic Awards (C.N.A.A.). Referring to the latter, the D.E.S. commented that they were 'designed to enable students to pursue coherent courses which draw on a number of related disciplines and, while not narrowly vocational, have high relevance to the world of work'.[99] From the point of view of fitting manpower production to manpower requirements in a continually developing economy, such courses have, or may have, the advantage of providing parts of the existing manpower pool with the capacity to adapt to new needs — rather than having to produce the fresh manpower from scratch.

At the same time, if the human capital approach to education is to be effectively implemented a change is necessary in the student role. The 1972 White Paper *Education: A Framework for Expansion*[100] makes a ritual obeisance to the traditional notion of the student role when it says 'the Government consider higher education valuable for its contribution to the personal development of those who pursue it',[101] but it then goes on to develop a thoroughgoing economic interpretation of that role which to all intents and purposes invalidates its initial statement. It continues:

at the same time they [the government] value its [higher education's] continued expansion as an investment in the nation's human talent in a time of rapid social change and technological development. If these economic, personal and social aims are to be realised, within the limits of available resources and competing priorities, both the purposes and the nature of higher education, in all its diversity, must be critically and realistically examined. The continuously changing relationship between higher education and subsequent employment should be reflected both in the institution's and in individual choices. The Government hope that those who contemplate entering higher education — and those advising them — will the more carefully examine their motives and their requirements; and be sure that they form their judgement on a realistic assessment of its usefulness to their interests and career intentions.[102]

There is little doubt here that the government, or the D.E.S., is

sufficiently confident and secure in its beliefs to lay its ideology
on the line, where it hurts most, at the level of individual
choice. Students are being asked to base their decisions about
the type of higher education they want on future employment
criteria — while bearing in mind that these are continually shifting. In this context, the student becomes part of the process
of the 'efficient' distribution of human capital, a necessary linkage
between economic demand and human supply. Institutions can
obviously help in this matter by the appropriate selection of
students, by the manipulation of entrance requirements for particular courses, and by course restructuring. But life is much
easier for the planners if people direct themselves towards the
suitable employment opportunities.

The process of self-legitimation employed by the D.E.S. ideology
relies heavily on its claim to be directly, objectively and uniquely
in touch with reality. This style is also evident in its legitimation
of the 'rational economic student'. With almost telepathic assurance, but no evidence, it asserts: 'not far from the surface of
most candidates' minds is the tacit belief that higher education
will go far to guarantee them a better job'.[103] Maybe, and there
again, maybe not — but such reservations are apparently not for
the D.E.S. It is as if it assumes that any extension of the logic
of its ideology must be a description of 'what is'. Alternatively,
if we hypothesise that the D.E.S. is sophisticated enough to realise
that others do not necessarily have the same economically-oriented
view of the world as itself, then their statement can be construed
as straightforward propaganda.

While the human capital approach asks for a redefinition of
the student role, its output budgeting context and the premium
this places on efficiency both imposes constraints on the student
role and asks for a redefinition of the institutional role. In the
belief that it would save money, the government has recently taken
to advocating home-based study for students in higher education.
In the 1972 White Paper it stated that it 'shared the frequently
expressed view' (another self-justifying assumption) 'that it is unrealistic and unnecessary for such a high proportion of students
to reside and study at a distance if equally acceptable courses
are available to them within daily travelling distance of their
homes'.[104] It therefore proposed to examine 'what steps might
be taken to reverse the present trend and thus encourage more
students to base themselves at home while studying'.[105] The implications of such a policy are clear. For the student it would mean
the restriction of, first, his freedom of choice of course, and second,
his capacity to engage in his own life-style; and for the institution
it would mean an undermining of the traditional reliance on

campus residence as one of the means of fostering a sense of community. The attack on the traditional university ideal, intentional or otherwise, could not be more evident.

Moreover once the efficiency criterion is applied at a more general level the possibility of the D.E.S. ideology responding to pleas for the consideration of such educational and cultural factors is shown to be a non-starter. In 1975 Reg Prentice, then Secretary of State for Education and Science, said: 'In essence part of what I have been saying about priorities in further and higher education

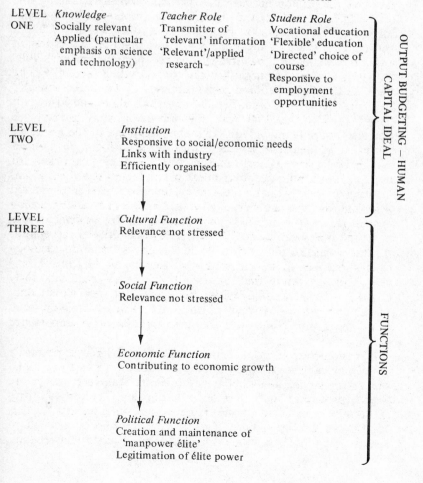

MODEL TWO   The Economic Ideology of Higher Education and its Cultural, Social, Economic and Political Functions

LEVEL ONE

Knowledge
Socially relevant
Applied (particular
   emphasis on science
   and technology)

Teacher Role
Transmitter of
   'relevant' information
'Relevant'/applied
   research

Student Role
Vocational education
'Flexible' education
'Directed' choice of
   course
Responsive to
   employment
   opportunities

LEVEL TWO

Institution
Responsive to social/economic needs
Links with industry
Efficiently organised

LEVEL THREE

Cultural Function
Relevance not stressed

Social Function
Relevance not stressed

Economic Function
Contributing to economic growth

Political Function
Creation and maintenance of
   'manpower élite'
Legitimation of élite power

OUTPUT BUDGETING — HUMAN
CAPITAL IDEAL

FUNCTIONS

is that in achieving our targets, higher and further education has got to consider its unit cost problems — just as have other areas of our national life. Just as we have got to become more efficient in industry, so we have in education.'[106] When this is compared with the protective statement by Robbins that educational investment cannot be 'measured adequately by the same yardstick as investment in coal or electricity',[107] the wheel can indeed be said to have turned full circle. Model Two sums up the overall result.

Piggy in the Middle

If Models One and Two are compared, the incompatibility of the two ideologies of education is self-evident. A structural illustration of the tension between the two has been the changing role of the U.G.C., the body responsible for dispensing government funds to the universities, over the past two decades. Caught between the old and the new, it has exhibited all the signs of a split personality as it has struggled to reconcile the irreconcilable.

We have already touched on the long-standing recognition by the U.G.C. of the national responsibilities of the universities.[108] In similar vein, the Committee of Vice-Chancellors and Principals (C.V.C.P.) stated in 1946 that 'the universities may properly be expected not only individually to make proper use of the resources entrusted to them, but collectively to devise and execute policies calculated to serve the national interest'.[109] They then asked for more guidance from the government in conducting that task. Commenting on this, Niblett writes 'unless there had been fundamental trust that any British government would have *a close understanding of what university ideals were*, no such request for guidance could or would have been made'.[110] And here is the crux of the matter. At this stage the universities could assume a common ideology to exist between themselves and other sections of the élite. Thirty years later they know that it does not. Then they could talk airily of their national responsibilities, believing that they would only be required to act in ways which suited themselves. Now they do so more warily and with frequent appeals to the importance of university autonomy.

The protection afforded them by the U.G.C. is likewise primarily an ideological one based on tradition. After all, when the U.G.C. was set up in the 1920s, élite homogeneity was such that more formal protective mechanisms for a university sector still with substantial sources of private income were unnecessary. Consequently, as Robbins pointed out, 'there is no absolute safeguard against interference with the distribution of grants to universities.

It is a convention that the Government abstains. But it cannot bind its successors; nor is its agreement likely to imply abstention in the face of major difficulties.'[111] The U.G.C., therefore, had no structural means to ensure the preservation of its own identity. Once fragmentation in the élite educational ideology occurred the U.G.C. was bound in the long run to succumb to the stronger protagonist — the government.

But the process was not a straightforward one, nor is it yet complete. Part of the reason is that, as we have shown, the D.E.S. ideology was not static but continually evolving. Thus we can see the reflection in U.G.C. reports of the ideological themes already identified. For example, in the mid-sixties, and in the wake of the Dainton, Jones and Swann Reports, the U.G.C. wrote:

> But there is no doubt that it would be valuable if the universities collectively made a further deliberate and determined effort to gear a larger part of their 'output' (sic) to the economic and industrial needs of the nation, for few things could be more vital to the national economy at the present time than the proper deployment of highly qualified scientific manpower and the application of research to the solution of current technological and economic problems.[112]

It then recommended a shift to more vocational postgraduate courses and a greater emphasis on applied research. A little later we find the committee advocating closer links with industry: 'Over and above general exhortation and general provision within the block grant, we have called special attention to the desirability of university–industry collaboration, and in some particular cases we have made special provision for it.'[113]

Yet at the same time, and in the same report, doubts are expressed. It points out that it is not easy to translate general expressions of national need into particular numbers and types of output or into particular types of education and training required of the universities.[114] With an air of unease the committee adds that 'the whole field is ... one of particular difficulty and sensitivity from the Committee's standpoint, though they have always stood ready to advise universities wherever possible on particular features of the situation'.[115] Being at the sharp end of an alleged manpower planning approach to education brings an awareness of its deficiencies. We find the comment: 'Nor is it apparent that to any significant extent the size and balance of the flow of candidates for university admission are directly related to the size and balance of the national needs for graduate manpower.'[116] Then again, at another point the committee pre-empts the whole issue by stating that in its experience, the precise nature of the qualifications of the university graduate is seldom directly related to the category of employment which he pursues as his life's career, except in the specifically vocational fields of university training[117] — which rather leaves manpower planning high and dry. Clearly the U.G.C. was not very happy and not a little confused.

The confusion at this time was compounded by the then still considerable influence of the traditional university ideal. In discussing the differences between universities and polytechnics, the freedom of universities 'to determine their own fields of academic activity, their curricula and courses, their degree standards and their research activities'[118] is stressed. And it was argued that provided they were 'duly responsive to broad national needs' and operationally efficient 'their proper freedom would be respected and safeguarded by the inter-position between them and the Government of an independent University Grants Committee in *a buffer role*'.[119] The problem with this traditional definition of the U.G.C. role is that it is completely incompatible with the new ideology. Not surprisingly, the U.G.C. subsequently contradicts itself when forced to redefine its role to fit the new ideology.

First comes the concern with the efficiency of the institutions in its care: 'The sheer number of universities, their decreasing homogeneity and the correspondingly increasing variety of their offerings, together with national considerations of the kind which have been mentioned, demand some central appraisal if uneconomic duplication is to be avoided and a reasonable degree of differentiation of function is to be achieved.'[120] This is accompanied by the use of words and ideas such as 'cost consciousness', 'plant utilisation' and 'unit cost'.[121] Second comes the recognition that, as the U.G.C. puts it, 'we are now inescapably involved in making positive judgements, *an activity which goes far beyond the capacity of a buffer or a shock-absorber*'.[122] The committee members have increasingly seen themselves as becoming more 'dirigiste', to use their own terminology, as the result of the necessity of being aware of the 'broad strategic picture'. Indeed, Lord Wolfenden, chairman of the U.G.C. from 1963 to 1968, has described its evolution into what he has called a 'strategic planning agency'.[123] With the U.G.C.'s self-confessed change of role to a stance more in keeping with the new ideology's conception of social control, the question naturally arises as to who decides the nature of the central strategy. Is it a case of he who pays the piper (that is, the government) calling the tune or does the U.G.C. retain its traditional independence despite the more obvious signs of an ideological takeover having occurred? Paul Johnson has few doubts. He argues that 'the U.G.C. has gradually aligned itself with the D.E.S., adopting its planning techniques, its methods of calculation and its terminology'.[124] In doing so, he echoed an earlier article by John Pratt which argued that the U.G.C. is fast becoming a branch of government.[125] The more obvious signs are certainly there. The transfer of financial responsibility for the U.G.C. from the Treasury to the D.E.S. was followed in 1968 by Parliament's decision that the accounts of the universities and U.G.C. should be open to scrutiny by the Comptroller and Auditor General. This issue had been a bone of contention between the U.G.C. and the government for a number of years and the decision was reached despite outright U.G.C. opposition which was based on the argument that such an innovation would be an infringement of university autonomy. So the traditional university ideal may be going under, but not without a struggle.

This is further evidenced, albeit in a negative fashion, by the failure of the U.G.C., so far, to fly one of the D.E.S. kites on the need for more home-based students in higher education. There is little doubt that this is an idea which in its present form basically stands Niblett on his head in that it pays little attention to the broader educative functions of the university. It is, therefore, antithetical to the traditional conception of the university and cannot be accepted while this conception retains a foothold in the U.G.C. Precisely how long the U.G.C. can maintain and manage the tension between the two élite ideologies of education (adopt 'a Janus-like posture' as the U.G.C. typically phrases it),[126] it is difficult to say.

The Future Conflict

One of the problems in evaluating the future nature of the conflict is that the position of the economic ideology of higher education is not quite so secure and unshakeable as we have perhaps implied. Although there can be no doubt that the élite is irretrievably split on this issue and that the new ideology now dominates the main resource allocating body, the D.E.S., it has also had its setbacks. The traditional university ideology may be under siege but it has managed to mount one or two largely unconscious counter-attacks.

In particular, it has seduced at least some polytechnics away from the straight and narrow path of D.E.S. thinking — not surprisingly, given the D.E.S.'s failure to spell out the role of the polytechnics in precise terms, and its lack of direct administrative control over their development. (At the present time, polytechnics are first and foremost responsible to the L.E.A. which funds them.) Two ex-champions of the polytechnics, Pratt and Burgess, are convinced that the process of 'academic drift', as they call it, has rendered polytechnics little more than 'bowdlerised universities' as they move away from both public control and their original social objectives.[127] A similar opinion is held by the Select Committee on Science and Technology. In its 1976 report it states that 'the transformation of the C.A.T.s into universities, and the present tendency of the polytechnics to seek "parity" with the universities, reflect the distressing British habit of attempting to bestow status and prestige on institutions and individuals by changing their names rather than encouraging them to do well the things for which they are best suited'.[128] It argues that in its treatment of the C.A.T.s the university system has attempted 'to eliminate a potential threat to its traditional freedom and independence by turning that threat into an asset to be deployed in defence of the freedom of the universities from direct state control'.[129] Clearly this is a regrettable turn of events so far as any manpower ideology is concerned since it means rebuilding the C.A.T.s in 'the image of the institutions [that is, the universities] which were regarded as having failed to provide the manpower which the nation required'.[130]

The judgement of the Select Committee, an all-party committee, that the C.A.T.s and polytechnics have in some sense failed, provides two important pointers regarding the future conflict: first, that the D.E.S. is not having it all its own way but second, that the manpower ideology is now strongly rooted not only in the D.E.S. and upper echelons of the government but also in important sections of the major parties. It is undoubtedly broadening its base and influence in the political structure. This impression is confirmed by the policy recommendations made by the Committee, which included: the appointment of a Minister of State within the D.E.S. with special responsibility for science and technology; the revival and implementation of the concept of SISTERS (Special Institutions for Scientific and Technological Education and Research); the consideration of the introduction of higher maintenance grants for students in the applied sciences and engineering; and preferential treatment by the U.G.C. of the applied sciences and engineering.[131] It is significant also that the Committee was not afraid to urge the D.E.S. to be more directive in its relationship with the U.G.C. and research councils. At present, it said, the attitude of the D.E.S. to this question is 'far too passive'[132] — a criticism the D.E.S. will almost certainly welcome since it validates any further intervention in higher education it may be contemplating.

So although the economic ideology of education has suffered certain reverses in its attempts at policy implementation, these have not damaged its own institutional security. Indeed, these reverses may well have enhanced it since in a time of economic crisis they provide the opportunity for the proponents of this ideology to argue that its detractors are being fundamentally unrealistic.

Assessing the future of the conflict is complicated further by its extension into the upper stratum of the secondary sector. Here is the area where the student demand for higher education originates and, as we have demonstrated, the economic ideology of education is naturally concerned with the relationship, or lack of it, between the input into higher education (that is students) and the desired output as defined by national economic demand. So far it has concentrated its efforts on influencing the structure of the opportunities available to potential students by encouraging the development in higher education of certain courses rather than others. However, the insensitivity of student demand to the opportunity structure of the courses available in higher education has meant that the D.E.S. was bound to desire, if not seek, other ways of shaping this demand. We have already noted its opinion that potential students should base their decisions 'on a realistic assessment of its [higher education's] usefulness to their interests and career intentions'.[133]

The chance for the manpower ideology to assert itself publicly in the hitherto sacrosanct secondary sector came in May 1976 when Mr Callaghan called for a memorandum from the then Education Secretary, Fred Mulley, on what he discerned as four major areas of public concern: the basic approach in primary schools to the teaching of the three 'R's; the curriculum for older children in comprehensives; the exam system; and the problems of sixteen-to nineteen-year-olds who have no prospect of going on to higher education yet who seem ill-equipped even for the jobs they find.[134] For a year prior to this Her Majesty's Inspectorate had been preparing an enquiry into curriculum and standards, paving the way, according to *The Times Educational Supplement*, for a more direct intervention by the Department.[135] From the latter's point of view, therefore, Mr Callaghan's timing could not have been better.

The resultant confidential report to the Prime Minister in October 1976 — the infamous and heavily leaked *Yellow Book*[136] — is littered with the easily discernible themes of the new ideology: employers' complaints about school-leavers lacking sufficient mathematical skills to benefit from technical training; the need for a core curriculum (particularly in maths and science); for more and better teachers of maths and science; for better links between the school and the world of work; the tendency of some teachers to overemphasise 'the importance of preparing boys and girls for their roles in society compared with the need to prepare them for their economic role'; and of course the need for more central government control in the educational process.[137] Many of these themes were subsequently taken up by the Prime Minister in his speech at Ruskin College and in the ensuing so-called 'Great Debate' on education.

The implications of these events for the traditional university ideal is that it finds itself in an entirely new ball-game. The bargaining power of the universities *vis-à-vis* the D.E.S., and hence their capacity to maintain effectively their own ideology of higher education, rests primarily on their control over the supply of graduates to the economy. If the economic ideology of education can structure this supply as it leaves the secondary sector then clearly the universities will have been both politically and ideologically outflanked. The traditional university ideal will find itself increasingly isolated as potential students concern themselves more with the career relevance of a university education and less with its social and cultural purposes. Even the more status-conscious polytechnics may begin to feel they are backing the wrong horse, that the university ideal is less seductive than they had perhaps thought, and that their technical college tradition should not be too hastily shrugged off.[138]

Much depends on whether or not the issues raised in the course of the 'Great Debate' will have any lasting impact, whether the interventionist intentions of the D.E.S. in secondary education are realised, and whether the traditional university ideal is still further ideologically isolated. Because the conflict has now extended beyond the domain over which they have immediate influence the universities cannot do a great deal to help themselves. They can only sit and wait — a strategy which previously they have chosen but which now is forced upon them.

Chapter 8

Social Stratification in Higher Education: the Preservation of Traditional Patterns

Although the educational élite is undeniably split in its conception of what higher education is, or should be, about, it is another question altogether whether this has any significant de-stabilising functions for the system as a whole. Intra-class conflict of this nature may be a periodic necessity endured by the élite as it shifts its posture towards a changing environment, while at the same time resting assured of ongoing support mechanisms. On the other hand, an emergent educational ideology may serve to undermine the efficacy of these mechanisms in a too hasty redefinition of élite needs. There is little doubt that many of the upholders of the traditional university ideal were wary of the expansionist implications of the manpower planning approach to higher education for precisely this reason. The Niblett Report, for example, was as we have shown expressly concerned with the desirability of keeping a close rein on the students from non-university backgrounds.[1]

But expansion could not be avoided. Economic theories such as 'maximising the use of the nation's talent' and 'keeping up with Britain's international competitors' irresistably combined with the notion of 'equality of educational opportunity' already formally sanctioned in secondary education by the 1944 Education Act. The numbers in full-time higher education rose from 131,700 in 1961 to 351,400 in 1973.[2] Mass higher education has apparently arrived. But which masses? Have the fears of the old guard been realised and the floodgates opened to the working class? Or have the social control mechanisms continued to function in their traditional manner, preserving the class patterns of higher education intact? In this chapter we provide some answers to these questions drawing on a range of data sources including previously unpublished material. To place this data in context, we first examine the position of class in the policies stemming from the new economic ideology of education.

Ideological Myths

It is one of the more accepted fallacies of current educational thought that higher education was at least partly expanded to achieve greater equality for the working class.[3] As we shall demonstrate, this is in fact not so. As far as it is possible to tell, the origins of the myth lie in the tendency of writers to deduce class implications from formal statements of policy in a way which can best be described as wishful thinking. The resulting fallacy is then used as a rod with which to beat the backs of the supposedly wayward policy-makers.

The manpower planning approach to education from which many such policy statements flow is after all concerned with ensuring that education serves the needs of the economy; not with social justice. It is quite prepared, however, to accept limited alliances with social justice themes such as 'equal educational opportunity' and 'higher education on demand' when it is convenient for it to do so. Thus the massive expansion of educated manpower in the early and middle sixties could be justified by such an alliance, for a while. Come the rigours of the economic squeeze, however, and formal commitment to the dispensable ideas of social equality soon waned — as Chapter 7 has shown.[4] The fact that, in official eyes, these ideas were not only secondary to the emerging manpower ideology but also contingent for their appearance upon their tactical contribution to the success of this ideology, meant that they were never developed by the D.E.S. in any great detail. Certainly there was little point, and a great deal of potential embarrassment, in spelling out the class ramifications of such ideas. Such a step would in any case have been quite contrary to the British tradition of keeping explicitly political questions out of education where at all possible. Vague obeisances to egalitarianism are one thing, but specific and measurable statements of intent expressed in class terms are quite another.

Nevertheless, two particular innovations in higher education policy have been subsequently construed as being for the benefit of the working class: the creation of the polytechnics and the Open University (O.U.). The polytechnics, first of all, were officially inaugurated in 1966 with the publication of the White Paper, *A Plan for Polytechnics and Other Colleges*.[5] This contained no reference whatsoever to social and political goals, only educational ones, but this in itself is not surprising. One could expect an implementation document of this kind to avoid areas of discussion more appropriately left to the politician sensitive to his electoral audience. Two speeches made by Antony Crosland while Secretary of State for Education and Science have been regarded as central in this respect: those delivered at Woolwich Polytechnic, 27 April 1965 and Lancaster University, 20 January 1967. At Woolwich, Crosland publicly stated the case for the binary policy for the first time and was not afraid to use some fairly vivid egalitarian phrasing — for example: 'Let us now move away from our snobbish caste-ridden hierarchical obsession with university status'. But he did not mention the working class. Nor did he mention them in his later speech at Lancaster. Admittedly he emphasised 'the historic and invaluable F.E. tradition of providing opportunities for educational and social mobility', but when it comes to the question of 'mobility for whom?' he is less than direct and identifies them as follows: 'Perhaps they left school early, perhaps they were late developers, perhaps they were first generation aspirants to higher education who were too modest at the right moment to apply to a university, perhaps they had started on a career and thought that a traditional college course would more directly improve their qualifications for doing it.' In their book *Polytechnics: A Report*, Pratt and Burgess decide that all this is 'really' an 'extended circumlocution for "working class students"'.[6] Precisely how they arrive at this insight is unclear. Nor is it substantiated in their examination of speeches on the binary policy by other Labour Secretaries of State for Education (Patrick Gordon Walker, Edward Short), or Ministers of State for Education (Shirley Williams, Gerald Fowler).[7] Nowhere, it seems, are the working class explicitly mentioned.

This can scarcely be regarded as a chance omission. Labour politicians are well aware of the fact that, although the majority of their electoral support comes from the working class, a significant minority of the middle class also votes for them.[8] To assume that this middle-class support would wholeheartedly accept an educational policy which specifically excluded them would be placing an undue strain on their altruistic social conscience. As competent politicians, Crosland and his successors obviously had to take account of this in their policy statements. When coupled with the manpower ideology's lack of interest in such social concerns, this pragmatic constraint on overt commitment to the working class became not only necessary but respectable. Hence the socio-political content of Labour policy on the polytechnics was kept at the general level of 'increased educational opportunity leading to more social mobility'.

So far as Pratt and Burgess are concerned, this is just not good enough. They maintain that 'though a coherent alternative to the conventional view of the development of higher education could be easily substantiated, the policy documents fall sadly short of this in practice'.[9] Could it? Substantiated by whom, Pratt and Burgess? So far as the economic ideology of education was concerned, the policy documents *were* coherent; *and* they represented a substantial departure from the traditional university conception of higher education. What Pratt and Burgess are doing, therefore, is judging government policy by their own conception of what polytechnics should have been (a perfectly legitimate procedure) and then implying that government policy was in fact aiming at this very conception all along, but in some way fell down on the job (which is an illegitimate procedure). Such an approach denies both the capacity of the government and D.E.S. to think out their own ideas on higher education, and the presence of the manpower ideology as a potent formative influence on policy creation.

The insistence that the polytechnics were officially intended disproportionately to benefit working-class mobility stems in large part from the myth of the technical colleges as the saviours of the working class. Eric Robinson, for example, insists that 'many of the technical colleges . . . were set up to give vocational instruction to the less academic (usually working class) young people'.[10] Hence the L.E.A.s have already 'weakened the elitist stranglehold on our children' through the comprehensive reform of secondary education: 'they now have the opportunity to extend this revolution into education beyond school and their springboard for this is the F.E. system'.[11] Expand a working-class dominated technical college sector, the argument runs, and you can expect to increase the proportion of working-class students in higher education as a whole — hence Robinson's book *The New Polytechnics* was subtitled *The People's Universities*. Subsequent research then reinforces the myth by examining the extent to which the original promise of the polytechnics has been fulfilled.[12]

However, the difficulty with this thesis is that it almost certainly exaggerates the traditional role of the technical colleges as avenues of social mobility for the working class. Although the data in this field is sparse, what there is has been comprehensively ignored by the protagonists of this myth. Robbins, first of all, provides an overview of the situation — see Table 8.1.[13]

TABLE 8.1 Social Class (Father's Occupation) of Full-time and Part-time Students in Further Education, Great Britain, 1961-2 (%) (Robbins)

	Non-manual	Manual	Not known	All
Full-time	58	38	4	100
Part-time day	42	55	3	100
Evening	41	54	4	99

It is true that students from manual or working-class backgrounds in the part-time categories (the major part of the technical colleges' traditional function) are in the majority — but only just. Cotgrove's figures, based on a survey of two polytechnics conducted in 1955, present an even bleaker picture — see Table 8.2[14] — with the students from working-class backgrounds in the minority — but this may be attributable to the localised nature of his sample.

TABLE 8.2 Social Class (Father's Occupation) of Full-time and Part-time Students at Two Polytechnics (%) (Cotgrove)

	Non-manual	Manual	All	N
Full-time	88	12	100	130
Part-time day	63	37	100	116
Evening	63	37	100	476

What is more important about Cotgrove's work is the light it sheds on the process by which students actually arrive at a technical college. He concludes:

It is the original choice of occupation, and the factors influencing this choice which largely decides whether a boy or girl will go on to evening classes in vocational subjects after leaving full-time education. It is only those who enter occupations where attendance carries with it expectations of occupational rewards who are likely to attend under such circumstances, and there is comparatively little effort to break into such occupations by evening study from those not already engaged in them.[15]

Since such occupations are primarily lower middle and middle class, this is reflected in the current occupational status of the students — see Table 8.3.[16]

TABLE 8.3 Occupations and Social Status of Evening Students at Two Polytechnics (%) (Cotgrove)

Professional, managerial, executive	Inspectional, supervisory	Routine clerical	Skilled manual	Semi-skilled, unskilled	All	N
8	73	8	10	1	100	539

This means that the impetus for social mobility occurs before the student attends a technical college — when he selects his occupation — and therefore that, as Glass points out in his classic study of social mobility, the technical college 'appears generally as a reinforcing, rather than as a critical agent' in the process.[17] It was instead the grammar school which exerted the significant influence on occupational choice and hence on the chances of an individual going on to further education.[18] For the most part, the socially mobile working class were those who had not been weeded out by the time they left grammar school. The reinforcing role of the technical colleges is further evidenced by Cotgrove's findings on the relationship between occupation and type of course: 'Nearly four-fifths of students in university, G.C.E. and professional courses were in non-manual occupations, while nearly 90 per cent of the students in City and Guilds courses were manual workers.'[19] In effect, then, the technical college made the working-class students better qualified to stay where they were.

Not to put too fine a point on it, these figures indicate that Robinson, Pratt and Burgess have got it wrong. The technical colleges never were the means by which the local working-class boy and girl made good to the extent that they claim. Hence an expansion of the F.E. sector, and in particular its higher education component in the shape of the polytechnics, could not be expected to increase significantly the proportion of working-class students in higher education as a whole (including the universities) assuming the take-up of educational opportunities in this area remained constant in class terms.

Precisely parallel discrepancies between myths and reality also exist in the case of the Open University. Firstly, the politicians were equally careful to avoid pinning down the function of the O.U. in class terms. In a speech at Scarborough in September 1963, Harold Wilson proposed the idea of the O.U. and defined its purpose as being 'to offer opportunities to those, who for one reason or another, have not been able to take advantage of higher education'.[20] This was reiterated in similarly vague terms in the Report of the Planning Committee on the O.U. in 1969[21] and by Lord Crowther Hunt, the O.U.'s first Chancellor, in his inaugural address in the same year. He stated: 'The first and most urgent task before us is to cater for the many thousands of people, fully capable of higher education, who, for one reason or another, do not get it, or do not get as much of it as they discover, sometimes too late, that they need.'[22] By expressing the policy objectives purely in terms of increased educational opportunities, the politicians thereby ensured that in terms of their internal logic there really was no way in which these objectives were not going to be fulfilled. So long as the new opportunities were taken up by someone or other, it would be possible to argue that this individual had previously been denied the chance of a higher education that he rightly deserved. How could you decide otherwise unless criteria regarding the subsequent *users* of the opportunities were explicitly included in the initial policy statements (social class criteria, for example)?

In the event, it transpires that 6 per cent of Open University students in the 1971 intake were members of the manual working class[23] and that the working class also have the highest drop out rate[24] — scarcely the beginnings of a social revolution, one feels. On the other hand, when it comes to fathers' occupation, 52 per cent of the students originate from manual backgrounds[25] — demonstrating that like the technical colleges, the Open University has a reinforcing effect on a social mobility already initiated elsewhere. The explanation advanced for this parallels exactly Cotgrove's argument, though oddly it fails to mention him. McIntosh and Woodley argue that it is those who can 'see the direct benefit of obtaining a degree *in the context of their present jobs* (teachers, for instance, receive a salary increase and also improve their chances of obtaining a headship)' who are most likely to attend the O.U.[26] And conversely, of course, it is for instance the labourer on the building site who is least likely to see a degree from the O.U. as a means of bumping up his weekly pay packet.

In his scathing and (up to a point) perceptive analysis of how the Open University discriminates against the working class, Pratt concludes by polarising the issue around the technical college myth: 'The tasks the O.U. has to undertake are those of an institution in the technical college tradition, but it was itself established in the university tradition.'[27] Clearly, this was a mistake, he writes, since 'a university is an inappropriate institution to use to try to redress social class imbalance in educational opportunity'.[28] But as we have shown, the technical college also has its limitations in this respect — a fact which Pratt ignores in his subsequent advocacy of technical college expansion. By adhering blindly to the myth of the technical college as an active promoter of the working class, he obscures the striking parallels between the technical college and the Open University in terms of their role as social control institutions — a strange irony. Furthermore, his ·championship of this myth introduces a false dichotomy into the ideological arena through its implication that the polytechnics, unlike the universities, were formally supposed to assist the working class. So far as the dominant manpower ideology is concerned, such class specificity in terms of educational objectives is not only unnecessary but also potentially dysfunctional.

Challenge or Continuity?

The idea of formal élite commitment to the conscious advancement of the working class in higher education — be it in polytechnics or universities — is, then, a figment of the imagination. Nowhere does the élite commit itself to anything more than the doctrine of increased educational opportunity as expressed, for example, in the Robbins principle of higher education for all those qualified to receive it. However, there was always the chance that in the headlong rush for educated manpower the traditional mechanisms for ensuring the preservation of particular class patterns in higher education might be brushed aside.

In examining this question, we have to rely on fairly gross measures since the main source of data, government-sponsored surveys, are not in the habit of making such questions their primary objective.

The Universities

At the beginning of the expansion, the situation had changed very little from pre-war days — see Table 8.4.[29]

TABLE 8.4 Undergraduates with Fathers in Manual Occupations (%) (Robbins)

	Men	Women	Men and women	
1928–47	27	13	23	(England and Wales)
1955	27	19	25	(Great Britain)
1961	26	23	25	(Great Britain)

Despite the 10 per cent increase in women from manual backgrounds between 1928–47 and 1961, their small numbers meant that this had a negligible effect on the overall proportion from manual backgrounds.

To the best of our knowledge, no relevant national figures are available for the years immediately following Robbins. From 1968 onwards, however, the Universities Central Council on Admissions (U.C.C.A.) regularly produced a breakdown of the parental occupation of the yearly student intake — see Table 8.5.[30]

TABLE 8.5 Parental Occupation of Accepted Home Candidates, 1968–74 (%) (U.C.C.A.)

Occupation group (order no.) of parent	1968	1969	1970	1971	1972	1973	1974
I–XX Manual and agricultural	28	29	29	29	29	28	28
XXI–XXIII,XXVI Other non-manual	28	27	27	28	26	26	25
XXIV Administrators and managers	14	15	15	14	14	14	15
XXV Professional, technical	30	29	29	29	31	32	32
All	100	100	100	100	100	100	100

Note: The Registrar General's classification of occupations employed by U.C.C.A. is not strictly comparable with that used in Table 8.4 since groups I–XX, although predominantly manual workers, are not exclusively so.

The remarkable stability over time of the parental occupation of successive intakes of students could not be more evident and demonstrates fairly conclusively the failure of the university expansion to shake the class pattern of higher education. The significance of these figures and the power of the social control mechanisms to perpetuate the middle-class hegemony is made more obviously apparent if we compare the above occupational distributions with those of the appropriate age group in the population as a whole — see Table 8.6.[31]

TABLE 8.6 Occupation of Economically Active Males, aged 45–69, Great Britain, 1966 and 1971 (%) *(Census of Population)*

Occupation group (order no.) of parent	1966	1971
I–XX Manual and agricultural	64	62
XXI–XXIII, XXVI Other non-manual	22	21
XXIV Administrators and managers	6	7
XXV Professional, technical	8	9
All	100	99

The continuing dominance in this respect of the manual and agricultural category throws its derisory presence in universities into sharp contrast and thus illustrates powerfully the general irrelevancy of increases in educational opportunity to any redistribution of class take-up of these opportunities.

In a thoughtful analysis of Scottish university entrants in 1962 and 1972, Hutchison and McPherson demonstrate that this may in fact be an overgeneralisation regarding non-redistribution — see Table 8.7.[32]

Although the extent of the redistribution is not over-impressive, it is in an interesting direction: 'women from middle-class homes . . . have tended to displace manual working-class men'.[33] The former have increased their share by 8 per cent to 31 per cent and the latter have dropped back by 7 per cent to 18 per cent. Overall, the working-class proportion has declined from a heady 36 per cent in 1962 to 29 per cent ten years later. It would appear that as a result of expansion, Scottish universities are operating more efficiently than ever on behalf

TABLE 8.7   The Sex and Social Class Composition of the Entry to the Scottish Universities in 1962 and 1972 (%) (Hutchison and McPherson)

	Social class	1962	1972
Men	Non-manual	42	40
	Manual	25	18
Women	Non-manual	23	31
	Manual	11	11
All		101	100
N		2097	6033

TABLE 8.8   Students from Manual Backgrounds at Particular Universities (%)

University	Year	% of students from manual backgrounds	Source
Cambridge	1961	8	Marris
Oxford	1962	9	Zweig
Edinburgh	1964	15	Abbott
Keele	1962/3	18	Perkins
Newcastle	1964	20	Abbott
Warwick	1966	20	Perkins
Durham	1964	21	Abbott
L.S.E.	1967	22	Blackstone
Sussex	1966	23	Blackstone
East Anglia	1965/6	24	Perkins
Kent	1965/6	24	Perkins
Stirling	1967	24	Perkins
Lancaster	1966	27	Perkins
Essex	1966	29	Blackstone
Southampton	1962	30	Marris
Leeds	1962	30	Marris
Bath	1966	32	Couper
Manchester	1962	32	Zweig
Manchester	1963	33	Blackstone
Brunel	1960	38	Jahoda
Brunel	1964	34	Marsland
Bradford	1966	41	Musgrove

of the middle class and improving the position of its previously underprivileged female members. It is just bad luck for the working-class males that they happen to be competing with them.

Although national figures provide evidence of a continuing stability in the middle-class dominance of the universities, this, of course, does not necessarily mean that working-class students are evenly distributed between them. In fact the scattered studies which are available on this question indicate quite the opposite — see Table 8.8.[34]

They demonstrate instead that a not entirely unexpected hierarchy exists with the arts-dominated Oxbridge at one end of the continuum and the ex-Colleges of Advanced Technology at the other.

The Polytechnics

The implications of Table 8.8 for the position of the working class in the polytechnics are relatively favourable. It is those institutions which have recently moved out of the F.E. sector (that is, Bradford University, Brunel University and Bath University) which tend to have the highest proportion of students from manual backgrounds. One could expect, therefore, that polytechnics would exhibit similar characteristics. In fact, again working from a very limited data base, this does not appear to be the case — see Table 8.9.[35] Rather, the polytechnics here approximate more to the university norm than to that of the ex-C.A.T.s.

The discrepancy may be explained by the timing of the data collection as the polytechnic surveys were conducted more recently,

TABLE 8.9   Students from Manual Backgrounds at Particular Polytechnics (%)

Polytechnic	Year	% of students from manual backgrounds	Source
Middlesex	1968–70	21	Crutchley
Kingston	1971–72	24	Pratt
Kingston	1970	25	Pratt
North-East London	1971	30	Pratt
North-East London	1970	33	Pratt

after they had succumbed to the temptation, according to Pratt, to turn increasingly into university type institutions and so 'to close the route to working and working-class students'.[36] This assumes that the polytechnics, and their forerunners the technical colleges, ever were 'open' to the working class — which, we have argued, is a false assumption. It is more accurate to say that the technical colleges provided an avenue of social mobility mainly for the lower middle class, were of limited use to the working class and not particularly attractive to the upper echelons of the middle class because of their vocational emphasis. However, once they moved more into the mainstream of liberal education as polytechnics with substantial commitments to the humanities and social sciences, they swept over the educational horizon of the middle class and were welcomed with open arms. As degree-awarding institutions, they became part of the middle class's opportunity structure — an honour which as mere technical colleges they had previously been denied. In such a competitive situation the working class were bound to lose out since they do not count degree-awarding institutions as part of *their* opportunity structure. The exceptions to this argument are those polytechnics which, like the ex-C.A.T.s, retain their vocational and scientific bias and where, as a consequence, the working-class student is not in such fierce competition with the middle-class student. This is one of the questions to which we now turn in a more detailed look at the role of class in higher education.

A More Detailed Examination

In this section we employ data gathered in the course of the Student Accommodation Project, based at the University of Kent, in the spring term of 1975.[37] It consists of random surveys of students in two areas of England, both of which contained one representative of the three types of institutions then constituting higher education — that is, a college of education, a polytechnic and a university. Since then the map of higher education has been redrawn with colleges of education merging with polytechnics or becoming institutes of higher education; and there may be more changes to come. Thus, the data presented here is of considerable historical interest in that it represents a last look at the impact of class under the old tripartite system of higher education. For the purposes of analysis, the data from the two surveys is combined (see Appendix II for the details of the surveys).

An initial look at the distribution of the working and middle classes at the three types of institutions holds no surprises (Table 8.10).[38]

TABLE 8.10   Higher Education Institution by Social Class (%)
(Kent Project)

	Social class			
Institution	*Middle class*	*Working class*	*All*	*N*
Universities	76	24	100	1025
Polytechnics	71	29	100	768
Colleges of education	64	36	100	337

Arranging the institutions by their commonly accepted status hierarchy results in the appearance of a parallel hierarchy in their class composition as the middle class is better represented in the higher status institution. As usual, they dominate the selection and entry mechanisms of the higher education opportunity structure. The question Figure 8.1 raises, however, is whether this overall class affect at point C on the route in and out of higher education is present in a more detailed fashion at other points in the process.

FIGURE 8.1   The Class Effect on the Route to Higher Education

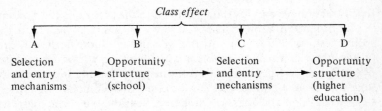

The effect at point A has already been dealt with, reiterating the well-established findings that the middle class are heavily over-represented in public and grammar schools.[39] Assuming the class effect is present across points B and C, one can expect the latter schools to do disproportionately well in the higher education race by having better access to the universities — which is in fact the case (Table 8.11).

TABLE 8.11 Type of School by Higher Education Institution (%)
(Kent Project)

| Type of school | Higher education institution | | | | |
	Universities	Polytechnics	Colleges of education	All	N
Private/Independent	57	33	10	100	587
Grammar	48 -	32	20	100	843
Comprehensive	45	37	18	100	384
F.E./Other sec.	39	47	14	100	443

Delving deeper, the next question is whether social class has an influence on access to higher education not only between school types but also within school type at point B (Table 8.12).

TABLE 8.12 Type of School by Higher Education Destination,
by Social Class (%) (Kent Project)

| Type of school | Higher education destination | Social class | | | |
		Middle class	Working class	All	N
Private/Independent	Universities	86	14	100	314
	Polytechnics	86	14	100	175
	Colleges of education	87	13	100	54
	All	86	14	100	543
Grammar	Universities	75	25	100	382
	Polytechnics	66	34	100	262
	Colleges of education	62	38	100	157
	All	70	30	100	801
Comprehensive	Universities	66	34	100	166
	Polytechnics	63	37	100	136
	Colleges of education	60	40	100	64
	All	64	36	100	366
Further education/ Other state sec.	Universities	69	31	100	156
	Polytechnics	68	32	100	187
	Colleges of education	52	48	100	61
	All	66	34	100	404

By controlling for type of school, we can see that with the exception of the public schools, the hierarchically organised link between status of higher education institution attended and the social class background of the student is clearly present within school type. Apart from the private sector, the middle class do consistently better than the working class regardless of school background. However, it is interesting to note that this class effect is smallest (again, apart from the public schools) in the comprehensive group where the class variation in the take-up of the different types of higher education opportunities is restricted to a range of 6 per cent compared to 13 per cent in the grammar schools and 17 per cent in the F.E. sector.

If the effect of class on the route to higher education is so finely apparent, what of its relevance to the position of students within the opportunity structure itself and their possible routes out? Our data in this respect is limited and we are restricted to an examination of (a) type of course studied, and (b) subject studied.

TABLE 8.13   Higher Education Institution by Course, by Social Class (%) (Kent Project)

| Institution | Course | Social class | | | |
		Middle class	Working class	All	N
Polytechnics	Post-grad.	77	23	100	517
	First degree/Dip.A.D.	73	27	100	102
	Dips and Certs	66	34	100	43
	H.N.D.	65	35	100	32
	Non-degree prof.	62	38	100	71
Colleges of education	B.Ed.	71	29	100	73
	Cert.Ed./Dip.Ed.	63	37	100	252

The difference in course status is clearly reflected in their class composition in that the middle class are disproportionately represented on degree level courses and above — see Table 8.13.[40] They are once again making the better use of whatever opportunities are available in their progress through higher education. In the case of subject studied, however, the picture is less clear (see Table 8.4[41]) for two reasons. First, the traditional tendency for the working class to favour the sciences and the middle class the liberal arts is apparent only in the polytechnics. Second, the implications of this pattern for the future position of the individual in the social structure are in any case dubious. While higher education was the preserve of a small élite it could be argued that a university liberal arts education was more likely than a science background to lead to the important decision-making posts in government and industry. With the arrival of 'mass' higher education, however, such a neat generalisation became less tenable because a much smaller proportion of the vastly expanded numbers of arts graduates would subsequently take up these posts.

TABLE 8.14   Higher Education Institution by Subject Studied, by Social Class (%) (Kent Project)

| Institution | Subject studied | Social class | | | |
		Middle class	Working class	All	N
Polytechnics	Science	65	35	100	369
	Humanities	83	17	100	124
	Social science, Arch./Planning	74	26	100	249
Universities	Science	75	25	100	343
	Humanities	79	21	100	267
	Social science, Admin.	75	25	100	391

Conclusions

If members of the educational élite were worried about the effect of higher education expansion on the stability of the system they dominate, then this chapter should have gone some way to reassuring them. Despite the trebling of student numbers in the period since the late fifties, no significant change has occurred in the social class composition of the higher education intake. The social control mechanisms have maintained the pattern intact.

With hindsight, one might argue that this was almost bound to be the case. All that was changed by the expansion — and according to our policy analysis all that it was intended to change — was the size of the higher education opportunity structure. Few significant alterations were made to the means of selection since the primary concern of the expansionist policy was increased output of graduates, not a radically different type of student body. There was consequently no reason why the *laissez-faire* system of higher education application and selection, dominated by the middle class, should be restructured. To do so in order to implement effectively an egalitarian policy worked out in specific social class terms would have required a politically unacceptable level of state intervention. Hence the selection system was left as it was and the social control mechanisms embedded within it have functioned in their traditional manner. They have expanded along with the structure of higher education through the normal process of disproportionate middle-class take-up of whatever opportunities are available — provided, of course, that these are commensurate with middle-class goals.

Chapter 9

Education and Political Change in Britain

The Breakdown of Consensus

The central purpose of this book has been to present a political perspective of the British educational system. Up to the present, political scientists — in contrast to sociologists, psychologists and economists — have devoted little of their attention to formal education. The study of political socialisation contains most of what political scientists have to say on this topic but, given their concentration upon the family, this has not amounted to much, and in any case we are sceptical of the theoretical foundations of this literature. This reticence is ironic in view of the fact that many social scientists have recognised the ultimately political purpose of formal education — to reinforce established patterns of political power. In the course of this book we have tried to show how the British educational system fulfils this task, and equally important, what constraints prevent its successful accomplishment.

Our task has been aided by the intensity of the contemporary debate which has made it patently clear that education and politics are two interwoven forces. The disguises of the political functions of formal education have been stripped away, and thus educational issues are no longer outside the political arena. Of course formal education has been a subject for political debate in the past, but there are aspects of the contemporary conflict that make it distinctive. The educational system that emerged from the 1944 Education Act (and it must be remembered that this only modified prevailing arrangements), has been under continuous siege since the mid-1950s, when the attacks on intelligence testing proliferated. As time passed the number of issues drawn into the conflict expanded, and it has reached the point where some, following in the footsteps of Illich, are prepared to question whether we need an educational system as such at all.[1] Although educational and political élites have taken the lead in most of the controversies, this has not always been the case. The Auld Report on the William Tyndale junior school portrays a timid authority (the Inner London Education Authority) responding far too belatedly to the damage caused by the conflict between the teachers, managers and parents of the pupils.[2] A more widespread example of this is the mobilisation of groups, either opposed to or in support of local plans for comprehensive education. As Hargreaves has commented: 'Ours is an age of growing dissensus about education — its structure, its roles, its content. . . *The Black Papers*, *Hard Cheese*, and *Rank and File* are examples of the pressure groups which are fighting for particular forms of structure, roles and content in education.'[3] Finally, we would maintain that the educational issues being raised have great significance for the overall character of society which naturally makes it impossible to contain the debate at the purely pedagogical level.

Although past educational issues have resulted in bitter controversies — none, for example, more bitter than the teaching of religious education in schools — they appear to have been successfully contained in terms of their duration, the range of the interested parties involved, the confining of the debate to established élites, and the limitation of its wider societal impact. This is in direct contrast to the present situation for the conflict is continuous, it is not confined to the élite levels of a few interested parties, and the issues being raised have direct implications for the overall character of the society.

Behind the myth that education and politics were separate entities lay the fact that educational institutions were influenced by only a narrow range of political pressures. A liberal consensus formed the umbrella that sheltered responsible educational opinion, and views outside that framework made very little headway. As the educational camouflage of the social control functions of schooling have been stripped away so the range of political intrusion into the debate has widened. The first question we want to consider is why this has taken place. It is possible to stress the importance of various specific, contemporary and rather superficial factors: the widespread malaise with the performance of established élites, the more limited disenchantment with the character of the political system, the need to ensure that the new eighteen-year-old voter has sufficient political literacy to exercise his franchise in a meaningful way, and the alleged decline in the literacy and numeracy of school-students in spite of an educational budget that, until quite recently, has expanded rapidly. The more directly political aspects of these pressures have been used for their own purposes by those who would place the teaching of politics in British schools on a more formal basis. From the point of view of established élites it is in their interests to characterise the problems as essentially fortuitous and contemporary, and to hope that they can be dealt with at a superficial level by tinkering with the curriculum without changing the structures within which it is set. Innovation of this kind is unlikely to challenge the power of the élites or to demand the commitment of resources that they may prefer to use elsewhere.

The message of this book is that the contemporary crisis in education is a consequence of fundamental societal weaknesses. The most significant of these is the continuing failure of the British economy to perform either as well as its nearest rivals or with sufficient proficiency to meet the demands that it is expected to fulfil. This is a pressing problem for contemporary élites for, as we have argued, the maintenance of their power is increasingly dependent upon the élite manipulation of resources rather than their perpetuation of a crumbling cultural hegemony. Foremost amongst those resources are goods and services, and if the economy is not providing these in sufficient abundance this jeopardises the power of established élites — they simply have less available with which to make their manipulations. For a long time Britain has suffered from a split personality: on the one hand politically stable (and even this may be disappearing) and on the other hand socially and economically stagnant. We would argue that the two halves of the split personality are causally related: the forces that have led to political stability are also those that have resulted in economic and social stagnation. If there are successful class patterns of social control, presumably within which the educational system plays a crucial part, then one can expect political stability and a superficial social harmony. At least no overtly class-based challenges to political authority should emerge, and socially class relations should rarely deteriorate below the level of sullen hostility on the part of the workers and paternalism on the part of the bourgeoisie. As long as Britain was a world power, in control of the resources of a huge empire, the economic impact of the class patterns of social control was limited. However, with the steady erosion of these advantages we are beginning to feel the full economic burden of our class structure, for much of our dismal economic record stems from socio-political attitudes that reflect a society fragmented culturally along class lines.

Even if one rejects the above arguments, it is clear that within the D.E.S. a body of opinion has emerged which accepts the gist of this case, and it looks to the educational institutions to provide part of the solution to the present economic ills. The critical question is whether this is a realistic strategy in view of the fact that the character of the educational system is so dependent upon wider societal structures. But as we shall see, the D.E.S. is orchestrating a sophisticated campaign to influence the wider structures while exerting maximum pressure in its own backyard.

A further incentive for change is that, besides the struggling economy, some of the political and social cleavages have an air of permanence about them. The political movements associated with regionalism and nationalism may come and go but the ultimate stimulus for those movements (the presence of vividly contrasting regions and nations in the United Kingdom) is permanent. The limited but highly contentious levels of coloured immigration in the past two decades have raised — on both sides of the colour line — the question of whether it is possible to reconcile being 'black' and being 'British'. These regional, national and racial cleavages (which incidentally are not class-based) pose serious problems for both the official and the cultural definitions of citizenship. It is natural to expect that the schools, given their pivotal position in the transmission of culture, should assist in the reconciliation of these tensions.

The Academic and Political Ramifications

The breakdown of consensus regarding both the goals of formal education, and how those goals should be achieved, has immense political and academic ramifications. We will deal with the latter first. The predominant explanation of the stability of the British polity, contained in the mainstream political science literature, was dependent upon the belief that the behavioural and attitudinal characteristics of the citizenry were distributed according to a particular pattern.[4] Political stability is allegedly the consequence of a widespread moral consensus that embalms the political order — in the terms of the political socialisation literature, most citizens support the political community, the established regime norms, and the legitimacy of the political authorities.[5] These high levels of support for the political *status quo* are reinforced by the acceptance of a division of political labour. Most individuals accept the political leadership of the minority but assume if the occasion warrants it they can mobilise their opinions and make their influence felt. The end result is a judicious balancing amongst the citizenry of 'participant' (or 'citizen') roles and 'subject' roles which result in the correct blending of social forces (for example, between consensus and cleavage or conservatism and change) to ensure political stability.[6] Although those who have been prominent in presenting these ideas have not had much to say by way of accounting for this fortunate balance of citizen predispositions, they have made a few cursory comments on the importance of the educational system in this respect. One of the clear themes of our book is that, even if the educational system could be relied upon to perform this function in the past, there is very little prospect of its fulfilling the same task (at least in the same way with identical legitimating themes) in the future.

The notion that a stable polity is dependent upon a citizenry balanced according to behavioural predispositions has certain affinities with our belief that political stability is a consequence of the successful legitimation of inequality. In both cases it is the willingness of individuals at least to comply with political inequality that brings about this stability. But this superficial similarity conceals critical distinctions: legitimating inequality brings into full view the explicit nature of this process and the power structure that benefits from it — both factors are rarely commented upon by those who base stability upon the correct mix of political behaviour; and we have continually stressed the precarious nature of the process, in direct contrast to the 'consensus' theorists who believe that individuals readily internalise the behavioural characteristics that accompany inequality.[7] Besides stressing the constraints which prevent the successful legitimation of inequality (whereby individuals fully accept their inequality by acting in ways that are commensurate with its demands) we have also argued that even when it appears that this state of affairs has been reached, it is much more likely that individuals respond to the dictates of established mechanisms of social control rather than accept that their inequality is legitimate. The situation has now been reached where not only is there widespread rejection of inequality, but also the social control mechanisms are under severe pressure. Where compliance with social control mechanisms is the norm then the established power structure is not jeopardised, even though this may not signify a fully legitimate regime, but few societies can expect to remain stable if their means of social control are under continuous scrutiny. Part of the efficacy of social control mechanisms is dependent on their not being challenged.

The contemporary educational crisis also makes a mockery of those who would have us believe that formal education is part of a cultural hegemony that serves to perpetuate the power of a tightly-knit ruling class. Pronounced political protest is emerging within the educational system, and at its various levels individuals are using it as a political base to challenge the character of the *status quo*. Within institutions of both higher and secondary education the recipients of knowledge, students and pupils, have started to question the political implications of that knowledge — its content, its method of transmission and its ultimate purpose. They have been joined by some of the transmitters of knowledge, teachers and lecturers, in this quest to expose the political biases of the prevailing educational institutions. As important as the fact that educational institutions can provide radical critics of society with a permanent base for their protests, is the public esteem in which formal education has been held as a legitimator of the general character of society. Many believe that all is right with the world if it has the approval of those who are supposedly qualified to know what is 'right' and what is 'wrong'. Comfort could be found in the belief that it was only a minority of students who were advocating revolution, but this still had to be explained, and it was not made any easier by the suspicion that perhaps they acted with the support of some of the faculty and the connivance of those formally in charge of the institution.

We have placed the challenge to the *status quo* that can emerge within educational institutions on a more fundamental basis than the chance emergence of oppositional behaviour on the part of their clientele. We see a tension between the social control mechanisms of formal education and its potential for liberating individuals. Education can be organised in ways that maximise the former function and minimise the latter, but it is our contention that this is a precarious balance that can be upset by wider societal forces. At present the British educational system is in a state of crisis because wider societal pressures are disturbing the equilibrium established between these opposing forces. Sharp and Green have argued that Durkheim overstressed the integrative role of education and failed 'to appreciate the implications of education's involvement in role allocation in the division of labour'.[8] All industrialised societies have in fact used their educational systems to reconcile social integration with a division of labour. Whether they have succeeded or not, and for how long, are further issues, but it is part of our understanding of formal education that the attempt has always been made. This is central to our notion that the primary political purpose of an educational system is to legitimate inequality. What British society is experiencing is a breakdown of this process for the legitimating ideologies have lost their potency and their consequences are seen — both by certain élite groups as well as many who lose out in the struggle for scarce resources — as intolerable. The society is experiencing a double challenge to its ideological basis with some élites attempting to place inequality on a new foundation and others challenging the right to manipulate the educational process for this purpose. This is, therefore, a period of transition, and what will finally emerge is uncertain, but what can be said is that the longer it takes to make the leap the greater is the likelihood of societal instability.

The very slow changeover from selective to comprehensive secondary education illustrates perfectly both the magnitude of this procrastination as well as its ramifications. There is no consensus as to what comprehensive schools are accomplishing or what they are supposed to accomplish. Some have doubted if they will actually stratify individuals along different lines from the selective secondary schools for it is possible to repeat the old class patterns of pupil differentiation within schools that are nominally comprehensive. Others have suggested that even if they create new patterns of social stratification they will not establish different forms of social control unless they also succeed in organising knowledge along less traditional lines. Past forms of cultural domination could be maintained thus ensuring the perpetuation of the prevailing hierarchy of political power. At the other end of the ideological spectrum many believe that the comprehensive schools represent the most fundamental attack to date upon academic standards and that they could destroy all that is worthwhile in British education. Proponents of this viewpoint argue that the pressures behind the comprehensive movement are political rather than educational, by which it is usually meant that they believe that their real aim is not to spread knowledge but to erode social inequality. They might accept that the way knowledge is controlled has profound socio-political consequences, but feel that to tamper with the established organisational forms has a definite negative impact upon educational standards with, at best, dubious social gains. Somewhere between these two viewpoints are to be found those who look upon comprehensive schools in more or less positive terms: as a step towards the equalisation of educational opportunity, as providing an institutional framework within which more members of a wider range of the social class scale can interact with one another, as creating an educational environment which is conducive to experimentation in the control of knowledge, and above all, as a distinct improvement — no matter what their own limitations may be — upon selective secondary education. With any major educational innovation one would have expected this kind of debate, but what is surprising is the length of time it has been progressing, the intensity with which the partisan positions are held, and the complete failure to work out a compromise which will satisfy all the major parties. Given this kind of debate, and it should be remembered that this is only one of the many contemporary issues, it is impossible to maintain the idea of formal education as a coherent and malleable instrument of social control.

In view of the kinds of functions it has performed for the state, and as the state is the main provider of the resources that enable it to flourish, it is to be expected that those who control the state apparatus will show more than a spectator's interest in the present turmoil that surrounds the educational system. The main political response to the crisis has been towards increased and more explicit state intervention in the affairs of formal education. Miliband has placed this development in a more general theoretical context by claiming that as the 'crisis of capitalism' deepens so the barriers between state and society are steadily eroded.[9] With the state no longer able to rely upon purely societal institutions to maintain the hegemony of the ruling class, so they are incorporated into the state itself to become, in Althusser's words, part of the ideological state apparatus.[10] In spite of the political opposition emerging within educational institutions the main pressure the agents of the state are exerting upon formal education concerns its economic functions. Just as the superimposed moral consensus that underlies the political order is starting to crumble so élite groups are trying to create a more viable and widely accepted basis for the nation's economic structure.[11] In view of the prevailing economic crisis they have no choice, but it would be ironic if success in this respect was matched by the increasing fragmentation of the political order. Their gamble is realistic, however, for it is certain that without a viable economy the political power of established élites is in jeopardy — and in the not too distant future.

We have shown considerable scepticism at attempts to change the character of society through the manipulation of the educational system. It is easy to see, however, why efforts to do this should persist. Because of its unique relationship to the economic, political and social structures of society the educational system appears to be in a strategic position to influence the character of all three. In the first place educational institutions are the society's main transmitters of cultural values which gives them a special part to play in regulating the pattern of class relations. At the same time they provide the raw recruits for the economic system as well as reinforcing the skill distributions that determine the forms and intensities of political participation. In spite of the fact that formal education links the various societal structures we would agree with Sharp and Green that 'comparative and historical studies suggest that attempts to bring about radical solutions to a variety of social problems through education are likely to fail — unless systematic attempts are made to alter the structure of incentives and manipulate and control other aspects of social structure through direct political intervention'.[12] However, the élite-sponsored attempt to use the educational system to assist in the resolution of the nation's economic ills is not an especially radical approach to the problem, and it is gaining increasing political support for more direct state intervention in educational affairs.

As we have clearly documented in our chapter on the changing ideology of higher education, the D.E.S. is pushing for the educational system to be based upon the ideology of manpower planning. What is remarkable about the British educational system is the tenacity of its past ideological biases so that mutually exclusive legitimations of inequality coexist. The continuing presence of the public schools is still one of the most evident symbols that Britain remains a firmly class-based society. Although their preservation can be justified in terms other than the need to perpetuate class stratification, all the alleged benefits of private education cannot disguise the fact that its privileges are distributed along class lines in institutions that owe their pre-eminence to the assumption that different classes should be exposed to different educational experiences. Even today these institutions continue to prosper because there are still sufficient persons who are prepared to buy class advantages for their children. This may not be openly approved on the grounds that class inegalitarianism is beneficial for individuals, classes or societies at large, but it is hard to avoid the impression that this is what many defenders of the public schools still in their hearts believe.

With the passage of the 1944 Education Act it was expected that Britain would move rapidly from a class-based society, with a class-directed distribution of educational resources, to a meritocratic society with a resource allocation pattern based upon the individual characteristics of age, ability and aptitude. The aim was to provide equality of opportunity commensurate with the individual's talents rather than his class position. In reality this ideal was undermined by the official sanctioning of some talents as opposed to others, and the use of intelligence tests to decide who had the most desired talents, with the allocation of a disproportionate share of educational resources to promote the development of the favoured few. Inequality was therefore based on supposedly objective criteria like 'merit' or 'intelligence', which could be measured in an allegedly scientific fashion. Although a great deal of rage was expressed at legitimating inequality in this fashion, it should be remembered that it was the technique rather than the principle of segregation that was under attack. The use of intelligence testing depended upon the willingness of those who controlled the policy-making process to accept the evidence of the so-called experts. With the passage of time, counter-expert opinion has grown stronger within the relevant disciplines (especially educational psychology), it has penetrated the guiding administrative structure (the D.E.S.), and it has gained a foothold in policy-initiating institutions (most noticeably the Labour Party).

Both class and meritocratic legitimations of inequality are not explicitly tied into the assumption that educational institutions should cater directly to societal needs. The education of a member of the upper class was meant to confirm his status as a gentleman, which many would claim was quite the opposite to providing an education that was useful in a societal sense. None the less even members of the upper class had to secure a living, and the education they received directed them towards those careers — usually in one branch of the public service or another — that it was deemed acceptable for them to pursue. In the late nineteenth century, when Britain was still the foremost industrial power and a large empire had to be administered, such luxury was permissible. One of the common complaints levelled at public schools is that they still convey a cultural experience which is best suited to the interests of a leisured upper class — a dangerous illusion to nurture in a world in which Britain has to compete aggressively for its economic survival. Although the post-1944 educational system has defined talent narrowly, and rewarded certain of its forms much more generously than others, once an individual was labelled as meritorious he had a wide range of personal choice as to what academic career he pursued. Given the cultural biases, it was to be expected that many of the technologically oriented subjects would be starved of talent.

The move towards making the educational system a major instrument of manpower planning is the most explicit and precise attempt to date to ensure that it serves a definition of the nation's economic needs. At the same time it provides a theme which can be used to legitimate inequality: status, income and power should be distributed on the basis of the individual's ability to meet this definition of economic need. As an ideological theme this argument is already well established and if the economic crisis continues it will grow stronger. It has considerable superficial attraction for, if one of the major weaknesses of our industrial society has been its failure to develop certain manpower skills, then the obvious remedy is to see that they are trained in the future. Since they have the responsibility of supplying the economy with its raw recruits, and since they help to mould the cultural biases that determine career choices, this can only mean reshaping educational institutions. The potency of the ideology is reinforced by the location of its main source, the D.E.S. Not only does the D.E.S. have ultimate responsibility for the educational system but also it has the resources which make it hard to resist its will in the long run. It has close ties with several departments of government as well as other vital economic and political power centres. Now that the U.G.C. reports directly to the D.E.S. its influence is felt in the sphere of higher education, and through its inspectorate — whose powers in the near future may be increased — it extends its tentacles into the schools.[13] The dependence of the local education authorities upon central government for much of the finance that keeps their educational systems running makes local defiance of the central will not impossible, but very precarious. So the move towards this new ideological legitimation of inequality is multi-faceted: it has a permanent and powerful institutional base, it provides a simple and logical answer to the pressing economic crisis, and if it so desired economic resources can be readily manipulated to ensure the appropriate strategies for its implementation.

In spite of the formidable weapons at its disposal we are sceptical as to whether this ideology will totally replace the more established legitimations of inequality. Besides all the technical problems of predicting future manpower demands there is the central political question as to whether the kind of society implicit in this ideology is desirable. It may be that we have no choice and the best we can hope to do is to passively meet the demands of the advanced industrial society. But even if educational resources can be manipulated to encourage the differential supply of skilled manpower, this does not guarantee that the values built into this distribution will be confirmed by the wider society. It is entirely possible that the legitimations of educational resource allocations could run directly counter to the values that are supportive of occupational inequality. Several times in the past, ritualistic claims have been made to the effect that the schools would solve our technological shortcomings. For example, some argued that the comprehensive schools would stimulate a new technological revolution by enabling talent that had been stifled in the selective system to blossom. What we may now be experiencing is a more determined version of this ritual, and in spite of the economic crisis, it may remain little more than this. The problem for the advocates of change is that past forms of inequality retain a powerful hold on how people think and act, and in Britain neither power, prestige, not even income and wealth has ever been in the hands of those with specific technological skills. In fact quite the contrary, for up until the present the nation has been dominated — culturally, politically and economically — by those whose education most closely follows that designed to produce the gentlemanly ideal.

Even though the present move towards manpower planning is likely to fizzle out, leaving as its legacy only a more complex ideological and institutional maze, it is none the less an important landmark in the development of British educational thought. It represents a struggle to complete the bourgeois revolution in education; to destroy those last vestiges of aristocratic influence that have so dominated formal education. Furthermore, in the past knowledge has been organised in ways that are meant to reinforce existing patterns of power rather than shape the overall character of the society, and in particular the industrial structure. Obviously patterns of power are the central feature of the societal character, but this is a long way from saying that they are its only important feature. Due to the United Kingdom's privileged industrial position the general character of the economy could be left to take care of itself, but the growing power of the proletariat made the question of who was to control the power centres more uncertain. Formal education was another instrument in the class struggle and it was used effectively by those who controlled the state to shore up their power base. We have now reached a point where the limitations of our structures and processes, particularly in the economic sector, are as pressing a concern as the question of who controls power. Very little is to be gained from holding power in a bankrupt nation that is socially stagnant and ungovernable. The realisation is growing that no matter who exercises power, or in whose name it is wielded, the constraints upon élite behaviour remain more or less constant, and the strategies that will best resolve the problems are fixed.

As befits a bourgeois revolution the members of the bourgeoisie will stand to gain most from it. The ideology of manpower planning could bring to an end that out-moded ideal of the gentleman scholar that has pervaded our consciousness. In future the bourgeoisie will no longer have to pretend to be what it is not. For the more elevated stratum of the bourgeoisie this is not a dramatic development, as ever since the 1950s the public schools have complemented their increasing emphasis upon science subjects with a willingness to compete aggressively with the prestigious grammar schools in the G.C.E. rat-race. By forcing some of the more prestigious grammar schools into the private sector, the movement towards comprehensive secondary schools brought about a formal reconciliation between the two dominant types of educational institutions that served the interests of the upper middle class. The working class, thanks partly to the misguided influence of progressive, bourgeois academics and teachers, is as unprepared as ever, which suggests that if one is serious about furthering the interests of the working class, the revolution should be made *before* ones pedagogical influence is felt.

In educational terms the influence of manpower planning is likely to be regressive. Recently some industrialists have complained that many school-leavers lack the basic skills to be considered for jobs that they have to offer.[14] In both the highest educational and political circles the concern at apparently declining standards of literacy and numeracy is growing. The Schools Council, which has been responsible for several of the important innovations in teaching methods, is on the defensive, and it has even been suggested that it be wound up. At least for a time the progressive impulse in education is likely to wane and perhaps even come to an untimely end. Educational opportunities may be extended in order to tap talent from a wider range of the class scale, but the limited social mobility this is likely to promote will be through traditional educational processes within the established structures. It is this very conservatism — pedagogically, socially and politically — of the manpower planning ideology that is its best guarantee of success, limited though it may be.

Inequality in the Advanced Industrial Society

Williamson has argued, 'It is just as woolly-headed to seek a solution to educational inequality in different learning situations as it is to attempt the discovery of a power structure through a school syllabus. . . Both in the end, have the same problem and for as long as this society needs dustmen and shop assistants, and so long as some people have more power than others to ensure that their children don't get such jobs, the problem will not change.'[15] We would like to suggest that the problem would still be with us even if *no one* had sufficient power to ensure that their children were neither dustmen nor shop assistants in a society that still required both. It is possible to manipulate the economic and status rewards of society so that the differentials in terms of these variables are not as great as in our present society. But while the division of labour in the economic sector results in different forms and lengths of training in the educational sector, an equalisation of these rewards is hard to contemplate. The educational stratification works against economic and status equality. Furthermore, even if status and economic differentials are eroded, there is still the question of how political power is to be distributed. It is our contention that in the advanced industrialised society power stems from knowledge as measured by exposure to formal education. Power is dependent upon control of the vast bureaucratic organisations that supervise so many facets of our lives; without formal education it is more and more difficult to obtain positions of power within those institutions. Of course once power differentials are established they will be complemented by status and economic inequalities. As we have already suggested, although the legitimations of this inequality may change, its ultimate source continues to reside within the class structure for it is that which still best accounts for the pattern of access to, and ability to make use of, educational resources.

If the educational system is to be reshaped better to fulfil certain economic goals then the forms of inequality associated with advanced technology will intensify. Those who control the state apparatuses are not helpless in the face of these pressures but their scope for action is limited by the fact that advanced technology has to be organised in certain ways and serviced by appropriate skill patterns if it is to yield its greatest rewards. The demands made of educational institutions are likely to increase in the future for not only do they have to ensure the maintenance of minimum educational standards but also they have the responsibility of refining patterns of training more carefully than in the past. The more complex forms of inequality this will cause runs up the political problems engendered by a growing awareness of the rights of citizenship. T. H. Marshall has noted the tension induced by 'the impact of a rapidly developing concept of the rights of citizenship on the structure of social inequality'.[16] This tension has been created partially by the extension of formal education amongst the population at large so that established forms of inequality come under challenge as their legitimations wear thinner. The evidence we have considered suggests that it will be difficult for educational institutions to legitimate new patterns of inequality successfully, and that the role differentiation function of formal education will increasingly become more pronounced than its social integrative function. In the future, élites will have to rely upon other institutions and other strategies to retain their power. Whatever moral consensus buttressed societal stability in the past is no longer with us, and rather than creating a new, even more precarious, consensus, social order in the future is likely to be further dependent upon explicit forms of control, complemented by an ever more frantic manipulation of societal resources.

We have tried to improve upon our original goal of increasing the amount of space devoted to the analysis of political education by offering an explanation of the contemporary crisis in education. In the process of making this explanation we have placed the sociological interpretations of formal education within a broader political context. It is our contention that whereas the past decade has been dominated by attempts to expand the theory and practice of formal education — very much in response to clientele rebellion within the educational institutions — the immediate future will see a concerted attempt by a powerful grouping of élites to tie formal education more closely into a particular economic definition of reality. The conflict this will stimulate has already commenced and now the political battle can be expected to start in earnest.

Appendix I

The Secondary Schools Survey

Given the fact that there has been very little overt discontent among school and technical college students, the research necessarily focused on the attitudinal level and deals with what can be termed 'latent' rather than 'active' discontent. A population survey was conducted at the beginning of 1972 and the data was gathered by means of self-administered questionnaires to 990 school and technical college students in a single locality in southern England. Six schools (four grammar schools, a public school and a comprehensive) and one technical college were surveyed with an overall response rate of 61 per cent. In the secondary schools, the survey focused on members of the sixth forms and in the technical college on their equivalent — that is, those students in the sixteen- to nineteen-year-old age group.

Appendix II

The Higher Education Survey

In the spring term of 1975, the Student Accommodation Project based at the University of Kent conducted a random survey by self-administered questionnaire of all full-time students in higher education in four areas of the United Kingdom. Two of these areas, Brighton and Leicester, contained a representative of each institution type in higher education — a college of education, a polytechnic and a university — and it is with the data from these areas that this chapter is concerned. The data from the Brighton and Leicester areas is combined so that comparisons can be drawn between the three types of institutions. A sampling fraction of 1:4 was employed, producing a target sample of 3527 respondents. In the event, 2284 questionnaires were returned — a response rate of 65 per cent and an unusually high one for a postal survey. Detailed comparisons by individual institution of the characteristics of achieved sample and population demonstrated that the achieved sample is highly representative.

Notes and References

Chapter One

1. B. R. Cosin (ed.), *Education: Structure and Society* (Penguin, 1972) p. 173.

2. Although it must be admitted that much of this literature is American. See G. Almond and S. Verba, *The Civic Culture* (Little, Brown, 1965) pp. 315–24; L. Milbrath, *Political Participation* (Rand McNally, 1965) pp. 57, 122–4; and S. Verba and N. Nie, *Participation in America* (Harper and Row, 1972) pp. 97–100, 129–33.

3. For the impact of social mobility (rather than formal education per se) upon party preference patterns, see D. Butler and D. Stokes, *Political Change in Britain* (Macmillan, 1969) pp. 95–101, pp. 95–102 (2nd edn, 1974). For the impact of schools upon party preferences see pp. 102–6 of the second edition.

4. See pp. 27–36.

5. See pp. 27–36.

6. Milbrath, *Political Participation*, pp. 110–14.

7. This has been changing in recent years and the vogue, in both Britain and the United States, is to encourage the development of the 'politically aware' citizen. For a discussion of these trends see pp. 75–84.

8. We are referring here to the Politics Association. For a consideration of some of its activities see pp. 68–84.

9. See pp. 72–4.

10. See R. Miliband, *The State in Capitalist Society* (Weidenfeld and Nicolson, 1969) chs 7 and 8.

11. For the formal controls exercised by the state see H. C. Dent, *The Educational System of England and Wales* (University of London Press, 1966) ch. 3.

12. Note, for example, the elaborate attempts to create a consensus upon which educational policy can be based. This is best seen in the long and painstaking negotiations between the interested parties which preceded the 1944 Education Act. This partially accounts for the longevity of the Act and why its dismemberment was so bitterly resisted.

13. Consider the following quotation: 'The advocates of comprehensivization make no secret of their intentions: they have long ceased in the face of irrefutable facts, to argue that a fully comprehensive system would be *academically* superior to our present arrangements. Their whole campaign is now concentrated on a single issue: the use of education as a means of breaking down the country's social structure and creating "equality of opportunity" — which is expected to lead inexorably to an egalitarian, possibly even "classless" society.' See T. Szamuely, 'Russia and Britain: Comprehensive Inequality', in *The Black Papers on Education*, eds C. B. Cox and A. E. Dyson (Davis-Poynter, 1971) p. 121.

14. L. Althusser, 'Ideology and Ideological State Apparatuses', in *Education: Structure and Society*, pp. 242–80.

15. For the strengths and weaknesses of this argument see pp. 48–56.

16. Jean Floud and A. H. Halsey are rightly seen as the major figures in this development.

17. B. Bernstein, 'The Sociology of Education: A Brief Account', in *Class, Codes and Control*, ed. B. Bernstein, vol. 3 (Routledge and Kegan Paul, 1975) p. 151.

18. I. Davies, 'The Management of Knowledge: A Critique of the Use of Typologies in the Sociology of Education', in *Knowledge and Control*, ed. M. F. D. Young (Collier-Macmillan, 1971) p. 268.

19. Young, 'Introduction', in ibid. p. 6.

20. J. Ford, *Social Class and the Comprehensive School* (Routledge and Kegan Paul, 1969); D. N. Holly, 'Profiting from a Comprehensive Education: Class, Sex and Ability', *British Journal of Sociology*, vol. 16 (1965) pp. 150–58; T. Tapper, *Young People and Society* (Faber and Faber, 1971).

21. Davies, in *Knowledge and Control*, p. 273.

22. Although in response to the growing interest in the social control of knowledge, this has been changing.

23. P. Bordieu, 'Cultural Reproduction and Social Reproduction', in *Knowledge, Education and Cultural Change*, ed. R. Brown (Tavistock Publications, 1973) p. 72.

24. This is as true of socialist as capitalist economies and the debate is about the range of available opportunities, the definitions of merit, and the patterns of inequality.

25. C. Jencks *et al.*, *Inequality: A Reassessment of the Effect of Family and Schooling in America* (Basic Books, 1972). For reactions to Jencks, see 'Perspectives on *Inequality*', *Harvard Educational Review*, vol. 43, no. 1 (1973) pp. 37–137.

26. Bordieu, in *Knowledge, Education and Cultural Change*, pp. 78–9.

27. Bernstein, 'Sources of Consensus and Disaffection in Education', in *Class, Codes and Control*, ed. B. Bernstein, vol. 3, pp. 48–9.

28. This is clearly seen in the debate on comprehensive education.

29. A discussion of this topic is taken up in greater detail in the third chapter. For an application of this perspective to the British educational system see, T. Benton, 'Education and Politics', in D. Holly (ed.), *Education or Domination?* (Arrow Books, 1974) pp. 9–37.

30. Of course they have not lacked allies outside the educational system, especially within the Conservative Party, which helps to explain the success of their rearguard action.

31. Davies, in *Knowledge and Control*, p. 269.

32. I. Davies, 'Knowledge, Education and Power', in *Knowledge, Education and Cultural Change*, pp. 322–3.

33. See pp. 61–5.

34. Care should be taken here to distinguish between 'education' and 'schooling' and it should not be assumed that there is a natural working-class antipathy towards education.

35. R. H. Tawney, *Secondary Education for All* (Allen and Unwin, 1922) p. 33.

36. See extracts from the Report of the Commissioners appointed to enquire into the State of Popular Education in England (Newcastle Report) in J. Stuart Maclure, *Educational Documents, England and Wales, 1816–1963* (Chapman and Hall, 1965) pp. 70–8; and R. Lowe, 'Democracy, alas, now educate the masters', in *Education and Democracy*, eds A. E. Dyson and J. Lovelock (Routledge and Kegan Paul, 1975) pp. 203–8.

37. For a discussion of differing views see S. Wiseman (ed.), *Intelligence and Ability* (Penguin, 1967); and P. Vernon, *Intelligence and Cultural Environment* (Methuen, 1969).

38. H. Rosen, 'Language and Class', in *Education or Domination?*, p. 62.

39. Controversy has broken out on this very issue. See T. Burgess, 'How it is decided which children go to which schools', *The Times*, Tuesday, 18 Jul 1972, p. 12; and S. Jessel, 'Many head teachers critical of school transfer system', *The Times*, Wednesday 19 Jul 1972, pp. 1–2.

40. For a sympathetic consideration of these educational advantages, see R. Lambert, 'The Public Schools: A Sociological Introduction', in *The Public Schools: A Factual Survey*, ed. G. Kalton (Longmans, 1966) pp. xi–xxxii.

41. B. Jackson and D. Marsden, *Education and the Working Class* (Routledge and Kegan Paul, 1962).

42. Although the transition was not inevitably smooth for it left its scars in a number of cases. See ibid. pp. 155–89.

43. D. Hargreaves, *Social Relations in a Secondary School* (Routledge and Kegan Paul, 1967) pp. 108–39.

44. B. Bernstein, 'On the Classification and Framing of Educational Knowledge', in *Class, Codes and Control*, ed. B. Bernstein, vol. 1 (Routledge and Kegan Paul, 1971) pp. 202–30.

45. Ibid. pp. 207–9, for a brief comparative statement on the organisation of different education codes.

46. Young writes, 'The Council [the Schools Council] has accepted the stratification of knowledge and produces most of its recommendations for reform in the low-status knowledge areas. These tend to be associated with curricula which are for younger and less able children and are not linked to the interests of those who are in positions of power in the social structure.' See 'Curricula and the Social Organization of Knowledge', in *Knowledge, Education and Cultural Change*, p. 355.

47. W. Taylor, *The Secondary Modern School* (Faber and Faber, 1963) pp. 82–102.

48. The information on the University of Sussex is based on our personal observations; for the Summerhil experiment, see A. S. Neill, *Summerhill, A Radical Approach to Education* (Victor Gollancz, 1969) pp. 3–92.

49. Amongst the other favourable factors we would include the newness of the educational institutions. The more recent British universities were supposed to break the Oxbridge stranglehold over the British university system, and Summerhill was set up as a planned educational innovation.

50. The Black Papers represent the broadest and best-known attack on many of these educational innovations. See Cox and Dyson, *The Black Papers*, and C. B. Cox and Rhodes Boyson, *Black Paper 1975: The Fight for Education* (J. M. Dent and Sons, 1975).

51. Consider this quotation from Bordieu's work: 'Those sections which are richest in cultural capital are more inclined to invest in their children's education at the same time as in cultural practices liable to maintain and increase their specific parity; those sections that are richest in economic capital set aside cultural and educational investments to the benefit of economic investments: it is to be noted, however, that heads of industry and commerce tend to do this much more than do the new "bourgeoisie" of the managers who reveal the same concern for rational investment both in the economic sphere and in the educational sphere.' Bordieu, in *Knowledge, Education and Cultural Change*, p. 72.

52. This reflects a wider debate — whether power is dependent upon the ownership or the control of the means of production. For some comparative perspectives on educational systems located within differing patterns of property ownership see O. Banks, *The Sociology of Education* (Batsford, 1976).

53. It should be stressed that the conflict is not only about the nature of society but also about important pedagogical issues, and the latter should not be seen as simply disguises for the former.

54. Davies writes, 'The central feature of an educational system is the control of knowledge. This control is both societal and international as well as internal to the educational institutions themselves. What a system of pedagogy and research misses out is as significant as what it puts in, because the omissions will largely illuminate the operations of the power mechanisms.' See Davies, in *Knowledge, Education and Cultural Change*, p. 331. Davies is claiming that controlling knowledge is also a means to defining knowledge through the manipulation of curriculum content.

Obviously there are international standards as to what is knowledge, but the wider the social base amongst which consensus is sought the greater the likelihood of conflict as to definitions of knowledge.
55. See a report by Ken Rowat on the new B.A. degrees in art in *Education Guardian*, Tuesday, 10 Feb 1976, p. 15.
56. The resurgence of Marxist studies in British universities is a clear sign of a widening of the knowledge boundaries.
57. But as we shall document in a later chapter, this appears to be breaking down. See pp. 97–102.
58. For example, note how the ideological backing of Lysenko held back the development of Soviet agriculture. See Z. A. Medvedev, *The Rise and Fall of T. D. Lysenko* (Columbia University Press, 1969).
59. B. Berstein, 'On the Curriculum', in *Class, Codes and Control*, ed. B. Bernstein, vol. 3, (Routledge and Kegan Paul, 1975) p. 81.

Chapter Two

1. This chapter derives some of its ideas from our paper entitled, 'An Obituary to Political Socialization', presented to the Political Studies Association Conference, Nottingham, 1976.
2. H. Hyman, *Political Socialization* (The Free Press, 1959).
3. F. Greenstein, 'A Note on the Ambiguity of "Political Socialization": Definitions, Criticisms, and Strategies of Inquiry', *Journal of Politics*, vol. 32 (1970) pp. 969–70.
4. Ibid.; as Greenstein acknowledges, this information was provided by Jack Dennis.
5. J. Dennis, 'Future Work on Political Socialization', in J. Dennis (ed.), *Socialization to Politics*, ed. J. Dennis (John Wiley and Sons, 1973) pp. 493–4.
6. Ibid. p. 501.
7. For a biting critique of this view of man and society see D. Wrong, 'The Oversocialized Conception of Man in Modern Sociology', *American Sociological Review*, vol. 26 (1961) pp. 183–93.
8. G. A. Almond, 'A Functional Approach to Comparative Politics', in *The Politics of Developing Areas*, eds G. Almond and J. Coleman (Princeton University Press, 1960) pp. 3–64; and D. Easton, 'An Approach to the Analysis of Political Systems', *World Politics*, vol. 9 (1957) pp. 383–400.
9. Almond, in *Politics of Developing Areas*, pp. 26–31; and D. Easton, *A Framework for Political Analysis* (Prentice-Hall, 1965) pp. 124–5.
10. Hyman, *Political Socialization*, p. 25.
11. F. Greenstein, *Children and Politics* (Yale University Press, 1969) pp. 45–6.
12. The most impressive sample is that which forms the basis of both Easton and Dennis's and Hess and Torney's works. See R. D. Hess and J. V. Torney, *The Development of Political Attitudes in Children* (Aldine,

1967) pp. 226–32, 248–53; and D. Easton and J. Dennis, *Children in the Political System* (McGraw-Hill, 1969) pp. 420–25.

13. H. Hyman, *Political Socialization* (The Free Press, 1969) p. vii.

14. Ibid.

15. D. Easton and R. Hess, 'The Child's Political World', *Midwest Journal of Political Science*, vol. 6 (1962) p. 235.

16. Hess and Torney have been the strongest advocates in favour of the school's influence. See *Political Attitudes in Children*, p. 101.

17. It is likely that a saturation point is being reached but the expansion in the past two decades, in many different kinds of societies, has been impressive.

18. D. Easton, 'The Function of Formal Education in a Political System', *The School Review*, vol. 65 (1957) p. 311.

19. Easton and Dennis, *Children in the Political System*, pp. 62–3.

20. For examples of the acceptance of the systems framework see: F. Greenstein, *Children and Politics*, pp. 10–15; B. Massialas, *Education and the Political System* (Addison-Wesley, 1969); and F. Wirt and M. Kirst, *The Political Web of American Schools* (Little Brown, 1972). For an attack on the use of this approach see, S. S. Wolin, 'Politics, Education and Theory', in *State, School and Politics*, ed. M. Kirst (D. C. Heath, 1972) ch. 1.

21. Easton, *The School Review*, p. 313.

22. For a restrained recognition of this bias see J. Dennis, 'Major Problems of Political Socialization Research', *Midwest Journal of Political Science*, vol. 12 (1968) pp. 105–8.

23. Hess and Torney, *Political Attitudes in Children*, p. 108.

24. E. Litt, *The Public Vocational University: Knowledge and Public Power* (Holt, Rinehart and Winston, 1969) ch. 8; R. Merelman, *Political Socialization and Educational Climates: A Study of Two School Districts* (Holt, Rinehart and Winston, 1971) ch. 8; and Massialas, *Education and the Political System*, ch. 3.

25. For a discussion of this point see T. Tapper, *Political Education and Stability* (John Wiley and Sons, 1976) pp. 51–3.

26. Massialas, *Education and the Political System*, p. 49.

27. For an example of such reluctance see, F. Greenstein, 'The Case of the Reluctant Consultant: On Moving from What We Know to What We Ought to Do', *The School Review*, vol. 77 (1969) pp. 41–53.

28. Merelman, *Political Socialization*, p. 231.

29. On this see pp. 70–84.

30. For the ineffectiveness of the civics curriculum see: K. Langton and M. Kent Jennings, 'Formal Environment: The School', in Langton, *Political Socialization* (Oxford University Press, 1969) pp. 84–119; and G. Mercer, *Political Education and Socialization to Democratic Norms*, University of Strathclyde, Survey Research Centre, Occasional Paper No. 11 (1973).

31. Langton and Kent Jennings, ibid. pp. 117–8. For middle-class blacks exposure to civics training increases their patriotism but not their participatory dispositions, which Langton and Kent Jennings put down (rather lamely) to their greater realisation of the limits to effective black participation in American political life.

32. E. Litt, 'Civic Education, Community Norms and Political Indoctrination', *American Sociological Review*, vol. 28 (1963) pp. 69–75.

33. Merelman, *Political Socialization*, p. 147.

34. D. Jaros and B. Canon, 'Transmitting Basic Political Values: The Role of the Educational System', *The School Review*, vol. 77 (1969) p. 95.

35. Wirt and Kirst, *Political Web*, p. 39.

36. H. Eulau, 'Introductory Essay — Political Science and Education: The Long View and the Short', in *State, School and Politics*, pp. 1–9.

37. For examples see, Langton and Kent Jennings, in *Political Socialization*; and Mercer, *Political Education and Socialization*.

38. For the most explicit claim that this was the end product of the American political socialisation process, see Hess and Torney, *Political Attitudes in Children*, pp. 217–9. The studies of subcultural political learning processes have undermined this convenient view of the socialisation process.

39. Easton, *The School Review*, p. 309.

40. D. Easton and J. Dennis, 'The Child's Image of Government', *The Annals*, vol. 36 (1965) p. 41.

41. Easton and Dennis, *Children in the Political System*, p. 7.

42. F. Greenstein *et al.*, 'Queen and Prime Minister: The Child's Eye View', *New Society*, no. 369 (1969) p. 638. An interpretation he scarcely modifies in an extended and more recent version; see F. Greenstein *et al.*, 'The Child's Conception of the Queen and Prime minister', *British Journal of Political Science*, vol. 4 (1974) pp. 285–7.

43. J. Dennis *et al.*, 'Support for Nation and Government among English Children', *British Journal of Political Science*, vol. 1 (1971) pp. 45–8. This article stimulated some reaction: see I. Budge, 'Support for Nation and Government among English Children: A Comment', *British Journal of Political Science*, vol. 1 (1972) pp. 389–92; A. H. Birch, 'Children's Attitudes and British Politics', *British Journal of Political Science*, vol. 1 (1972) pp. 519–20; and D. Kavanagh, 'Allegiance among English Children: A Dissent', *British Journal of Political Science*, vol. 2 (1972) pp. 127–31. For a different perspective on Dennis' article, see Tapper, *Political Education and Stability*, pp. 121–3.

44. C. Merriam, *The Making of Citizens: A Comparative Study of the Making of Citizens* (Chicago University Press, 1931). This volume is Merriam's overview of an eight-nation study of civics training undertaken under his overall supervision in the 1920s.

45. N. Masters *et al.*, *State Politics and the Public Schools* (Alfred Knopf, 1964) pp. 3–7.

46. Tapper, *Political Education and Stability*, p. 42.

47. T. Parsons, 'The School Class as a Social System: Some of its Functions in American Society', in *Education, Economy and Society*, eds A. H. Halsey *et al.* (The Free Press, 1961) pp. 439–41.

48. E. Greenberg, 'The Political Socialization of Black Children', *Political Socialization*, ed. E. Greenberg (Atherton Press, 1970) pp. 178–90; and S. Lyons, 'The Political Socialization of Ghetto Children: Efficacy and Cynicism', *Journal of Politics*, vol. 32 (1970) pp. 297–305.

49. T. H. Marshall, 'Citizenship and Social Class', in T. H. Marshall,

Sociology at the Crossroads and Other Essays (Heinemann, 1963) ch. 4.

50. For the best empirical evidence see, P. Abramson, 'The Differential Political Socialization of English Secondary School Students', *Sociology of Education*, vol. 40 (1967) pp. 246–69; and Tapper, *Young People and Society*, chs 5–9.

51. W. G. Runciman, *Sociology in its Place* (Cambridge University Press, 1970) pp. 110–11.

52. For the pattern of class recruitment into higher education, see Chapter 8.

53. Hess and Torney, *Political Attitudes in Children*, p. 171.

54. Although, as we have already discussed, this initial proposition grew hazier over time.

55. For a further elaboration of this point, see pp. 66–7.

56. This is the general theme of Chapter 7.

57. See Eulau, in *State, School and Politics*, p. 5, for an interpretation of this distinction.

Chapter Three

1. A. Giddens, 'Elites in the British Class Structure', in *Elites and Power in British Society*, eds P. Stanworth and A. Giddens (Cambridge University Press, 1974) p. 2.

2. S. Aaronovitch, 'The Ruling Class' in *Power in Britain: Sociological Readings*, eds J. Urry and J. Wakeford (Heinemann, 1973) p. 130.

3. Ibid. p. 127.

4. Ibid.

5. T. Bottomore, *Sociology as Social Criticism* (Allen and Unwin, 1975) p. 127.

6. W. Guttsman, *The British Political Elite* (MacGibbon and Kee, 1968) p. 356.

7. J. Rex, 'Power', *New Society*, 5 Oct 1972, p. 25 (our stress).

8. For a good explanation of why research in this area has flourished, see I. Crewe, 'Introduction: Studying Elites in Britain', in *British Sociology Yearbook: Volume 1, Elites in Western Democracy* ed. I. Crewe (Croom Helm, 1974) pp. 20–4.

9. This is substantiated by several of the contributions to the Urry and Wakeford, and Stanworth and Giddens texts.

10. Guttsman, *British Political Elite*, ch. 9; W. L. Guttsmann, 'The British Political Elite and the Class Structure', in *Elites and Power*, ch. 2; and R. W. Johnson, 'The British Political Elite, 1955–1972', *European Journal of Sociology*, vol. 14 (1973) pp. 35–77.

11. Crewe, *British Sociology Yearbook*, p. 15. Why either a 'ruling class' or 'power elite' is required to act conspiratorially to be defined as such is not at all clear.

12. See T. Lupton and C. Shirley Wilson, 'The Social Background and Connections of Top Decision-Makers', in *Power in Britain*, ch. 14.

13. Bottomore, *Sociology as Social Criticism*, p. 143.

14. For some empirical evidence in support of this, see A. H. Halsey, 'Theoretical Advance and Empirical Challenge' in *Readings in the Theory of Educational Systems*, ed. E. Hopper (Hutchinson, 1971) pp. 273–81.

15. J. Wakeford, *The Cloistered Elite* (Macmillan, 1969) pp. 134–59.

16. I. Weinberg, *The English Public Schools* (Atherton Press, 1967) p. 125.

17. For a somewhat dated, but still interesting study of the changing values of socially mobile working-class adolescents, see Jackson and Marsden, *Education and the Working Class*.

18. Giddens, in *Elites and Power*, p. 17.

19. For the most detailed analysis of the specialisation of élite careers, see S. Keller, *Beyond the Ruling Class* (Random House, 1963).

20. Bottomore, *Sociology as Social Criticism*, p. 142.

21. Here we are referring to the reforms instigated by the Northcote-Trevelyan report.

22. See T. Balogh, 'The Apotheosis of the Dilettante', in *The Establishment*, ed. H. Thomas (Anthony Blond, 1959) pp. 84–5.

23. R. K. Kelsall, 'Recruitment to the Higher Civil Service: How Has the Pattern Changed?', in *Elites and Power*, p. 180.

24. Ibid. p. 184.

25. Ibid. But it should be noted that the evidence is contradictory and for a different viewpoint see, Report of the Committee of Inquiry, *The Method 11 System of Selection*, (H.M.S.O., 1969).

26. Balogh, in *Establishment*, p. 94.

27. A. Sampson, *Anatomy of Britain Today* (Harper and Row, 1965) p. 254.

28. T. Bottomore, 'Ruling Elite or Ruling Class?', in *Power in Britain*, p. 276.

29. N. Poulantzas, 'Controversy over the State', *New Left Review*, no. 95 (1976) p. 75.

30. Ibid. p. 69 (our stress).

31. Ibid. p. 68.

32. K. Marx and F. Engels, *The German Ideology* (International Publishers, 1965) p. 39.

33. A. Gramsci, *Prison Notebooks* (Lawrence and Wishart, 1971). See especially the sections entitled, 'The Intellectuals', 'On Education' and 'State and Civil Society'.

34. Ibid. p. 263.

35. Althusser, in *Education: Structure and Society*, p. 254. Note that Miliband makes a distinction between class power and state power but he is less than clear in defining the boundaries between the two. For a discussion of this point see, E. Laclau, 'The Specificity of the Political: The Poulantzas–Miliband Debate', *Economy and Society*, vol. 4 (1975) pp. 99–101.

36. Althusser, ibid. p. 258 (stress in original text). It is difficult to know whether to admire Althusser for his courage or to condemn him for his foolhardiness.

37. R. Williams, 'Base and Superstructure in Marxist Cultural Theory', *New Left Review*, no. 82 (1973) p. 9.

38. See Ford, *Social Class and the Comprehensive School*, and Tapper, *Young People and Society*, ch. 1.

39. Miliband, *State in Capitalist Society*, p. 241.

40. P. Anderson, 'Origins of the Present Crisis', *New Left Review*, no. 23 (1964) p. 39.

41. Miliband, *State in Capitalist Society*, p. 181.

42. Williams, *New Left Review*, p. 10.

43. Miliband, *State in Capitalist Society*, p. 195.

44. F. Parkin, 'Working-Class Conservatives: A Theory of Political Deviance', *British Journal of Sociology*, vol. 18 (1967) p. 289 (stress in original text).

45. For a statement of the move towards the home-centred society see M. Abrams, 'Social Trends and Electoral Behaviour', *British Journal of Sociology*, vol. 13 (1962) pp. 228–42.

46. Parkin, *British Journal of Sociology*, p. 280.

47. This power of the headmaster is illustrated by the problems the Inner London Education Authority faced in handling the conflict at William Tyndale junior school. See p. 194.

48. G. Parry, *Political Elites* (Praeger, 1969) p. 83.

49. For an example of such eagerness, see Miliband, *State in Capitalist Society*, p. 239.

50. R. Williams, *The Long Revolution* (Columbia University Press, 1961) p. 126.

51. For élite manipulation of conflict situations in Britain see, Tapper, *Political Education and Stability*, chs 7–10.

52. J. Rex, 'Capitalism, Elites and the Ruling Class', in *Elites and Power*, p. 218.

53. Rex, *New Society*, p. 26.

54. For the recent growth of political opposition amongst school-students see, Chapter 5.

55. Almond and Verba's analysis of the British political culture contains few references to the possibility of class cleavages within the culture. See *Civic Culture*.

56. Marx and Engels, *The German Ideology*, p. 69 (stress in original text).

57. J. Merrington, 'Theory and Practice in Gramsci's Marxism', *The Socialist Register*, 1968, pp. 156–60.

58. For the empirical evidence that working-class Labour and working-class Tory voters share many political attitudes see, R. McKenzie and A. Silver, *Angels in Marble* (Heinemann, 1968) pp. 160–62.

59. R. Dahrendorf, *Class and Class Conflict in Industrial Society* (Stanford University Press, 1959) pp. 280–9; and H. F. Moorhouse, 'Attitudes to Class and Class Relationships in Britain', *Sociology*, vol. 10 (1976) pp. 492–3.

60. See Anderson, *New Left Review*, pp. 41–2.

61. M. Mann, 'The Social Cohesion of Liberal Democracy', *American Sociological Review*, vol. 35 (1970) p. 435.

62. M. Mann, *Consciousness and Action Among the Western Working Class* (Macmillan, 1973) p. 29.

63. Ibid. p. 71.

64. For an example of this see J. Westergaard, 'Sociology: The Myth of Classlessness', in *Ideology in Social Science*, ed. R. Blackburn (Fontana, 1972) p. 151.

65. Williams, *New Left Review*, pp. 10–12; and Rex, *New Society*, p. 26.

66. On this see Miliband, *State in Capitalist Society*, pp. 270–72.

67. On this see pp. 148–54, 160–8, 171–3.

68. Mann, *Consciousness and Action*, pp. 29–30.

69. N. Harris, *Beliefs in Society: The Problem of Ideology* (Penguin, 1968), p. 111.

70. Of course this depends partially on definitions of 'class' and 'success' and that is why we have placed them in inverted commas.

71. R. Miliband, 'The Capitalist State: Reply to Nicos Poulantzas', in *Power in Britain*, p. 313.

Chapter Four

1. See, for example, Tapper, *Political Education and Stability*, p. 40. This is one of the themes found in much of the literature published under the auspices of the Politics Association, for a discussion of which see below.

2. The first issue of *Teaching Politics* appeared in May 1972. This statement is our assessment of its editorial opinion and the bias of many of its contributions.

3. The research project (A Programme for Political Education) is sponsored by the Hansard Society in association with the Politics Association and funded by the Nuffield Foundation. The principal investigators are professors B. Crick and I. Lister. The radio programmes were first broadcast in the spring of 1975 and repeated in the spring of 1976. Furthermore, a continental based journal, to be known as *The International Journal of Teaching Politics*, will appear in the near future.

4. E. Simon, 'The Aims of Education for Citizenship', in the Association for Education in Citizenship, *Education for Citizenship in Secondary Schools* (Oxford University Press, 1936) p. 9.

5. Ibid. p. 10. Note the foreword to this book was written by O. F. G. Stanley, President of the Board of Education, and in it he claimed that political education could act as a check upon the erosion of democracy in Britain.

6. I. Lister, 'The Aims and Methods of Political Education in Schools', paper prepared for the Conference on the Development of Democratic Institutions in Europe, April 1976, pp. 1–3; and D. Heater, 'A Burgeoning Interest: Political Education in Britain', in B. Crick and D. Heater, *Essays on Political Education* (The Falmer Press, 1977) pp. 58–78.

7. This is not too strained an interpretation of the tenor of the Newsom

Report. See, A Report of the Central Advisory Council for Education, *Half Our Future*, (H.M.S.O., 1963) pp. 111–27.

8. Tapper, *Political Education and Stability*, pp. 27–8.

9. This fudging of the issue is illustrated by this quote from Lister's work: 'Classroom research into political education programmes suggests that an essential pre-condition for the success of any programme is that it should be planned according to a coherent theory of politics.' Lister, 'Aims and Methods', pp. 4–5. But he provides no evidence as to what his classroom research may be and no inkling as to what 'coherent theory of politics' supports his own sponsored political education programmes. For another example of the same point, see G. Mercer, 'Political Interest among Adolescents: The Influence of Formal Political Education', *Teaching Politics*, vol. 11 (1972) p. 13.

10. For a fuller statement of these reasons see Heater, in *Essays on Political Education*, pp. 69–72, and Lister, 'Aims and Methods', pp. 1–3.

11. Lister, ibid. p. 3.

12. M. Oakeshott, 'Political Education', in M. Oakeshott, *Rationalism in Politics: And Other Essays* (Basic Books, 1962) pp. 111–36.

13. Ibid. pp. 132–3.

14. B. Crick and I. Lister, *Political Literacy*, Document No. 2 of a Programme for Political Education (Nov 1974) p. 1.

15. Ibid. p. 5. See also, B. Crick and I. Lister, *A Programme for Political Education: An Explanatory Paper*, Document No. 1 of a Programme for Political Education (Nov 1974) p. 1.

16. For a consideration of this criticism, see pp. 31–5.

17. B. Crick, 'On Bias', *Teaching Politics*, vol. 1 (1972) pp. 4–5. Note also this quote from Crick and Lister, *A Programme for Political Education*, p. 3: 'It would, however, be both intellectually and morally wrong to assume that there is a "consensus" in our society about political values (*even though there may be a consensus about procedures*)' (our stress).

18. He has argued that 'knowledge' rather than 'participation' restrains governments. See, B. Crick, 'The Introducing of Politics', in *Teaching Politics*, ed. D. Heater (Methuen, 1969) p. 17.

19. See, for example, Miliband, *State in Capitalist Society*.

20. P. White, 'Education, Democracy and the Public Interest', in *The Philosophy of Education*, ed. R. S. Peters (Oxford University Press, 1973) p. 227.

21. Ibid. p. 223.

22. See Heater, in *Essays on Political Education*, p. 59.

23. I. Lister, 'Political Education in the Schools', *New University*, vol. 3, no. 9 (May, 1969) p. 25.

24. D. Heater, 'Politics as a University Discipline and Political Education in the Schools', *Political Quarterly*, vol. 40 (1969) pp. 326–7.

25. This is reflected in the kinds of questions appearing on the examination papers. In response to this change of mood, and in order to stimulate it further, the Politics Association have produced a series of texts — known as the *Political Realities* series — intended to be used [primarily] as 'British Constitution' A level texts.

26. Heater, in *Essays on Political Education*, p. 60; Crick and Lister, *A Programme for Political Education*, p. 1; and D. Thompson, 'The Teaching of Civics and British Constitution', in *Teaching Politics*, p. 63.

27. Crick and Lister, *Political Literacy*, p. 6.

28. B. Crick, 'Basic Political Concepts and Curriculum Development', *Teaching Politics*, vol. 3 (1974) pp. 13–23.

29. Heater, 'Political Concepts and the Construction of a Syllabus', Exeter University Conference on Political Socialisation (1971) p. 4.

30. Ibid. p. 10.

31. Crick, *Teaching Politics*, pp. 13–18.

32. Oakeshott makes a distinction between 'the academic study of politics' and 'political activity'. The latter is not increased, in his opinion, by the former but by actual political participation. See, *Rationalism in Politics*, pp. 132–3.

33. E. Barker in a foreword to M. Stewart's chapter entitled 'Politics or Public Affairs' in *Education for Citizenship*, p. 108.

34. H. Entwistle, *Political Education in a Democracy* (Routledge and Kegan Paul, 1971) chs 4 and 5.

35. Ibid. pp. 38–42.

36. Tapper, *Political Education and Stability*, pp. 148–9.

37. Ibid. p. 148.

38. See, for example, the conflict which followed the appointment of Mr T. Ellis to the headship of William Tyndale junior school: *The Sunday Times*, 28 Sep 1975, and *The Sunday Times*, 25 Jan 1976, pp. 4–5.

39. W. Robson, *Politics and Government at Home and Abroad* (Allen and Unwin, 1967) p. 40.

40. Ibid. p. 40.

41. L. Freedman, 'Approaching Politics', *Teaching Politics*, vol. 3 (1974) p. 7.

42. Ibid. p. 10.

43. Lister, 'The Aims and Methods of Political Education', p. 15.

44. R. Wilkinson, *The Prefects: British Leadership and the Public School Tradition* (Oxford University Press, 1964); Wakeford, *Cloistered Elite*; and Weinberg, *English Public Schools*.

45. See, for example, White, in *Philosophy of Education*, pp. 233–6; and Entwistle, *Political Education in a Democracy*, pp. 5–6. For conflict in the educational experiences of public school pupils, see pp. 51–2.

46. A point made by one of the authors elsewhere. See Tapper, 'The Limits of Political Education: An Expanding Interest', *Teaching Politics*, vol. 4 (1975) pp. 11–14.

47. Robson, *Politics and Government*, pp. 40–44.

48. See Heater, in *Essays on Political Education*, p. 70; and D. Heater, 'Political Education in Schools — The Official Attitude', *Teaching Politics*, vol. 1 (1972) p. 29.

49. On this see Tapper, *Young People and Society*, pp. 103–6.

50. On this point see Tapper, *Teaching Politics*, p. 11.

51. For example, those students taking examination courses (in G.C.E. or C.S.E.), while in Scotland there is a Modern Studies programme.

224 *Notes and References to pages 84–92*

52. See pp. 14–15.
53. With the two strongest but radically different challenges coming from Christopher Jencks and Ivan Illich. See Jencks *et al.*, *Inequality*; and I. Illich, *Deschooling Society* (Harper and Row, 1971).
54. See pp. 27–36.
55. Lister, 'The Aims and Methods of Political Education in Schools', pp. 8–9.
56. As is the case with Crick and Lister's project on political education.
57. See Chapter 7.
58. This is reinforced by Langton's evidence on the effectiveness of civics courses in the United States which provide redundant information except for those from family backgrounds that are low in political awareness. See Langton and Kent Jennings, in *Political Socialization*, pp. 118–9.
59. As is most clearly exemplified by events in Northern Ireland where some have looked to the schools to provide a bridge between the two communities. See Tapper, *Political Education and Stability*, pp. 226–9.

Chapter Five

1. Entwistle, *Political Education in a Democracy*, ch. 3. For a full discussion of the reasons for the growing interest in political education in Britain, see pp. 70–5.
2. Much of this literature has been dissected in the previous chapter.
3. *Teaching Politics* has provided the main forum for this discussion.
4. A Report of the Central Advisory Council for Education, *Half Our Future*.
5. Schools Council, *Working Paper No. 2: Raising the School-leaving Age* (H.M.S.O., 1965).
6. D. Lawton *et al.* (for the Schools Council), *Working Paper No. 39: Social Studies, 8–13* (Evans/Methuen Educational, 1971). See also the General Studies Project of the Schools Council, directed by R. Irvine Smith of the University of York, for in progress working papers on the subject.
7. Heater, in *Essays on Political Education*, p. 72.
8. Some pioneering work in this area is being conducted by Professor Ian Lister of the Political Education Research Unit, University of York.
9. An assessment of the growing interest in political education in this country has been made in the previous chapter. See especially, pp. 75–84.
10. See, N. Berger, 'The Child, the Law and the State', in *Children's Rights*, eds P. Adams *et al.* (Panther Books, 1972) for a general discussion of the legal position of the child.
11. *The Times*, 11 Jan 1973, p. 3.
12. *The Times* 20 Jan 1973, p. 3.
13. See D. Lawton *et al.*, *Working Paper No. 39* and the Moral Education Project, *Lifeline* (Longmans, 1972).
14. Humanities Curriculum Project, *The Humanities Curriculum Project* (Heinemann Educational, 1970).
15. Schools Council, *Working Paper No. 2*.

16. P. Newell, 'Classroom Crunch', *Guardian*, 20 Jun 1972, p. 17.

17. For general ideological support for free schools see Illich, *Deschooling Society*. For a commentary on the British free school experience see P. Newell, 'A Free School Now', *New Society*, 15 May 1975, pp. 400–403.

18. G. Dennison, *The Lives of Children* (Penguin, 1971).

19. Quoted by Newell, 'Classroom Crunch', in the *Guardian*.

20. See the 1944 Education Act, Part III, Section 70.

21. Penguin in particular have published a number of books illustrating the various threads of progressivism. See, for example: P. Aries, *Centuries of Childhood* (1973); L. Berg, *Look at Kids* (1972); G. Dennison, *Lives of Children*; P. Goodman, *Compulsory Miseducation* (1971); J. Henry, *Essays on Education* (1971); J. Holt, *How Children Fail* (1969); H. Kohl, *36 Children* (1971); R. D. Laing and A. Esterson, *Sanity, Madness and the Family* (1970); A. S. Neill, *Summerhill* (1968); N. Postman and C. Weitgartner, *Teaching as a Subversive Activity* (1971); E. Reiner, *School is Dead: Essays in Alternatives in Education* (1972); and D. Rubinstein and C. Stoneman (eds), *Education for Democracy* (1972).

22. R. Sharp and A. Green, *Education and Social Control* (Routledge and Kegan Paul, 1975), p. vii.

23. See, R. Gagne, 'Learning Theory, Educational Media and Individualized Instruction' in *The Curriculum*, ed. R. Hooper (Oliver and Boyd, 1971) pp. 299–319; and J. D'Arcy, 'The Design of Learning Systems — Part 1', in *The Teacher as Manager*, ed. G. Taylor (Books for Schools Ltd, 1970) pp. 24–9. For an attack on the subject based curriculum see A. Hunt, 'The Tyranny of Subjects', in *Education for Democracy*, pp. 26–33.

24. *Humanities Curriculum Project*.

25. Rubinstein and Stoneman, *Education for Democraçy*, p. 20.

26. I. Goodson, 'The Teachers Curriculum and the New Reformation', *Journal of Curriculum Studies*, vol. 7 (1975) pp. 160–9.

27. I. Goodson, 'Towards an Alternative Pedagogy', in *Explorations in the Politics of School Knowledge*, eds G. Whitty and M. F. D. Young (Nafferton Books, 1976) p. 128 (his stress).

28. M. Armstrong, 'The Role of the Teacher', in *Education without Schools*, ed. P. Buckman (Souvenir Press, 1973) p. 51.

29. In a letter to *Radical Education*, no. 1 (1974) p. 15.

30. The 'Bust Book' gave practical advice to children tangling with the law. Michael Duane and Leila Berg in fact objected to its publication in *Children's Rights*. All the articles mentioned appeared in the first five issues, 1971–2.

31. Quoted in Rubinstein and Stoneman, *Education for Democracy*, p. 11.

32. Crick and Lister, *A Programme for Political Education: An Exploratory Paper*, paragraphs 1–5.

33. Crick and Lister, *Political Literacy*, p. 6.

34. For an elaboration of this point, see pp. 78–9.

35. The information on which this section is based was collected from a variety of sources: interview with Michael Wolf, ex-activist of the Schools Action Union; interviews with Simon Emerson and David Paterson, presi-

dents of the N.U.S.S. in 1974–5 and 1975–6 respectively; back issues of *Vanguard* — the national journal of the S.A.U.; a dissertation by Anne Wilson, former undergraduate at the University of Sussex; a paper by Nigel Seal (N.U.S.S. member) on the history of the N.U.S.S.; and *The Times* and *Guardian* for the period 1968–75.

36. 'Pupil Power Sequel to Student Revolt', *The Times*, 30 Sep 1968, p. 3.

37. 'Report on the National Conference', *Vanguard*, 15 Jan 1969, p. 3.

38. As its title indicates the 'Broad Left' is an umbrella political organisation for a section of the student left.

39. *Hansard*, Volume 787, No. 151 (17 Jul 1969) p. 855.

40. Ibid.

41. See the report of a speech by Rhodes Boyson, *The Times*, 3 Jan 1975, p. 3.

42. *The Times*, 19 May 1972, p. 17.

43. See a special report by Adam Hopkins and Mark Jackson in *The Sunday Times*, 25 Jan 1976, pp. 4–5, for an analysis and synopsis of the enquiry and its background. See also the report itself: R. Auld, *The William Tyndale Junior and Infant Schools Public Inquiry* (I.L.E.A., 1976).

44. *The Times*, 6 Oct 1972, p. 15.

45. Butt, *The Times*, 19 May 1972.

46. *The Times*, 19 May 1972, p. 15.

47. Butt, *The Times*, 19 May 1972.

48. Ibid.

49. Ibid.

50. A recent example of this was the proposal put to the National Association of Head Teachers' conference in May 1975 that a General Teaching Council should be set up to control entry into the profession and to expel 'undesirables'. See the *Guardian*, 28 May 1975, p. 6.

51. *The Times*, 17 May 1972, p. 2.

52. *Guardian*, 24 May 1972, p. 2.

53. 'Wots Rong with the Evening News', *Vanguard*, 1 Jan 1969, p. 3.

54. *Guardian*, 18 May 1972, p. 5.

55. J. Killigrew, 'Rebellion in the Classroom', *The Sunday Times*, 20 Jul 1969, p. 9.

56. *Guardian*, 12 May 1972, p. 12.

57. Quoted in *The Times*, 17 May 1972, p. 2.

58. Ibid.

59. C. Price, 'Little Red Schoolkids', *Guardian*, 28 May 1972, p. 16.

60. *Guardian*, 26 May 1972, p. 16.

61. *Times Educational Supplement*, 16 Jul 1971, p. 6.

62. Goodson, in *Explorations*, p. 133.

63. Ibid. p. 225.

64. Ibid. p. viii.

65. *School Student* (Spring 1976) back page (our stress).

66. Ibid.

67. Ibid.

68. Ibid.

69. Ibid.

70. For a more detailed discussion of the organisational problems faced by the N.U.S.S. see, B. G. Salter, 'What Price a Piece of the Action?', *Guardian*, 17 Jan 1976, p. 17.

Chapter Six

1. For a summary of the explanations of student revolt see B. Salter, 'Explanations of Student Revolt: An Exercise in Devaluation', *British Journal of Sociology*, vol. 24 (1973) pp. 329–40.

2. The only directly relevant work is American and concerned mainly with particular subcultures. See P. Ritterband and R. Silverstein, 'Group Disorders in the Public Schools', *American Sociological Review*, vol. 38 (1973) pp. 461–7; A. M. Orum and R. S. Cohen, 'The Development of Political Orientations among Black and White Children', *American Sociological Review*, vol. 38 (1973) pp. 62–74; and J. W. Clarke, 'Family Structure and Political Socialization among Urban Black Children', *American Journal of Political Science*, vol. 17 (1973) pp. 302–15.

3. M. K. Maykovich, 'Political Activism of Japanese American Youth', *Journal of Social Issues*, vol. 29 (1973) pp. 167–85. His typology is as follows:

	Attitude toward traditional values	
Social-issue behaviour	*Acceptance*	*Rejection*
Involved	Liberated	Militant
Non-involved	Conformist	Anomic

See also, J. Block *et al.*, 'Activism and Apathy in Contemporary Adolescents', in *Understanding Adolescence: Current Developments in Adolescent Psychology*, ed. J. F. Adams (Allyn and Bacon, 1968) pp. 198–231. Their categories are: (a) Politically apathetic youth — low involvement, high acceptance of social values; (b) Alienated youth — uninvolved, rejection of social values; (c) Individualist youth — involved in politics, accepts the *status quo*; (d) Activist youth — involved in politics, rejects traditional values; (e) Constructivist youth — similar to those in category (d) except that the rejection of the traditional values is not as pronounced (e.g. Peace Corps volunteers).

4. The question was: How do you feel about school discipline? Is it — far too strict, a little too strict, just right, or not strict enough?

5. F. Greenstein, 'The Benevolent Leader: Children's Images of Political Authority', *American Political Science Review*, vol. 54 (1960) pp. 934–43; F. Greenstein, 'More on Children's Images of the President', *Public Opinion Quarterly*, vol. 25 (1961) pp. 648–54; and R. D. Hess and D. Easton, 'The Child's Changing Image of the President', *Public Opinion Quarterly*, vol. 24 (1960) pp. 632–44.

6. D. Jaros *et al.*, 'The Malevolent Leader: Political Socialization in

an American Subculture', *American Political Science Review*, vol. 57 (1968) p. 574.

7. E. Greenberg, 'Children in the Political Community: A Comparison Across Racial Lines', *Canadian Journal of Political Science*, vol. 2 (1969) pp. 471–92; E. Greenberg, 'Black Children and the Political System', *Public Opinion Quarterly*, vol. 34 (1970) pp. 333–45; E. Greenberg, 'Children and Government: A Comparison Across Racial Lines', *Midwest Journal of Political Science*, vol. 14 (1970) pp. 249–75; and S. R. Lyons, *Journal of Politics*.

8. R. Flacks, 'The Liberated Generation: An Exploration of the Roots of Student Protest', *Journal of Social Issues*, vol. 23 (1967) pp. 52–75.

9. R. Flacks, 'Student Activists: Result, Not Revolt', *Psychology Today* (Oct 1967) p. 20.

10. For a selection of ideas on this explanatory theme see R. Coles, 'Serpents and Doves: Non-Violent Youth in the South', in *Challenge of Youth*, ed. E. Erikson (Basic Books, 1963) pp. 188–216; J. Ehle, *The Free Men* (Harper and Row, 1965); H. Draper, *Berkeley: The New Student Revolt* (Grove Press, 1965); J. R. Fishman and F. Soloman, 'Youth and Social Action: An Introduction', *Journal of Social Issues*, vol. 20 (1964) pp. 1–28; P. Heist, *Intellect and Commitment: The Faces of Discontent* (Berkeley, Centre for the Study of Higher Education, 1965); K. Keniston, *The Young Radicals* (Harcourt, Brace and World, 1968); F. Soloman and J. R. Fishman, 'Youth and Peace: A Psycho-Social Study of Student Peace Demonstrators in Washington D.C.', *Journal of Social Issues*, vol. 20 (1964) pp. 54–73; D. L. Westby and R. G. Braungart, 'Class and Politics in the Family Background of Student Political Activists', *American Sociological Review*, vol. 31 (1966) pp. 690–2; and H. Zinn, *S.N.C.C., The New Abolitionists* (Beacon, 1965).

11. Social class is measured by the Hall–Jones scale. See J. Hall and D. C. Jones, 'Social Grading of Occupations', *British Journal of Sociology*, vol. 1 (1950) pp. 31–55.

12. See for example, R. Lane, *Political Life* (Glencoe Free Press, 1959) pp. 220–34.

13. The question was: 'With regard to the making of decisions in your family, what kind of relationship do you have with your parents? Do they —?'

14. J. Katz and N. Sandford, 'Causes of the Student Revolution', *Saturday Review*, 18 Dec 1965, pp. 64–6. See also, R. Middleton and S. Putney, 'Student Rebellion against Parental Political Beliefs', *Social Forces*, vol. 41 (1963) pp. 377–83.

15. The question was: 'How well do you get on with your father/mother?'

16. For a review of much of this research see Chapters 2 and 3.

17. Almond and Verba, *Civic Culture*, pp. 352–62.

18. Abramson, *Sociology of Education*, pp. 261–5.

19. See for example, S. M. Lipset and S. S. Wolin (eds), *The Berkeley Student Revolt* (Anchor Books, 1965) Part II; J. W. Scott and M. El-Assal, 'Multiversity, University Size, University Quality, and Student Protest, An Empirical Study', *American Sociological Review*, vol. 34 (1969) pp. 702–9;

D. R. Brown, 'Student Stress and Institutional Environment', *Journal of Social Issues*, vol. 23 (1967) pp. 92–107; and E. E. Sampson, 'Student Activism and the Decade of Protest', *Journal of Social Issues*, vol. 23 (1967) pp. 1–23.

20. But see Wakeford, *Cloistered Elite*, pp. 155–9 for another example of this.

21. The chi-square figure in this table is unreliable because some of the frequencies in the 'Grammar School' and 'Comprehensive' row cells are less than 5.

22. See for example, S. M. Lipset, 'University Student Politics', in *Berkeley Student Revolt*, p. 7.

23. An initial problem, prior to the cross-tabulation, was how to collapse the large number of different courses into manageable, yet meaningful, categories. The choice was whether to stick simply to a purely academic grading — thus all city and guild courses, craftsmen and technicians, would be in the same category — or whether the occupational destination of a course should be the criterion instead. The latter was chosen — partly because it seemed the most important anyway, and partly because it was practically impossible to construct a compact categorisation using the academic criterion. The three categories thus indicate the future niche in the social structure that people taking certain courses are likely to assume.

24. The different types of responsibility were classified as follows: (a) 'disciplinary' — prefect or equivalent; (b) 'social activity' — officer of school social club, e.g. secretary; (c) 'both' — both 'disciplinary' and 'social activity'.

25. R. Flacks, *Psychology Today* (Oct 1967) p. 62.

26. Ibid. p. 62.

27. See B. G. Salter, 'Student Militants and Counter Culture', *Universities Quarterly*, vol. 28 (1974) pp. 455–69; R. Dunlap, 'Radical and Conservative Student Activists; A Comparison of Family Backgrounds', *Pacific Sociological Review*, vol. 13 (1970) pp. 171–81; J. W. Clarke and J. Egan, 'Social and Political Dimensions of Campus Protest Activity', *The Journal of Politics*, vol. 34 (1972) pp. 500–21; H. C. Finney, 'Political Libertarianism at Berkeley; An Application of Perspectives from the New Student Left', *Journal of Social Issues*, vol. 27 (1971) pp. 35–62; R. Kann, 'Rank and File Student Activism: A Contextual Test of Three Hypotheses', paper presented at a meeting of the American Sociological Association, San Francisco, August 1969; D. Kirby, 'A Counter-Culture Explanation of Student Activism and Family Socio-Economic Status', *Pacific Sociological Review*, vol. 14 (1971) pp. 121–8.

28. See D. Horowitz, N. Lerner, C. Pyes (eds), *Counterculture and Revolution* (Random House, 1972); T. Roszak, *The Making of a Counterculture* (Anchor Books, 1969); J. M. Yinger, 'Counter-Culture and Sub-Culture', *American Sociological Review*, vol. 25 (1960) pp. 625–35.

29. Keniston, *Young Radicals*, p. 341. See also K. Keniston, *The Uncommitted: Alienated Youth in American Society* (Dell Publishing Co., 1965).

30. J. S. Coleman, *The Adolescent Society* (The Free Press, 1961) p. 4.

31. L. Stenhouse, *Culture and Education* (Nelson, 1967) pp. 18–19.

32. G. Murdock and G. Phelps, 'Youth Culture and the School Revisited', *British Journal of Sociology*, vol. 23 (1972) pp. 478–9.

33. J. Bernard, 'Teen-Age Culture: An Overview', *The Annals of the American Academy of Political and Social Science*, vol. 338 (1961) pp. 2–12.

34. See for example, W. F. Whyte, *Street Corner Society* (University of Chicago Press, 1943); S. M. Miller and F. Riessman, 'The Working Class Subculture', *Social Problems*, vol. 9 (1961) pp. 86–97; R. Hoggart, *The Uses of Literacy*, (Chatto and Windus, 1957); A. K. Cohen and H. M. Hodges, 'Characteristics of the Lower-Blue-Collar-Class', *Social Problems*, vol. 10 (1962) pp. 303–34; H. Gans, *The Urban Villagers* (The Free Press of Glencoe, 1962); S. M. Lipset, 'Working Class Authoritarianism' in *Social Controversy*, ed. W. Petersen and D. Matza (Wadsworth Publishing Co., 1963) pp. 242–55.

35. B. M. Berger, 'On the Youthfulness of Youth Cultures', *Social Problems*, vol. 11 (1963) p. 342.

36. K. Polk and D. S. Halferty, 'Adolescence, Commitment, and Delinquency', *Journal of Research in Crime and Delinquency*, vol. 3 (1966) pp. 84–95.

37. B. Sugarman, 'Involvement in Youth Culture, Academic Achievement and Conformity in School', *British Journal of Sociology*, vol. 18 (1967) pp. 151–64. See also his 'Social Norms in Teenage Boys Peer Groups', *Human Relations*, vol. 21 (1968) pp. 41–58.

38. The findings of Polk and Pink are very similar. See K. Polk and W. T. Pink, 'Youth Culture and the School, a Replication', *British Journal of Sociology*, vol. 22 (1971) pp. 160–71.

39. Murdock and Phelps, *British Journal of Sociology*, p. 479.

40. The question was 'How do you feel about . . . ?' For the purpose of this table 'strongly approve' has been collapsed with 'approve'.

41. The questions were: (a) 'What, if anything, do you think is wrong with society's values today?'; and (b) 'How important is it to you to "get on" and be successful in life by making a lot of money?' 'Anti-materialism' is defined as that group of respondents who indicated in their reply to question (a) that they considered society too materialistic. 'Anti-success' is that group which ringed 'not very important' or 'irrelevant' in their reply to question (b).

42. F. Musgrove, *Ecstasy and Holiness: Counter Culture and the Open Society* (Methuen and Co. 1974) p. 22.

43. Ibid. p. 152.

44. Hargreaves, *Social Relations in a Secondary School*, chs 6 and 8; and Whyte, *Street Corner Society*.

45. For evidence of this see Musgrove, *Ecstasy and Holiness*, pp. 26–7.

Chapter Seven

1. A. H. Halsey, 'A Pyramid of Prestige', *Universities Quarterly*, vol. 15 (1960–1) pp. 341–5.

2. A. H. Halsey, 'The Universities and the State', *Universities Quarterly*,

vol. 23 (1968–9) p. 137.

3. Ibid.

4. K. Mannheim, *Ideology and Utopia* (Harcourt, Brace, 1936) p. 52.

5. H. T. Betteridge, 'Academic Freedom', *Universities Quarterly*, vol. 23 (1968–9) pp. 189–202.

6. Sir Sydney Caine, *British Universities, Purpose and Prospects* (The Bodley Head, 1969) p. 27.

7. B. Truscot, *Redbrick University* (Faber, 1943) p. 49.

8. Ibid.

9. H. C. Dent, *Universities in Transition* (Cohen and West, 1961) p. 121 (stress in original text).

10. V. H. Green, *The Universities*, (Penguin, 1968), p. 319.

11. Sir Charles Grant Robertson, *The British Universities* (Methuen, 1944) p. 9 (stress in original text).

12. A. H. Halsey, 'The Changing Functions of Universities', in *Education, Economy and Society*, eds Halsey *et al.*, p. 456.

13. Quoted by Dent, *Universities in Transition*, p. 115 (our stress).

14. Quoted by G. H. Bantock, 'T. S. Eliot and Education', *Universities Quarterly*, vol. 19 (1964–5) p. 113.

15. Ibid.

16. Williams, *The Long Revolution*, p. 142.

17. Ibid. p. 142.

18. This is the last of the six principles that Sir Walter Moberly thought the university of today should incorporate. Quoted by Dent, *Universities in Transition*, p. 116, and taken from Moberly's *The Crisis in the University* (S.C.M. Press, 1949).

19. J. Brothers and S. Hatch, *Residence and Student Life* (Tavistock Publications, 1971) pp. 40–41.

20. Reprinted in the *Times Higher Education Supplement*, 7 Mar 1975.

21. See, for example, the report of Lord Bullock's speech in the *Times Higher Education Supplement*, 2 Apr 1976, entitled ' "Universities" ' Role Unrelated to Manpower Planning'.

22. Ministry of Education, *Higher Technological Education* (H.M.S.O., 1945). For a review of these developments up to 1963 see, M. Argles, *South Kensington to Robbins* (Longmans, 1964) chs. 7 and 8.

23. Ministry of Education, ibid. paragraph 2.

24. Ministry of Education, *Technical Education* (H.M.S.O., 1956). This theme is frequently reiterated in other reports — see for example Ministry of Education, *Education in 1958* (H.M.S.O., 1958) p. 36.

25. Ibid. p. 37 (our stress).

26. S. Cotgrove, *Technical Education and Social Change* (Allen Unwin, 1958) p. 186.

27. Ibid. p. 81.

28. See, A. Sampson, *Anatomy of Britain* (Hodder and Stoughton, 1962) p. 224; R. K. Kelsall, *Higher Civil Servants in Britain* (Routledge and Kegan Paul, 1955) pp. 135–45; and C. D. Dodd, 'Recruitment to the Administrative Class, 1960–1964', *Public Administration*, vol. 45 (1967) p. 80.

29. Halsey, 'The Changing Functions of Universities' in *Education, Economy and Society*, eds Halsey *et al.*, p. 461.

30. Lord President of the Council, *Scientific Manpower* (H.M.S.O., 1946). This report recommended the training of 70,000 qualified (that is, graduate and equivalent) scientists by 1950 and 90,000 by 1955.

31. See Argles, *South Kensington to Robbins*, pp. 91–2, and Cotgrove, *Technical Education*, pp. 168–75.

32. Parliamentary and Scientific Committee, *Memorandum on Higher Technological Education* (H.M.S.O., 1954).

33. According to Argles, De Witt's *Soviet Professional Manpower* (National Science Foundation, 1955) had considerable influence.

34. Ministry of Education, *Circular 305/56*.

35. *Education in 1958*, p. 38 (our stress).

36. Ibid. p. 57 (our stress).

37. An unlikely event since it would be anathema to the traditional university ideal.

38. *Education in 1958*, p. 57.

39. Ministry of Education, *The Supply and Training of Teachers for Technical Colleges: Report of a Special Committee* (H.M.S.O., 1957), which is quoted in *Education in 1958*, p. 51.

40. Ministry of Labour, *Industrial Training: Government Proposals* (H.M.S.O., 1962) p. 4 (our stress).

41. Ibid.

42. To name but a few: Ministry of Education, *Liberal Education in Technical Colleges*, Circular 323/57; Ministry of Education: National Advisory Council on Education for Industry and Commerce, *Report of the Advisory Committee on Further Education for Commerce* (H.M.S.O., 1959); Ministry of Education: National Advisory Council on Education for Industry and Commerce. *A Report on the Wastage of Students from Part-time Technical and Commercial Courses* (H.M.S.O., 1959); Ministry of Education, *Better Opportunities in Technical Education* (H.M.S.O., 1961); and Ministry of Education, *General Studies in Technical Colleges* (H.M.S.O., 1962).

43. Committee on Higher Education, *Higher Education* (H.M.S.O., 1963–4).

44. Ministry of Education, *Education in 1963* (H.M.S.O., 1963).

45. Reprinted in the *Times Higher Education Supplement*, 7 Mar 1975, p. 15.

46. Ibid.

47. Ibid.

48. Ibid.

49. Ibid. This is reminiscent of the relationship that was supposed to exist between the various strata of secondary education.

50. Ibid.

51. Ibid.

52. Department of Education and Science, *A Plan for Polytechnics and Other Colleges — Higher Education in the Further Education System* (H.M.S.O., 1966).

53. Reprinted in the *Times Higher Education Supplement*, 7 Mar 1975, p. 15.

54. Committee on Higher Education, *Higher Education*.

55. Universities Grants Committee (U.G.C.), *University Development 1957–62* (H.M.S.O., 1964) p. 70.

56. Ibid. p. 73.

57. U.G.C., *Report of the Subcommittee on Halls of Residence* (H.M.S.O., 1957).

58. Ibid. p. 9.

59. Ibid. p. 35.

60. Ibid. p. 9 (our stress).

61. Ibid. p. 5.

62. *University Development 1957–62*, p. 109. A. H. Halsey has pointed out that the 'new' universities were in fact never really new: 'They accepted established definitions of the conditions of entry and they chose curricula and a balance of learning between research and teaching from within the practices current in the existing western universities.' In the same article, referring to the new universities, he writes: 'The policy that eventually emerged was a comic pattern of return to medieval symbols.' See, A. H. Halsey, 'Ancient Grip on New Universities', *Times Higher Education Supplement*, 5 Jul 1974, p. 5.

63. Quoted in *University Development 1957–62*, p. 153.

64. Ibid. ch. 7.

65. Ibid. p. 198.

66. Ibid. p. 198.

67. Sir Robert Aitken, 'The Vice-Chancellors Committee and the U.G.C.', *Universities Quarterly*, vol. 23 (1968–9) p. 185.

68. U.G.C., *University Development 1962–67* (H.M.S.O., 1968) p. 49.

69. Committee on Higher Education, *Higher Education*, pp. 6–7.

70. Ibid. p. 170.

71. Ibid. p. 8.

72. Ibid. p. 204.

73. Ibid. p. 205.

74. Ibid. p. 205.

75. Ibid. p. 228.

76. Ibid. p. 228.

77. See above, p. 142.

78. Committee on Higher Education, *Higher Education*, pp. 7–8.

79. Robbins envisaged a three-fold increase in the university population from 118,000 students in 1962/3 to 350,000 in 1980 — Committee on Higher Education, *Higher Education*, pp. 87, 284.

80. For the details of the recommendations see Committee on Higher Education, *Higher Education*, ch. 17.

81. For a review of manpower forecasting in the 1960s see K. G. Gannicot and M. Blaug, 'Manpower Forecasting Since Robbins—A Science Lobby in Action' in *Decision Making in British Education*, ed. G. Fowler, V. Morris and J. Ogge (Heineman Educational Books, 1973) pp. 259–83.

82. See D. Hencks, 'Teacher Supply: A Case of Manpower Planning', *Higher Education Review*, vol. 8 (1975) pp. 17–31.

83. Council for Scientific Policy, *Enquiry into the Flow of Candidates in Science and Technology into Higher Education* (H.M.S.O., 1968).

84. Committee on Manpower Resources for Science and Technology,

The Brain Drain, Report of the Working Group on Migration (H.M.S.O., 1967).

85. Committee on Manpower Resources for Science and Technology, *The Flow into Employment of Scientists, Engineers and Technologists, Report of the Working Group on Manpower for Scientific Growth* (H.M.S.O., 1968).

86. *University Development, 1962–67*, p. 103.

87. Organisation for Economic Co-operation and Development, *Gaps in Technology Between Member Countries: An Analytical Report* (O.E.C.D., March 1970).

88. U.G.C., *University Development, 1967–72* (H.M.S.O., 1974) p. 25.

89. D.E.S., *Education in 1966* (H.M.S.O., 1966) p. 10.

90. Ibid.

91. Ibid.

92. D.E.S., *Education Planning Paper No. 1: Output Budgeting for the Department of Education and Science* (H.M.S.O., 1970).

93. D.E.S., *Education Planning Paper No. 2: Student Numbers in Higher Education in England and Wales* (H.M.S.O., 1970).

94. *Education Planning Paper No. 1*, reprinted in *Decision Making in British Education*, eds Fowler *et al.*, p. 310.

95. See V. Morris, 'Investment in Higher Education in England and Wales: The Human Capital Approach to Educational Planning', in *Decision Making in British Education*, eds Fowler *et al.*, pp. 284–308.

96. *Decision Making in British Education*, eds. Fowler *et al.*, p. 287.

97. See the Expenditure Committee, Session 1972–3, *Government Observations on the Report on Further and Higher Education* (H.M.S.O., 1973) Section entitled 'Higher Education and Manpower Needs', p. 1.

98. Reported in the *Times Higher Education Supplement*, 16 May 1975, p. 1 (our stress).

99. D.E.S., *Education: A Framework for Expansion* (H.M.S.O., 1972) p. 31.

100. Ibid.

101. Ibid. p. 34.

102. Ibid.

103. Ibid. p. 31.

104. Ibid. p. 37.

105. Ibid. A research project on student accommodation was subsequently funded by the D.E.S., and located at the University of Kent, with 'the feasibility of home-based study' included in its terms of reference. Similar statements to those quoted here appear in *Report from the Expenditure Committee; Further and Higher Education*, vol. 1 (H.M.S.O., 1972).

106. Reported in the *Times Higher Education Supplement*, 23 May 1975, p. 7.

107. See above, p. 157.

108. See above, p. 156.

109. From 'A Note on University Policy and Finance, 1947–56', a statement circulated by the Committee of Vice-Chancellors and Principals in 1946, quoted by W. R. Niblett, 'The Development of British Universities since 1945', *Year Book of Education* (Evans in association with the University of London Institute of Education, 1952) p. 168.

110. Ibid (our stress).

111. Committee on Higher Education, *Higher Education*, p. 237 (our stress).

112. *University Development, 1962–7*, p. 107.

113. Ibid. p. 181.

114. Ibid. p. 95.

115. Ibid.

116. Ibid. p. 97.

117. Ibid. p. 95.

118. Ibid. p. 81.

119. Ibid. p. 82 (our stress).

120. Ibid. p. 179.

121. Ibid. p. 178.

122. Ibid. p. 179 (our stress).

123. This phrase occurs in a *Times Higher Education Supplement* article by Lord Wolfenden, 'The U.G.C.: A Personal View', 2 Apr 1976, p. 5, which, in turn, is an extract from his autobiography, *Turning Points* (The Bodley Head, 1976).

124. Paul Johnson, 'Beware the Leviathan, its "Gifts", its Motives and its Friends', *Times Higher Education Supplement*, 24 Oct 1975.

125. John Pratt, 'Is the U.G.C. a Buffer or a Branch of Government?', *Times Higher Education Supplement*, 11 Apr 1975, p. 17. This is a condensed version of his 'The U.G.C. Department', *Higher Education Review*, vol. 7 (1975) pp. 19–32.

126. *University Development, 1962–7*, p. 180.

127. J. Pratt and T. Burgess, *Polytechnics: A Report* (Pitman, 1974) pp. 23–30 and pp. 172–4.

128. *Third Report of the Select Committee on Science and Technology*, (H.M.S.O., 1976), extracts of which were printed in the *Times Higher Education Supplement*, 26 Nov 1976, p. 17 from which this quotation was taken.

129. Ibid.

130. Ibid.

131. Ibid.

132. Ibid.

133. See above, p. 165. It is no coincidence that the D.E.S. is currently funding an investigation by Gareth Williams of Lancaster University into how courses for higher education are chosen. Not surprisingly, one of the hypotheses being examined is 'the possibility that a pupil's perceptions of the economic advantages of different courses of action would be an important consideration in career-related decisions'. See, 'Attitudes of Young People to School, Work and Higher Education', a preliminary report by Gareth Williams and Alan Gordon of Lancaster University's Institute for Research and Development in Post-Compulsory Education, summarised in the *Times Higher Education Supplement*, 27 Feb 1976, p. 7.

134. For an account of the politics behind this request and the resultant 'Yellow Book' see Adam Hopkins, 'Is Teaching too Important to be left to Teachers?', *Sunday Times*, 17 Oct 1976, p. 17.

135. 'A New Approach to the Public Curriculum', *Times Educational Supplement*, 15 Oct 1976, p. 1.

136. For extracts from this report see, 'Has Something Gone Wrong? How Is It To Be Put Right?', ibid. p. 2.

137. Ibid.

138. It is interesting to note that the Committee of Directors of Polytechnics welcomed Mr Callaghan's statement in his Ruskin speech on the need to fit children and students for a working life. 'Oxford Speech Soothes "Yellow Book" Critics', *Times Higher Education Supplement*, 22 Oct 1976, p. 3.

Chapter Eight

1. See p. 155.

2. 'Higher education' is defined in the accepted D.E.S. way as consisting of the universities plus advanced courses in further education (now mainly in the polytechnics). The sources for the totals arrived at here are: (a) *Statistics of Education, 1961*, Further Education, Table 29, p. 63 and *University Development, 1957–62*, p. 26 for the 1961 figure; (b) *Statistics of Education, 1973*, vol. 3, Table 12, p. 20, and vol. 6, Table 1, p. 2 for the 1973 figure.

3. Working class is defined in accordance with normal sociological convention as 'manual occupations' and middle class as 'non-manual occupations'.

4. See pp. 148–54.

5. D.E.S., *A Plan for Polytechnics and Other Colleges* (H.M.S.O., 1966).

6. Pratt and Burgess, *Polytechnics*, p. 6.

7. Ibid. pp. 45–8.

8. Although its title may suggest otherwise, the Labour Party has never been a vehicle for working-class interests alone.

9. Pratt and Burgess, *Polytechnics*, p. 172.

10. E. Robinson, *The New Polytechnics* (Cornmarket Press, 1968) p. 10.

11. Ibid. p. 171.

12. See for example, L. Donaldson, 'Social Class and the Polytechnics', *Higher Education Review*, vol. 4 (1971) pp. 44–68.

13. This is a composite table formed from the Committee on Higher Education, *Higher Education*, Appendix Two (B), table 102, p. 92, and table 135, p. 115.

14. S. F. Cotgrove, *Technical Education and Social Change* (Allen and Unwin, 1958) p. 115.

15. Ibid. p. 106. Cotgrove's figures at this stage in his argument are unfortunately available only for evening class students but there is no reason to assume that his thesis is not generally applicable. Certainly he believes this to be the case.

16. Ibid. p. 104.

17. D. V. Glass (ed.), *Social Mobility in Britain* (Routledge and Kegan Paul, 1954) p. 306.

18. Ibid. p. 307.

19. Cotgrove, *Technical Education*, p. 105.

20. The speech was called 'Labour and the Scientific Revolution'.

21. The Report stated that the main objects of the Open University were, 'To provide opportunities, at both undergraduate and postgraduate level, of higher education to all those who, for any reason, have been or are being precluded from achieving their aims through an existing institute of higher education' — quoted by N. E. McIntosh and A. Woodley, 'The Open University and Second Chance Education — An Analysis of the Social and Educational Background of Open University Students', *Paedagogica Europaea*, vol. 9 (1974) p. 85.

22. Speech delivered on 23 July 1969, reproduced in The Open University, Prospectus 1971, quoted here from McIntosh and Woodley, ibid.

23. McIntosh and Woodley, ibid. Table 4, p. 91.

24. N. E. McIntosh and V. Morrison, 'Student Demand, Progress and Withdrawal', *Higher Education Review*, vol. 7 (1974) p. 45.

25. McIntosh and Woodley, *Paedagogic Europaea*, Table 4, p. 91.

26. Ibid. p. 99 (our stress).

27. J. Pratt, 'Open, University!', *Higher Education Review*, vol. 3 (1971) p. 20.

28. Ibid. p. 21.

29. Committee on Higher Education, *Higher Education*, Appendix Two (B), table 6, p. 5.

30. This is a composite table formed from the following sources: The Universities Central Council on Admissions: (a) Statistical Supplement to the Seventh Report, 1968–9, table E2, p. 19; (b) Statistical Supplement to the Eleventh Report, 1972–3, table K4, p. 19; (c) Statistical Supplement to the Twelfth Report, 1973–4, table K4, p. 18.

31. *Census of Population*, 1966, Economic Activity Tables, Part I, p. 51; *Census of Population*, 1971, Economic Activity Tables, Part II, pp. 57–62.

32. D. Hutchison and A. McPherson, 'Competing Inequalities: The Sex and Social Class Structure of the First Year Scottish University Population 1962–1972', *Sociology*, vol. 10 (1976) table 3, p. 113. The 1972 figures were weighted by known population values to reduce response bias in terms of sex, achievement, and age.

33. Ibid. p. 111.

34. The sources for this table are: J. Abbott, *Students in a Class Society* (Pergamon, 1970) and 'Students' Social Class in Three Northern Universities', *British Journal of Sociology*, vol. 16 (1965) pp. 206–20; T. Blackstone, *Students in Conflict, L.S.E. in 1967* (Weidenfeld and Nicolson, 1970); M. Couper, G. Harris, 'C.A.T. to University: The Changing Student Intake', *Educational Research*, vol. 12, pp. 113–20; M. Jahoda, *The Education of Technologists* (Tavistock, 1963); P. Marris, *The Experience of Higher Education* (Routledge and Kegan Paul, 1964); D. Marsland, quoted in Blackstone, *Students in Conflict*, p. 21; F. Musgrove *et al.*, *Preliminary Studies of a Technological University* (Bradford University, 1967) mimeographed; H. Perkins, *Innovation in Higher Education—New Universities in the United Kingdom* (UNESCO, 1966); and F. Zweig, *The Student in an Age of Anxiety* (Heinemann, 1963).

35. The sources for this table are: J. Crutchley, J. Young, J. Grant, J. Gregory, B. Salter, *Student Culture* (SSRC Research Report, 1972) (This data in fact comes from a survey of Enfield College students, which since 1972 has been a part of Middlesex Polytechnic); and Pratt and Burgess, *Polytechnics*, p. 86.

36. Pratt and Burgess, ibid. p. 173.

37. The Student Accommodation Project was financed by the D.E.S. The members of the research team were Robert Flynn, Linda McDowell and Brian Salter, and the research directors were, in chronological order, Professor Murray Stewart, David Reason and David Morgan. Our thanks are due to David Morgan for permission to use the data.

38. The Registrar General's scale was used to classify social class.

39. See pp. 14–19.

40. The universities are excluded from this table because they do not have courses with markedly different statuses.

41. The colleges of education are excluded from this table because it was not possible to classify their courses in terms of the subject studied.

Chapter Nine

1. I. Illich, *Deschooling Society*.

2. R. Auld, *The William Tyndale Junior and Infants Schools: Report of the Public Inquiry*, pp. 290–9.

3. D. H. Hargreaves, 'Deschoolers and New Romantics', in *Educability, Schools and Ideology*, eds M. Flude and J. Ahier (Croom Helm, 1974) p. 208.

4. See especially G. Almond and S. Verba, *Civic Culture*, pp. 337–44.

5. On this see, pp. 27–36.

6. Some confusion exists as to whether the balance should be within individual citizens or the citizenry at large. On this see Almond and Verba, *Civic Culture*, pp. 344–54. Whether a nation which encourages non-participation (in order to ensure a balanced citizenry) can be described as a 'democracy' or said to have a 'civic culture' is just one of the questions raised by this issue.

7. We have termed them 'consensus' theorists, because of their belief that the political order rests upon a set of shared values.

8. Sharp and Green, *Education and Social Control*, p. 224.

9. See pp. 65–7 for our reinterpretation of his prediction.

10. See pp. 56–61.

11. For a consideration of some of the barriers that have to be removed before this can be accomplished see J. H. Goldthorpe, 'Social Inequality and Social Integration in Modern Britain', in *Poverty, Inequality and Class Structure*, ed. D. Wedderburn (Cambridge University Press, 1974) pp. 222–34.

12. Sharp and Green, *Education and Social Control*, pp. 226–7.

13. See 'Shake-up in the Inspectorate: Focus Switches to Centre', *Times Educational Supplement*, 4 Feb 1977, pp. 1 and 3.

14. For example, Sir Arthur Bryan, chairman of Wedgewood Pottery Company — see 'Education "Has Lagged Behind Social Change"' *The Times*, 7 Jan 1977, p. 3.

15. B. Williamson, 'Continuities and Discontinuities in the Sociology of Education' in *Educability, Schools and Ideology*, p. 12.

16. Marshall, *Sociology at the Crossroads*, p. 127.

Index